THE FIRST LADY OF DIRT

THE FIRST LADY OF DIRT

The Triumphs and Tragedy of Racing Pioneer Cheryl Glass

BILL POEHLER

ROWMAN & LITTLEFIELD
Lanham • Boulder • New York • London

Published by Rowman & Littlefield
An imprint of The Rowman & Littlefield Publishing Group, Inc.
4501 Forbes Boulevard, Suite 200, Lanham, Maryland 20706
www.rowman.com

86-90 Paul Street, London EC2A 4NE, United Kingdom

British Library Cataloguing in Publication Information available

Library of Congress Cataloging-in-Publication Data

Names: Poehler, Bill, 1977– author.
Title: The first lady of dirt : the triumphs and tragedy of racing pioneer
  Cheryl Glass / William Poehler.
Description: Lanham, Maryland : Rowman & Littlefield, [2024] | Includes
  bibliographical references and index. | Summary: "The First Lady of Dirt
  tells the incredible, little-known story of one of the most promising
  race car drivers in the United States who defied the odds as a Black
  woman in the sport of auto racing to find success, but whose life came
  crashing down after repeated run-ins with authorities and struggles with
  mental illness before her death at age 35"— Provided by publisher.
Identifiers: LCCN 2023034254 (print) | LCCN 2023034255 (ebook) | ISBN
  9781538184059 (cloth : acid-free paper) | ISBN 9781538184066 (epub)
Subjects: LCSH: Glass, Cheryl. | Women automobile racing drivers—United
  States—Biography. | Women drag racers—United States—Biography. |
  African American athletes—Biography. | African American
  Models—Biography.
Classification: LCC GV1032.G595 P64 2024 (print) | LCC GV1032.G595
  (ebook) | DDC 796.72092 [B]—dc23/eng/20231018
LC record available at https://lccn.loc.gov/2023034254
LC ebook record available at https://lccn.loc.gov/2023034255

CONTENTS

INTRODUCTION

Skagit Speedway

11:30 p.m., August 30, 1980

CHERYL GLASS WAS HAPPY.

For much of her first 18 years of life, Cheryl was paid to smile for cameras as a model.[1] This time the grin captured in the photo was genuine.

Her hair, cut short months earlier so she could more easily shove her head into racing helmets, had grown slightly. She wore a ring on the index finger of her left hand, but no other jewelry. She didn't wear her prescription eyeglasses or makeup. Her white fire suit had a couple black and orange stripes with her nickname "The Lady" embroidered on the chest. After a year of hard use racing on dirt tracks around the northwest, Cheryl's white fire suit was slightly dingy no matter how many times it was laundered.

Cheryl was a stickler for appearance. She didn't care this night. She was dressed perfectly for the moment.

She stood 5 feet, 5 inches tall, but she was physically towered over by the men on either side.

To her left, holding her helmet under his arm, was her father. Marvin Glass stood 6 feet, 4 inches and still looked every bit of the athlete that gave him his first notoriety. He wore the white pants required to be in the pit area and a slightly dingy white sweater to guard against the chill of the August evening. His hairline receding at age 45, Marvin has his free arm around his daughter in a moment of genuine fatherly pride.

Cheryl Glass (*third from left*) celebrates winning the 1980 season finale race at Skagit Speedway. She is flanked by her father, Marvin Glass (*right*), crew chief Jim Grantham (*holding trophy*), and Dan Murphy in front of her sprint car.
SHIRLEY GLASS COLLECTION

To her right is her crew chief, Jim Grantham, with a big smile on his face. He sacrificed a lot to help his friend's daughter achieve her goal that night. The sandy blonde Grantham wore a printed, button-up shirt, the cuffs rolled up to his elbows. The stains on the knees of his white pants demonstrated how much work he invested to help Cheryl. Grantham's blue athletic sneakers were the tell-tale sign of a working man. Cheryl handed off the trophy she earned that night to him, and he held it proudly at her side. Cheryl resented him for holding the trophy she earned, but she wasn't capable of holding it for a long period of time. It was too damn big.[2]

To Cheryl's far right is Dan Murphy. He occasionally worked on her race car, just as a number of other family friends had throughout the years. He wore the same style white pants as the other men, but his pants were held up with a brown belt, a shade darker than his brown shoes. His light blue button-down shirt was grease-stained, but his mustache and dark hair were immaculate. Murphy appears nowhere else in the story of Cheryl Glass.[3]

Cheryl's chariot rests behind her. It served her well through a full year of racing and especially well this night. A RAM chassis sprint car, the lime green frame is offset by the black and gold car body, as well as the aluminum silver of the wings and wheels. The car is splattered in the dirt of the speedway she had conquered, adding tan accents to the car's body.

In the background on the right are Jerry Day, who built the car, and his pit crew member "Crazy" Dave, both dressed in orange jackets, background characters in her tale.[4]

But Cheryl is the star on this night.

Cheryl Glass's life got more complicated from then on. She didn't know that this would be the greatest moment of her life, but she savored it.

Cheryl Glass was a winner. She always believed she could win, but this proved to everyone else she could, too.

For the next 17 years, this moment defined her.

Cheryl Glass was happy.

Chapter One

Raised to Excel

1961 to 1970

Marvin Glass and Shirley Robinson came from impoverished backgrounds in rural Tennessee. The Depression-ravaged South of the 1930s was not an ideal environment for anyone, least of all young Black people who wanted to rise above their station in life. Money was scarce and everything was segregated in the area: education, workplaces, restaurants, and nearly every service. Opportunities for Black people were limited. Two people who grew up in incredibly difficult situations found each other.

When Shirley Robinson was born in October 1936, her family set her up for a lifetime of disappointment. Helen Robinson was 14 years old when she got pregnant by 41-year-old Porter Price, and they married March 17, 1936.[1] The age of consent in Tennessee was 18 at that time, but Porter never faced repercussions. Helen Robinson didn't know she was already pregnant when they married. Eight months later, October 22, their first daughter, Shirley, was born in Nashville.[2] Three years later, another girl, Dorothy, was born. But the relationship between Helen and Porter was combustible and doomed to collapse. They divorced not long after Dorothy was born, though few people knew they were married, especially Porter's girlfriends.

"He was a contractor. Contractors were wine, women, and song," Shirley said.[3]

With two daughters, no job prospects, and no future, Helen moved from boyfriend to boyfriend, taking her daughters with her on every stop. Eventually she settled in Ohio.

For years, the girls didn't hear much about their father. When they did, it was not positive. Late at night on July 11, 1942, Porter Price was playing in an illegal dice game—and losing—at a house at 800 Church Street in Nashville against a group of men including 26-year-old William Bailey. Bailey won the game and the pot of 75 cents, which included all the money Price had. Price insisted Bailey had cheated. Bailey picked up his winnings from the table and they got into an argument. Price left the house, went to his home on Batavia Street and retrieved a pistol. When Price returned to the Church Street house, he pointed the gun at Bailey and called him a cheater once again. Price fired five shots at Bailey at point-blank range, killing him instantly. Price was convicted of murder and sent to prison.[4]

Helen Robinson met and dated Albert Reister, a known criminal who was out of jail on parole. They married and moved into a small apartment with Helen's two daughters in Mansfield, Ohio. Reister was a violent man. Even when her children were in the apartment, Reister repeatedly kicked and punched Helen on a near daily basis. On the night of June 15, 1945, Helen had enough. After drinking heavily that day, Reister undressed and crawled into bed for the night. Helen picked up a gun, pointed it at the sleeping Reister, and shot him dead. Helen left the apartment, stole a car, and sped away. Detective Howard Shuck was dispatched to track her down. She led the officer on a chase for a few miles through neighborhoods before stopping, and he arrested her. She told Shuck her getaway was "more of a thrill than killing Reister." Police found the gun she used to kill him under the carpet in the apartment after she told them where to look. Helen was found guilty of manslaughter and sent to prison.[5]

Shirley and Dorothy Robinson would only briefly see either parent from that day forward.

Shirley and Dorothy were sent to live with their maternal grandparents, James "Red" Terry and Louise Terry, who lived in Nashville, Tennessee. They were the only relatives who would take the girls. They had space for two young girls, but not much else to give them.

James was a light-skinned Black man with red hair[6] and Louise was of Native American descent. Their home was a three-room tenement with no plumbing, no electricity, and no central heating. The ramshackle house was so cold in winter that Louise would drape quilts over the windows to retain as much heat from the wood-fired stove as possible. In the summer, the house would swelter. To get around Nashville, Red and Louise often drove horse-drawn carriages. Red worked at a stove-making plant in Franklin, requiring a 20-mile bus ride each day to get to work. Though Louise worked as a cook in a school near the house, she didn't believe education was necessary. Neither she nor Red graduated high school, and they could barely read or write.

But the girls were bright. Both excelled in school. Shirley showed an aptitude in math and science; Dorothy was better at English. Shirley viewed education as her way out of the poverty of her situation. Everyone in her family was poor, but she didn't have to be, she reasoned. Pearl High School in north Nashville was the city's first high school solely for Black students and became a magnet for the best Black students and teachers. It took work for Shirley to gain admission as the school accepted few new students each year and was barely supported financially by the city's school system. But once she was accepted, Shirley excelled and graduated in 1955. Shirley was the first person to graduate high school in her family.

Shirley enrolled at Tennessee Agricultural & Industrial State College in Nashville, a Black college, and opted for the most challenging major it offered: engineering. Few Black men went into engineering; Black women weren't in the field at all. Shirley's engineering classes had a couple women and over a dozen men. The tuition was so expensive that Shirley took multiple low-paying jobs to afford it. And she didn't tell her grandparents she was in college.

"They didn't understand," Shirley said. "In Nashville, one of the places that I worked was Aladdin Industries. They could not hire me as an engineer, but they did give me a job cleaning up."

Professors at Tennessee Agricultural & Industrial State College saw the potential Shirley Robinson possessed and tried to help her succeed.

The first time Shirley met Marvin Glass in college, she knew she had found her high-achieving counterpart.

Marvin's father, Porter Glass, was born in 1916 in rural Dyersberg, Tennessee, 150 miles west of Nashville and dropped out of school after the third grade.[7] There weren't many options for a Black child at that time and Porter went to work in farmers' fields to help his family. The best thing that happened to Porter in school, however, was he met Florence Bonds, a striking girl. Her mother, Lucy Willingham, had an adventurous streak and raced horse-drawn buggies. Porter Glass and Florence Bonds married and on July 1, 1935, Marvin Glass was born.[8] Not long after they were married, Porter Glass left and wasn't heard from for years. Marvin was a large kid for his age, bright, personable, and able to make friends with everyone. He also excelled immediately at every sport he tried. His athletic ability gave him the chance to exceed the boundaries of his situation.

After graduating high school—he was the first person in his family to do so—Marvin received a scholarship to play football and compete in track and field in college. He excelled at sports, but it was academics in which he was most interested. After his first few years, Marvin transferred to Tennessee Agricultural & Industrial State College to major in engineering.

"And Marvin was a guy that grew up slashing cotton," said Jim Grantham, who would later befriend Marvin. "Earned his way through college, graduated with an electrical engineering degree and played college football. The Baltimore Colts wanted him, and he told them, 'I didn't get this degree to be a sweat hog.'"[9]

The engineering program at Tennessee Agricultural & Industrial State College was one of the few venues for secondary education for Black people at the time. The program drew the brightest students and the best professors together in an environment in which the students could gain the knowledge necessary for the field. A few professors from the University of Tennessee even taught classes at the school to its students at night. The program was challenging, but that was the type of challenge which helped Marvin and Shirley to thrive.

Shirley had a second job as a cook at a hospital, and a third as a checker at a drug store. She had little time for anything else. Marvin worked as a janitor at the college to pay for his schooling. In between his studies, he joined every group involved with academic excellence he could find. He joined the Institute of Radio Engineers, the Beta Kappa Chi National Scientific Honor Society, and the Omega Psi Phi fraternity.[10]

There were more than a dozen men in the engineering program at Tennessee Agricultural & Industrial State College; Shirley was one of a few women. When she first met Marvin in class, Shirley was taken.

"Tall, handsome," Shirley thought of him. "I wasn't no slouch."

They began dating, and Marvin and Shirley got engaged in their senior year of college. They were the "it" couple in their class.

Their relationship was also a boon to their future employment.

Boeing, an aircraft manufacturer based in Seattle, Washington, rapidly expanded post-World War II, largely because it secured government contracts to build planes and other technology.[11] In the 1950s, government rules for awarding contracts required a percentage of Black people on staff. And they couldn't work in minor roles like janitors. To get the lucrative business, Boeing needed Black engineers. Boeing aggressively recruited every Black engineer it could find in an effort to meet the government quota. There were few colleges that trained Black people to work as engineers in the United States, and Tennessee Agricultural & Industrial State College became a focal point for Boeing's recruiters. Before Marvin and Shirley graduated, they both accepted lucrative offers from Boeing. The jobs required a move across the country to a place of which they had previously only heard.

There was a problem when Boeing tried to verify Shirley's identity, however. As she would be working on top-secret government projects in her role in working with technology in classified fields, the government needed to perform a background check. When the agents did, the information they found indicated she didn't exist. Due to her transient childhood, Shirley had a number of surnames. She also struggled with spelling, which further compounded the government's troubles in verifying who she was.

"My grandmother was named Terry and her other name was Thompson before she got married," Shirley said. "And then Robertson, I didn't know how to spell it, whether it was Robertson, Robinson. So my grandmother had to go to court and swear I was the same person to come to work for Boeing to get a clearance. And I finally got a top clearance."

With new jobs awaiting them, the marriage plans for Marvin and Shirley accelerated. The day after Marvin and Shirley graduated in 1959 with bachelor's degrees in electrical engineering, they were married at Olivet Baptist Church in Nashville. Shirley went all out on her wedding dress. She hand sewed the gown from Chantilly lace, embroidering it with handsewn pearls and iridescent sequins. The dress was expensive. Marvin and Shirley had dozens of friends on hand for the ceremony, but not much family. Marvin's mother was there. Shirley's sister, Dorothy, was the maid of honor. And Shirley's grandparents, Red and Louise Terry, attended. The rest of the church was filled with friends.[12]

The wedding also served as a going-away party for the newlyweds; the next day Marvin and Shirley left for Seattle to begin their careers with Boeing.

Seattle boomed in the 1950s, growing by 38 percent in a decade. The new freeway, Interstate 5, was completed in Seattle in 1965, ensuring people no longer had to cross the Aurora Bridge to pass into north Seattle. It was on that then-deserted interstate where Shirley Glass first learned to drive a car. The city and areas surrounding it in the Puget Sound developed into a sprawling metroplex in a matter of years, with Boeing responsible for much of the area's growth.

Founded in Seattle by timber magnate and aspiring pilot William Boeing in 1916,[13] the company was a minor player in aviation until the early 1940s when the United States was involved in World War II. The Boeing workforce grew to 50,000 workers in 1944 from 6,000 workers in 1939 as airplanes were needed at a record pace. The company's workforce again spiked to 100,000 by 1957 as the United States entered the Cold War and had been involved in the Korean War.[14]

For many workers in the northwest, a job with Boeing represented stability. Much like the automobile manufacturers in Detroit in the 1930s, thousands of workers moved to Seattle in search of work at Boeing in one of its many manufacturing facilities. For unskilled workers, gainful employment at Boeing was a career.

A common joke in the Puget Sound is to ask a stranger if they know someone who worked at Boeing.

"They'll say they know two or three," said Jim Galasyn, who once worked for Boeing.[15]

For the highly skilled engineers Boeing hired to work on government contracts, such as the Saturn rocket boosters, the work ebbed and flowed. Once the project was completed, less-tenured employees would be laid off. But the company paid salaries that made that hassle worth it.

In its early years, jobs at Boeing were off limits for Black people. The population of people who identified as Black in Seattle in 1940 was .01 percent, slightly more than 4,000 people. But in its first decades as a company, Boeing refused to hire any of them. The union representing the company's workers and the local Communist Party were complicit in the company's refusal to hire them. Even after President Franklin Roosevelt's executive order prohibiting racial discrimination in 1941, the company refused to comply. It wasn't until a complaint was filed by the National Association for the Advancement of Colored People (NAACP) in 1942 that the union began admitting Black people. Boeing hired its first two Black employees, Florise Spearman and Dorothy West Williams, in 1942.[16]

Another executive order from President Roosevelt in 1943 gave a federal commission power to ensure defense contractors hired Black people for jobs in the defense industry. Companies like Boeing were late to comply, but eventually relented.

But the government contracts that brought Marvin and Shirley to Seattle were quickly fulfilled. Rival aircraft manufacturer Lockheed had won other government contracts. When Lockheed offered the Glasses more money to relocate to California, they accepted. A little over a year after moving to Seattle, the Glass family relocated to San Jose in 1960. They found a small apartment, not far from Lockheed's manufacturing facility.

Marvin and Shirley wanted a family and were overjoyed when Shirley found out she was pregnant in April 1961. Unlike many of the women in her family, Shirley's pregnancy was planned and coincided with a time of economic prosperity. On Christmas Eve, December 24, 1961, Shirley went into labor. She was rushed to the hospital in Mountain View, California. But something was wrong.

"I had to make a choice when they were delivering her whether I wanted them to save her or me. I said, 'Save her,'" Shirley said.

After hours of labor, the doctors didn't have to make the decision, and Cheryl Linn Glass was born.[17]

In their humble, scattered childhoods in Tennessee, both Marvin and Shirley struggled in every way. They worked long hours to earn everything they received. They were determined to give their daughter every tool to be successful.

They pushed Cheryl from a young age and instilled in her the importance of education and self-reliance. Cheryl Glass was groomed to be the best at everything. When she wasn't the best, she was instructed not to waste her time on it and find another activity.

Marvin and Shirley were such hot commodities in the field of electrical engineering that other companies offered increasing amounts of money to work for them. Shirley was offered a job for the Navy designing communication facilities, which required the family to move back to Seattle in 1962. Marvin got another job with Boeing. The money they were paid at the age of 26 enabled the couple to purchase their first house on Lake Washington Boulevard. Marvin left Boeing in 1963 for a similar engineering job at Pacific Northwest Bell. He started out as a supervisor in the engineering section and soon became vice president of planning and operations.

"He would have never been an executive at Boeing. Are you kidding?" Shirley said.

Soon after, Shirley left the Navy to return to another engineering position at Boeing.

Cheryl showed she was advanced at an early age. By age three, she could read, write, and had reasoning skills. Her parents decided to see if her intelligence could be measured. Cheryl was given the Stanford-Binet Intelligence Scale test. Often used to gauge if children have developmental disabilities, the test could also indicate if a child is average or advanced. Cheryl scored 151 out of a possible 160. That placed her in the "very gifted" or "highly advanced" categories. With such promise in academics, the Glasses enrolled Cheryl at the prestigious Evergreen School for Gifted Children and then at the private Helen Bush-Parkside School in Seattle.[18]

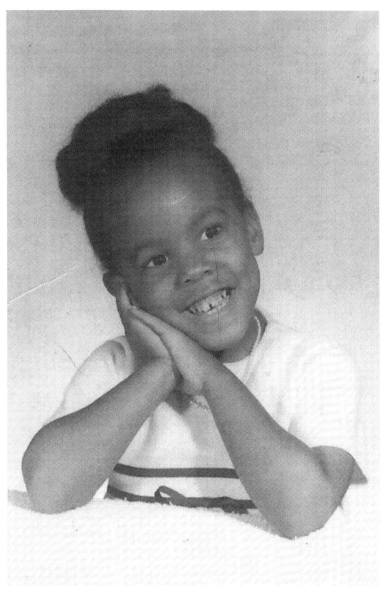

Cheryl Glass poses for a photo.

Within the span of a few years, Marvin and Shirley were earning more money than they could have previously imagined. They started buying houses in Seattle as investments. At one point they owned a half dozen. They rented some to tenants and let family members live in others. One of the houses they purchased was for Marvin's mother, Florence. She had moved to Seattle from Tennessee and assisted the family in raising Cheryl. While Cheryl's parents worked long hours in their lucrative jobs, Florence often was left alone to care for Cheryl.

"(Florence) didn't care too much for me because in that day, a lot of people felt like their sons were supposed to take care of (their wives)," Shirley said. "We had a difference of opinion."

There was another way Boeing's push for diversity in its workforce paid dividends for the Glass family: it helped them find a community.

In 1956, Eugene Young Sr. was successfully recruited to take a position at Boeing. The perk that drew him to the job was the high quality of fishing in Washington. He and his family became friends with the Glass family. Waymon Whiting moved to Seattle from Texas for a position at Boeing. After moving back to Seattle, Shirley brought her sister Dorothy from Tennessee. Dorothy met Waymon Whiting through the Glasses, and they married on March 21, 1961, and moved nearby to Bellevue. Their first daughter, Vicki, was born in September 1961.[19]

Seattle was relatively remote from the rest of the country, but it became a place where Black engineers could come together.

The affluence of the Glass family afforded them opportunities to get involved in community activities. Marvin Glass became involved in a fundraising drive to raise money to build a pool at a local elementary school, though not the one his daughter Cheryl was attending. Shirley participated by baking and selling cookies for $1 per dozen while Cheryl decorated them. Unlike their childhoods when their parents were scratching out a living and trying to survive, Cheryl was shown a different path.[20]

Decorating cookies brought something out in Cheryl. The freedom she found in the intricate designs on the cookies was new and exciting. She enjoyed creating something unique, and how she could combine the designs with a sense of precision to make something beautiful. She had little interest in cooking, but designing those cookies was a breakthrough.

A couple years later, Cheryl found another path where her creativity would be an asset. At age seven, Cheryl took her first modeling class at the Bon Marche's Cinderella Modeling Class. Her angular face, even at a young age, was striking and she almost immediately found work as a model for department stores throughout Seattle. She was quickly in demand to model clothes in advertisements for the stores. On some days she would appear in advertisements in multiple newspapers for multiple stores. Cheryl got a taste for attention at an early age.

Shirley and Marvin encouraged Cheryl's interests in ways only parents with financial means could. As soon as she showed an aptitude at design, they bought a complete set of tools and kilns for making ceramics, nearly enough to fill the garage of their home. Cheryl soon was making ceramic dishes. She rapidly expanded her line and was making items like bowls. People outside the family also recognized her talent.

Cheryl needed somewhere to sell them. She had contacts at department stores around Seattle from her modeling work, and her mother insisted she exploit them. On a Saturday afternoon in 1971, Shirley drove 11-year-old Cheryl from one Seattle department store to another, bringing samples of her work to potential buyers. Shirley coached her daughter on how she should talk to people in the purchasing department and advised her on what she needed to tell them. That afternoon, Cheryl was dropped off at department stores through downtown Seattle while her mother waited in the car.

"You go in there yourself and I'll wait out here in the car for you," Shirley told her.

That afternoon, Cheryl convinced buyer after buyer to sell her ceramic dishes, including the one at the prestigious Frederick & Nelson chain of department stores.

The profiles of multiple Glass family members rose.

Beyond his job at Boeing, Marvin Glass joined the National Urban League and the local chapter of the NAACP. He became the director of the Northwest Gifted Children's Association, a group in which Cheryl was a member. Marvin took another volunteer position on the board of the East Madison YMCA. At age 34, Marvin was spreading himself thin, but he knew how important his participation could be in Seattle's Black community, especially considering his highly regarded position at Pacific Northwest Bell.

Then a bigger opportunity came along. After three days of racial protests in 1969, Carl Dakn resigned from his position on the all-white Seattle Community College Board of Trustees. Washington Governor Dan Evans appointed Marvin to the position, making him the first Black person to hold such an important position. Marvin's presence wasn't universally appreciated. After his appointment to the board, a group of mostly white protesters marched outside the college, objecting to his presence. One of the protesters called Marvin an "Uncle Tom." Marvin tried to assure doubters he could work in harmony with the six white board members of the community college, but was "not adverse to creating a little friction if it's something I believe in."[21]

A week later, someone broke into the Glass's home, stole a television, savings bonds, and wedding rings. They also let the family's dog run away. Detectives from the Seattle Police Department who investigated the break-in said the front door may have been left open, but the family didn't believe it. After years of living in Seattle, the family was experiencing how the police treated Black people through a different lens.[22]

"We went to a hotel out of town and stayed because the FBI had got a report that the (Alabama) Governor George Wallace had a hit out on us," Shirley Glass said.

Then Cheryl did something that would forever define her life.

CHAPTER TWO

Finding Her Calling in a Small Arena

1971 to 1979

EVERY TIME CHERYL GLASS FOUND A NEW SPORT, ACADEMIC PURSUIT, or activity that she wanted to try, her family gave her their full support. They asked one thing in return: if she took part in something, she would give it everything she could and find a way to excel. Marvin and Shirley believed that supporting their only daughter in ways that they themselves had never been could lead her to future success. But their level of support also led Cheryl to believe that if she was to take on an activity, she had to be the best. She couldn't enjoy a sport for the sake of participation.

After trying ice skating, she soon was going to multiple practices each week at the few ice rinks around Seattle. When she wanted to try swimming, her family bought a house with a pool. She tried volleyball, gymnastics, soccer, and ballet. She worked hard at each, but gave them up when she realized she wasn't the best at them.

"There has to be something out there at which I can be the best. It's just up to me to find what that something is," Cheryl said.[1]

A newspaper article[2] or advertisement[3]—depending on which version of the story she told—set the direction of Cheryl's life. One of the Seattle newspapers published a piece about the relatively unknown form of auto racing known as quarter midgets—a small race car intended for children—in 1970. When the curious 10-year-old Cheryl Glass read about it, she decided it was something she had to do. She thought that this was the sport in which she could be the best.

In post-World War II America, people had children and they had money. They were dreaming up new ways to spend it. Innovative builders of full-size race cars like midgets and big cars—which would later be known as sprint cars—struck on the idea that miniature size vehicles with rudimentary mechanical workings could be an affordable, easy-to-maintain, and easy-to-transport solution to getting young people involved in their sport. Starting in the 1950s, enterprising builders created new classes of miniaturized race cars: three-quarter midgets, go-karts, quarter midgets, and mini sprints. There were slight differences in the size of the cars, their appearance, and the rules which governed them. But they shared similar ethos of using inexpensive components like lawn mower or motorcycle engines to power the tiny speedsters.

When quarter midget racing got its start in 1954, the scaled-down racers were an inviting way to get children involved. The bodies of the cars were modeled after the midget class. Where midgets were intended for adults to race, quarter midgets were aimed solely at children. On circle tracks a few hundred feet in length, they never had the distance to get up enough speed to seriously injure someone, but they offered oversized thrills to any child fortunate enough to drive one.[4]

Quarter midget racing quickly spread to every corner of the United States. Tracks were relatively cheap to build. There was no need for expensive officials as parents often took on the roles. And the cars were relatively inexpensive to operate.

The story Cheryl read described the racing at Paine Field as a permanent home for quarter midget racing. It painted a picture of dozens of children spending nearly every weekend in the summer with their families, racing wheel to wheel, lap after lap, and seeking the grand prize of a trophy at the end of the races. Cheryl was immediately drawn to the image of bringing home trophies.

Built as a military base in Everett as a Works Progress Administration project in 1936, Paine Field served as a U.S. Army Air Corps base during World War II due to its strategic position on the west coast. But in peacetime, it went years without being used. With the need to build larger jets for commercial air traffic, Boeing purchased the retired base in 1966 to build its newest aircraft, the Boeing 747. Boeing constructed a massive 98-acre building, the largest building by volume in the world at the time. In 1969, the first of a new class of luxury airplanes rolled out of the assembly plant.[5]

Though the airport was still used by Boeing, there were unused corners of the property, including a wooded area on the western border. In those woods, a group of parents built a ½₀-mile asphalt oval in 1969, and the races—the first of their type in the Puget Sound area—gained popularity. Races were held on Sundays. Race car drivers saw it as an easy way to introduce their children to racing.

In racing, most aspiring young drivers learn about the sport from family members. They tag along with their parents to races and get hooked on the sport. The children of racers can be found in the grandstands or the pits, running around in circles or racing toy cars against each other. They emulate a parent, usually a father, and dream of the day they will be the race car driver in the family.

Cheryl Glass had none of that.

Her family knew nothing about racing, a sport in which Black people infrequently participated from when it started nearly 100 years earlier. When Cheryl Glass announced to her parents she was going to race quarter midgets, they didn't understand.

"I was surprised because racing was the farthest thing from my mind at the time," Marvin Glass said. "I didn't know such a thing existed, and if it did, that she wanted to do it."[6]

It's difficult to get new people involved in driving race cars. The sport is prohibitively expensive and requires a massive amount of knowledge and money to get started. Cars, trailers, parts, tools, and fuel all cost money, no matter what size of cars being raced.

Unlike Cheryl's other endeavors, however, her parents weren't going to finance this one. For Cheryl to race, she needed money to pay for it.

She made a few dollars for her hard work on each ceramic dish she made, but by 1971 was already producing them at such a pace that it didn't take her long to earn $300. With that money in hand, Marvin found a quarter midget in her price range, and Cheryl purchased her first race car.

"It was something my father and I could do together," Cheryl said.[7]

Though her father had little experience with cars and none in racing, he threw himself into his daughter's newest pursuit. Cheryl and her father were close and shared similar temperaments and mannerisms. Unlike Shirley, Cheryl was more gentle when it came to getting her own way. Even at a young age, she could talk people into things they didn't know they wanted. Where Cheryl had coaches and other private instructors at other sports like swimming and tennis, she had to have someone by her side in order to compete in quarter midgets, and Marvin committed himself to filling that role in this endeavor.

The Washington Quarter Midget Racing Association's races at Paine Field grew so quickly that in a few years, children had to be broken into classifications based on how much power their cars had and how much experience the drivers possessed.

Second-generation youngsters competing at Paine Field like Kelly Tanner and Billy Kennelly had been hanging around racetracks all of their lives and had studied their parents closely. Tobey Butler also had a father who drove sprint cars and wanted to get his son involved in racing. Though he was a beginner as an 11-year-old in 1971, Tobey Butler knew the basics of racing. But he still needed seat time to excel.

Cheryl Glass had no idea how to drive a race car before she climbed in her quarter midget for the first time for a race in 1971. She had never been to a race before that day. Her inexperience showed, but she was also fast from the start.

"The first time I ever rolled over in my quarter midget, she's the one I hit. She hit me and I rolled," Tobey Butler said.[8]

There were few girls and no other Black drivers racing at Paine Field when Cheryl Glass started racing there. Most of the other drivers and families didn't know what to make of her at first. Some thought this was some kind of a stunt. They soon found out it was not.

And many of the young boys against whom Cheryl raced either were intimidated by her or developed crushes on her.

Developing the ability to perform even the basic skills of racing, such as sensing speed, takes time and effort. The hand-eye coordination needed in racing is more difficult. Figuring out where a driver's fear and courage intersect in the perfect combination to drive a race car quickly

Cheryl Glass prepares to race a quarter midget. She raced quarter midgets from 1971 to 1979.

requires the driver to repeatedly push beyond their perceived limits to find out how fast they can be. But Cheryl placed third in her first quarter midget race. That promise was enough to tell her this was the sport for her.

Once she found her limits, Cheryl progressed quickly.

She gained quick recognition for her ability as a driver as she improved with each race. She was voted the rookie of the year for the Washington Quarter Midget Racing Association in 1971 by her fellow competitors. That award gave Cheryl a sense of accomplishment: She found something she was immediately good at.[9]

Then in July 1971, her family got a surprise.

After the difficult birth of Cheryl, Shirley had been instructed by her doctor that she couldn't get pregnant again. She was warned another pregnancy could endanger her life and the potential life of the child. Because of that, Marvin and Shirley had lavished a great deal of attention and their focus on Cheryl, who they thought would be their only child. Then a second daughter, Cherry (pronounced Sherry), arrived.

"I thought I had an ulcer because I wasn't supposed to get pregnant again," Shirley said.[10]

Marvin and Shirley were making sizable salaries from their work at Boeing and with their growing family needed a bigger house than the one on Lake Washington Boulevard.

What the Glass family found was a house on 42nd Avenue, just north of the University of Washington with a view of Lake Washington. The house was essentially in the country as there were no other houses around and the area was heavily wooded. The most important feature of the house was that it had a large two-car garage, which would give plenty of room for Cheryl's quarter midget and all the necessary equipment. As soon as they moved in, the garage was quickly filled.

For Cheryl, winning races was her only option. As she turned lap after lap on Paine Field's 1/20-mile oval, she got faster. She showed no fear, crashing frequently and winning with increasing frequency. In one of her first years of racing, the Washington Quarter Midget Association presented her its rollover award as she was the most frequent driver to accomplish that dreaded accident in many of her races.

She once crashed a quarter midget so hard into a wall, that she was dragged the length of the front stretch, ripping the roll cage off the car, scraping her helmet, and grinding her leather driving suit on the pavement all the way to her arm. But after that wreck, she got back in the quarter midget 10 minutes later and placed second in the next race.[11]

The positive results came, too. She won the Novice class main event at the 1972 Northwest State championship race at Paine Field. That encouraged her to find more competition. She began travelling to other races hours away at tracks like Alpenrose Dairy in Portland, Oregon, and into British Columbia. These experiences also aided Cheryl's progress and she started to become a threat to win any race in which she drove. While the quarter midget competition at a track or in a region like the Northwest may be good, the only way to gauge a driver is when they compete against the best in the nation.

For quarter midgets, that competition is at the Grand Nationals.

Where a race at Paine Field could draw 100 kids with their quarter midgets to race for a day, a Grand National would draw hundreds of drivers from across the nation to one track, making the competition intense. Where a class like Heavy B Modified might have a half dozen entries at a local race, there would be three dozen of them at a grand national, most of them champions at their home tracks. The qualifying process for the ultimate main event would last for days, slotting the cars into races against those of similar skill levels. A driver who won race after race at home quickly found out that he or she wasn't as good as they had thought. Racing against drivers like P. J. Jones and Bobby Labonte was tougher than the competition they faced at home. Most quarter midget drivers wouldn't bother going to a Grand National until they had years of experience.

When Cheryl went to her first Grand Nationals in 1973 in Sunnyvale, California, she learned how tough it was, and she loved it. After dominating the competition in the Northwest, at the Grand Nationals the best Cheryl could do was make the semi-main event in the Heavy B Modified class, in which she placed eighth. She was the first Black person to compete at that level of racing, something that brought her recognition beyond her results.[12]

Shirley Glass (*left*), Marvin Glass, and Cherry Glass sit together in the pits at a quarter midget race.
SHIRLEY GLASS COLLECTION

And there was one competition at that level where Cheryl and the rest of the Glass family excelled.

Every year at the Grand Nationals, a contest was held for the "Best Appearing" crew. When it came to outfitting Cheryl and her crew, Shirley went all out, designing and sewing immaculate matching outfits for each person. She made a custom driver's suit for Cheryl, then made matching shirts and pants for Marvin, Cherry, and herself. The white shirts and pants were embroidered with their names in red stitching. When Cheryl got a new driving suit, Shirley would sew new outfits for the rest of the family to match. The family was awarded the Best Crew trophy at the 1973 Grand Nationals, their first of many. If the Glass family was going to participate in something, they had to be the best.

"She'd get out of the car and she'd have her leather jacket on with the tassels, full of style," Billy Kennelly said.[13]

Though Cheryl was finding ways to excel in racing, her parents pushed her to continue other pursuits as well. She competed in sports like swimming and volleyball in high school. She took advanced modeling classes at the John Robert Powers Advanced Modeling School and appeared in national magazines such as *Seventeen*, *Essence*, and *Jet*.

"I remember seeing Cheryl in middle school," said Lisa Kelsie, who would later become her hairdresser and a friend. "She drove to middle school in a convertible Mercedes. She was the coolest person."[14]

But it was quarter midget racing where Cheryl excelled the most. After winning races at Paine Field consistently in 1974, she won the consolation race at the Grand Nationals in Columbus, Ohio.

But there was something else going on at the racetracks, too. She transfixed many of the younger drivers at the track.

"We just had the biggest crush on Cheryl the whole time," Billy Kennelly said of himself and friend Rory Price. "There was always something about Cheryl, something about the way she carried herself off the track."

Cheryl had gone as far as she could artistically and financially making ceramic dishes. She decided to expand her line. Porcelain dolls were fetching a high price, so Cheryl started making reproductions of high-end dolls. It took her three months to make each one of the intricate dolls, but when she completed her first, Fredrick & Nelson purchased it for $250. Making the dolls took more time than the dishes, but she made enough of them that she was able to buy bigger and better quarter midgets to race.

When she outgrew some of her cars, she gave them to her cousins Vicki, Waymon III, and DeVonna Whiting so they could get into racing, too.

Marion Gartler, a woman who lived near the Glass family home, had co-authored several books for children and noticed the constant buzz of activity going on at the Glass's house. After stopping by the house several times and seeing the chaos of people working on quarter midgets, she decided this was a family she needed to write a book about. Gartler followed the Glass family to the final race of the 1975 season at Paine Field, which Cheryl won.

As Cheryl moved into bigger quarter midget classes, her talent became more apparent. She won Washington Quarter Midget Association championships in the Heavy B and Heavy AA classes in 1975 as she was racing two cars in each race program.

Gartler tagged along to the 1975 Grand Nationals at Portland's Alpenrose Dairy. Cheryl had damaged the engine in one of her cars in the final race of the season at Paine Field, though it wasn't discovered until shortly before the family was to leave for Oregon. The repairs needed were extensive and required the engine to be sent to an engine builder. Vicki Whiting, meanwhile, was racing with Cheryl's backup engine in her car.

The family still traveled to Portland for the race because Cheryl still had one of her cars ready to go. She managed to qualify her first car for the race. Cheryl decided to let Vicki race her back-up engine and hope her primary engine for her second car would be finished in time. At the last moment, Cheryl's primary engine was delivered by the engine builder and she was able to qualify for that race, too. Everything looked like it was going to work out.

But just as the final day of the race was about to get underway, the Oregon skies filled with rain. The only award handed out that day was the Best Appearing Crew, which went to the Glass family again. Retired Indianapolis 500 veteran driver Len Sutton, the 1962 runner-up, lived nearby in Portland. Wearing bellbottoms that seemed out of place for a 50-year-old driver of his generation, Sutton presented the trophy to the family. It was as close as Cheryl would get to winning a race that weekend.[15]

Cheryl took more courses in modeling at age 14, and work in the field was plentiful.

"I really enjoyed that," Cheryl said. "I got to meet a lot of different types of people. I just ran out of time for modeling. When I really got into racing I just ran out of time for some of the other things I did before. You have to be dedicated. It has to be something you really want to do."[16]

Cheryl spent most of her life attending private schools. But the private schools she attended wouldn't let her skip ahead. Cheryl opted to transfer to Nathan Hale High School, a public school not far from her home for her sophomore year. She immediately excelled.

"Well, I got bored," Cheryl said. "I had been in private school and I changed to a public school my last few years of high school and I wanted to just take the meaty courses, the math and sciences, and I wanted to kind of not have to take the PE and the Home EC and some of the things that I didn't really think I needed."[17]

Cheryl and the Glass family had found a level of acceptance in the quarter midget racing world that defied all the conventions of racing.

When eight-year-old James Grantham made a deal with his father, Jim, that if he would give up drinking, James would win every quarter midget race he entered, the father realized he needed to clean up. Jim Grantham never had a drink again. Marvin Glass and Jim Grantham became unlikely friends, a conservative white man who worked in blue-collar professions like construction and a Black white-collar executive in the technology sector. But the families were soon joined together all the time, travelling together to top races all over the nation.

"(James) really enjoyed Marvin. I trusted him to go with Marvin everywhere," Jim Grantham said.[18]

Cheryl won Washington Quarter Midget Racing Association championships in 1977 and 1978, but while she was busy racing quarter midgets near home and around the nation, a dramatic shift in racing was happening that made her think she could have a career in the sport.

Several women, including Lella Lombardo, Davina Galica, and Janet Guthrie, were accomplishing things previously thought impossible for women in racing, like racing in Formula One and the Indianapolis 500. Along with the accomplishments of women in other forms of racing in the 1970s, it suddenly didn't seem a stretch for a woman to become a professional race car driver. Reading about the exploits of other women drivers, Cheryl developed a dream of becoming an Indy Car driver and parlaying that into a Formula One career. But Cheryl also decided she needed to be successful at those levels, unlike the women who came before her.

"I give her (Janet Guthrie) credit for becoming the first woman at Indianapolis," Cheryl Glass said in 1980. "But I think she kind of left a bad name in racing as far as women were concerned. She hasn't done that well as far as winning races goes and a lot of sponsors aren't willing to back women drivers now."[19]

Though Janet Guthrie became the first woman to race in the Indianapolis 500, there was another first open to Cheryl that she could accomplish. No Black person had ever competed at the biggest race in the world. In its early days under the sanction of the Contest Board of the American Automobile Association, the Indianapolis race had excluded Black drivers. Though vestiges of the earlier racism and exclusion were removed—the "coloreds only" grandstand had been razed—the racism itself remained. Cheryl believed she could become the first person of her race to race at Indy.

Cheryl decided she was ready to move on to the ranks of professional race car driver and needed to make a drastic move.

For her to accomplish her new goal of becoming a professional driver, she was going to graduate high school early. At age 16 in 1978, she completed her junior and senior years at Nathan Hale by attending school during the day and returning for more classes at night so she could graduate two years early.[20]

"So because I was bored, I went on to college when I was 16," Cheryl said.[21]

She enrolled at the University of Washington for the fall semester in 1978, intending to major in electrical engineering.[22] Cheryl still raced quarter midgets at every opportunity, but she made time for other pursuits. Cheryl ran for the University of Washington's homecoming queen and was the runner-up. Outside of college, she competed in disco dancing competitions and continued to model.

The story of a Black female race car driver having success against white boys was too much to resist for the local media. Mainstream newspapers and magazines gushed about her success and held Cheryl up as a pioneer in racing.

Nearly every story mentioned she was a model. The mostly male writers and editors couldn't let that detail go without mention.

Some teenagers would have been overwhelmed by the attention. Cheryl excelled when it came to interviews. Her story was compelling and her delivery impeccable.

"I remember going out to (Seattle International Raceway) with everybody because they were doing a TV show, like an evening magazine," James Grantham said.[23]

In 1979, Cheryl transferred to Seattle University for her junior year "where I thought I could get a more meaningful education." Though she was a good student and held a B average, she was adrift. She took courses for electrical engineering then some in pre-med. College was failing to hold her attention.

Racing quarter midgets limited how far Cheryl's career could go. Drivers age out of quarter midgets as the level of racing plateaus as drivers in their teenage years move into full-size race cars.

But there were many types of racing that were closed to Cheryl because of her age. Many series for full-size race cars required drivers to be 18 years old. Midgets were an exception. At age 17, Cheryl secured a ride in a midget for a Washington Midget Racing Association race at Olympia-Tenino Speedway south of Seattle on the outskirts of Rochester for a race on July 22, 1979. The race was being officiated by Indianapolis 500 flagman Pat Vidan from nearby Portland, Oregon. While many people would compete in their first full-size car race at a far-flung track so they could learn before competing against the best, Cheryl was determined to compete in front of the biggest audience possible. It would become a pattern in her career.

While quarter midgets and midgets sound similar, the only thing they have in common is they are pushed to start. Everything else—weight, length, tire size, engine size, and power—is different. They look similar to jelly beans, but a midget is larger, more powerful, faster, and more difficult to drive. A push start in a quarter midget is far different than a push start in a full-size midget. In the quarter midget, one person pushes the car to get a little speed, then the driver hits the ignition switch and gives the car throttle to pull away. To start a midget, however, requires having a truck push it from behind to get it up to speed. The driver must turn on the fuel and ignition to start the engine, and then the driver can accelerate away. The midget is difficult to start for a novice.

Cheryl didn't get to practice in the car she was to race, not even a push start, before her first time on the ¼-mile asphalt oval at Olympia-Tenino.[24] To go out onto the track for the first practice session of the day, the push truck driver attempted to push her up the ramp and onto the track. Just as she crested onto the oval, however, another car that was already under its own power and circling the track hit her before she could get the car started. The midget she was supposed to race was wrecked and done for the day. Her time in that type of car came to a conclusion before she even drove a lap.

"And it really wasn't her fault," Jim Grantham said.[25]

After her first attempt in a midget, Cheryl needed to find another class to race in, and one that was a path to a professional racing career. Marvin and Cheryl did extensive research into what kind of racing she could compete in. As he did in many areas, Marvin networked with everyone he could find and discovered there was an advanced category that competed regularly around Washington that could give Cheryl the skills and visibility she craved. It was beyond her ability, but that was the point.

"I've been told I can't run sprint cars competitively, and that makes me want to do it," Cheryl Glass said. "I think I can beat them at their own game."[26]

Cheryl Glass was going sprint car racing.

CHAPTER THREE

Becoming a National Star at the Local Level

January to August 1980

CHERYL GLASS DIDN'T KNOW SHE WASN'T SUPPOSED TO BE A SPRINT CAR driver.

Standing five feet, five inches and carrying 110 pounds on her slender frame, Cheryl was the anthesis of what people thought of when they pictured a sprint car driver. Cheryl was young, pretty, feminine and still looked like a model, a profession she was in the process of giving up. The 18-year-old wore immaculately tailored driving suits that were impeccably clean and radiated her unique style, a style more closely associated with her role as a competitive disco dancer than with the grungy world of sprint car racing. She had a number of driving suits tailor-made; some matched her car and others were black with pink striping and white lettering, the nickname "The Lady" embroidered on the left chest.[1] Her helmet was painted to match her race car and her name was painted on the side of the helmet. That was something race car drivers didn't do in 1980.

Sprint cars date back to the original race cars in the early 1900s when street cars were stripped of most of their bodies, along with everything else that could possibly make them slower, and engines were enhanced as much as possible. While other classes of race cars advanced technologically, sprint cars rarely did, relying instead on the creativity of the car builders and mechanics to perfect and enhance the basic technologies. In the 1930s, sprint cars stopped being based on any other type of car and morphed into purpose-built machines at the hands of experienced race car drivers who wanted to go faster. The rules for the class were fixed to a simpler time when cars were built with items like solid front and rear axles, technology that was quickly outdated. Safety was an afterthought for much of the existence of sprint cars: seat belts were frowned upon until the 1950s and roll cages were thought of as unnecessary until the 1960s. Many drivers assumed they would be safer being thrown from a car in an inevitable crash; drivers who were thrown often died from those injuries. There were no creature comforts in a sprint car: drivers sat in a rigid aluminum seat and gripped a steering wheel with no padding. Racing a sprint car came with the inherent risk of death.

By 1980, sprint cars evolved into little more than a cage of small steel tubes wrapped around an engine and a driver, often complimented by large wings on top and up front. The class was filled with snorting V8 engines, based loosely on those found in American passenger cars, drinking methanol at a rapid rate of a few miles per gallon through an archaic yet efficient fuel injection system which contributed to producing hundreds of horsepower. The engine was linked as directly as possible to the rear tires by a driveshaft less than an inch in diameter for maximum efficiency. The ultra-wide rear tires were drastically different sizes with the right rear 10 inches or more taller than the left rear (forcing the car to turn violently to the left to better negotiate the turns of tight oval tracks). Sprint cars didn't have power steering until the late 1970s; since most drivers believed it would give them less feel of what the car was doing and thus make them slower (some would claim the power steering advancement is what made Cheryl's career possible). The rear tires of a sprint car do most of the steering. The small, lightweight brakes are used only to help it turn by sending it into a slide. Items like starters and transmissions are noticeably absent from this class of cars by tradition, requiring the car to be pushed by a truck or by another vehicle to start.

The result of the evolution of the sprint car is that they are the purest race car ever devised, blessedly simple and utterly difficult to drive.

The cars shoot out flames, lift the front tires off the ground at the slightest urging of the driver, sling dirt from the track's surface hundreds of feet in all directions and are prone to flip after only the slightest error from the driver. They skim over the top of the dirt surfaces at unbeliev-able speeds. The power-to-weight ratio is so high that the cars can circle a quarter-mile-dirt oval in under 10 seconds and a half-mile in 15 seconds.

That type of thrill is what attracted Cheryl Glass to them. That, and being told that she couldn't be good at it.

Racing a sprint car requires a lack of fear; by the 1980s, few women had dared to race sprint cars. They had been forbidden from racing them for years. Many people involved at dirt tracks assumed women didn't have the physical ability to race a sprint car.

Many early racetracks and sanctioning bodies for racing in the United States wouldn't allow women to compete; European racing was more progressive. Women like Camille du Gast, Odette Siko, and Maria Teresa Filippis competed in some of the biggest races the Continent had to offer, such as the 24 Hours of LeMans and what would become Formula One.[2]

But in America, organized racing was off limits to women. When French Grand Prix racer Helle Nice came to the United States to race against drivers like Indianapolis 500 winner Fred Frame in 1938, race organizers only allowed her to drive in exhibitions instead of in real races, despite her extensive experience and success in similar cars in Europe. When Irish flat rack motorcycle champion Fay Taylour applied for a license to the American Automobile Association (AAA was the sanctioning body that controlled all major racing in the United States) in 1952, she was denied a license.

"It was explained that the A.A.A. does not license women drivers," Robert Cromie wrote in the *Chicago Tribune*.[3]

The message was clear: men didn't want to race against women. But racing against men was the only way for a woman to race.

It wasn't until the 1970s that many dirt tracks allowed women in the pits, the area of a racetrack where cars are staged for the races and worked on. According to racing superstition, it was bad luck to have a woman in the pits. The few women who drove on dirt tracks were the wives or girlfriends of regular racers who competed in "Powder Puff" races where they competed exclusively against other women in lower classes of race cars. They were considered a sideshow or intermission between the real racing classes. After their races were completed, usually in their husband's or boyfriend's car, they were immediately sent back to the grandstands so the men could race uninterrupted.

A few women had attempted to race sprint cars, but most competed in a few races and gave up. In 1978, Cheryl Burgard—who was always referred to in the press and promotional material in a variation of the "lady sprint car driver"—of New Berlin, Pennsylvania, started racing a sprint car. She raced a few times near her home and ventured as far as the grand palace of sprint car racing, Knoxville Raceway in Iowa. But she suffered burns and injuries in a crash in her first year and never raced again.[4] A few other women tried through the years, but only a couple raced a sprint car more than a few times.

The only group in history that was prevented from racing more than women was Black people. In the early days of racing, Black people were banned from competing against white drivers by sanctioning bodies such as AAA. That precedent dated back to 1910 when Black heavyweight champion boxer Jack Johnson was denied a license in his attempt to compete in a match race against superstar driver, Barney Oldfield.[5] In the northwest, a few Black drivers like Rajo Jack had competed on dirt tracks in independent competition, but that was long before Cheryl Glass was born. Few people in the northwest had ever seen a Black person race.

In 1980, the world of racing sprint cars was very male and very white. It made Cheryl Glass want to conquer the discipline more, she would later say.

Sprint car racing isn't cheap. In 1980, Cheryl was a junior in college with a couple of sideline occupations. Making ceramic dolls and dishes had enabled her to pay for quarter midget racing for nearly a decade, but the only way she could race a sprint car was for her family to fund her efforts. By 1980, Marvin Glass had risen to Assistant Vice President of Planning and Operations at Pacific Northwest Bell Telephone Company and Shirley Glass was a senior electrical engineer at Boeing. The Glass family had the financial means to make sure their daughter had the necessary equipment to be competitive in a sprint car.

Jerry Day was one of the top sprint car drivers in the northwest, but he made even more of an impact by building sprint cars. Outside his day job as an ironworker, Day built sprint cars from the ground up out of his shop in Renton, Washington, under his RAM sprint car brand. It took a tremendous amount of work to build a sprint car as Day did, cutting and bending sticks of steel one at a time into the proper shape, then welding the steel bars together with precision into a tube-frame chassis. Though a competitive driver and consistent winner, it wasn't unusual for Day to step out of the seat of a sprint car. On occasion, he would bring in one of the country's best drivers, such as Jan Opperman, to drive one of his creations in the Northwest's biggest races. Day had also started his own touring series for sprint cars, Northwest Sprint Cars Inc., after disputes with track owners about the low amounts of money being paid out to drivers. By 1979, he was burned out on racing and needed a break.

When Jerry Day wanted to sell one of his race cars, he didn't bother to advertise. People found out through word of mouth and the car would be sold for whatever asking price he sought, no matter how steep. A RAM sprint car was going to be competitive. When Marvin Glass found out Day wanted to sell his current race car in late 1979, he saw it as the next step in his daughter's career. Between the car, a trailer, and all the necessary parts and pieces they thought they needed, the Glass family spent about $20,000 to purchase the equipment for Cheryl's sprint car racing career to get underway.

"They weren't hurting any," Jerry Day said. "They had great jobs. They paid for the car up front."[6]

Many racetracks had rules that required drivers to be 18 years old, but Cheryl's birthday wasn't until December 1979. Before turning the car over to the Glass family, Day raced it one more time. He listed Marvin Glass as the car owner for the Gold Cup race at West Capital Raceway in Sacramento, California, in October 1979. One of the highest paying and most prestigious races in the country, the Gold Cup drew some of the most accomplished sprint car drivers on the planet. Jerry Day did not do well—he placed 16th in the final B-Main event—but it showed that the car could be fast.[7]

Jim Grantham dedicated himself to learning as much about sprint cars as he could as quickly as possible to serve as Cheryl's crew chief. He stripped Jerry Day's former car down to the lime green frame and started to reconstruct it from the ground up. This was a common practice upon buying a used race car. The only component not included in the purchase from Day was an engine.

The body on Cheryl's car was painted black and gold—which offset the green chassis—and a local sign painter everyone knew as "Clifford" intricately painted the numbers and details on the car. He painted "Cheryl Glass" on the panel directly in front of where Cheryl sat. Nobody knew Clifford's last name, but they knew he had once been a vice president of a major marketing firm in Seattle. Clifford walked away from that career to become a sign painter at a fraction of the pay of his former job and lived an independent hand-to-mouth existence. And he similarly lettered Cheryl's helmet.

Everything about Cheryl's operation looked professional.

Before the season started, Marvin arranged a session for Cheryl and her new car with a professional photographer. Cheryl didn't know how to drive a sprint car, but she knew how to look like she did. Racers at the local short track level never thought about having professional photos taken. Those photos came in handy when the media inevitably took notice of her.

Skagit Speedway, about an hour's drive from the Glass's Seattle home in a valley outside of Alger, was the one venue in the area where sprint cars raced regularly. But it might have well been on a different planet.

Skagit Speedway was willed into existence by a group of 14 investors, most of whom had been racing jalopies at nearby tracks and wanted one of their own. They found an unwanted tree-covered plot of 17 acres along Highway 99 that was available for the steep price of $100 an acre. It took the large consortium to purchase the property in 1952, and two more years of clearing the trees and other vegetation in the layout they wanted for their oval to build their dream dirt track. They left a ring of trees around the oval, which forever made the track picturesque. The jalopy drivers volunteered their time and labor and after three years, the site finally bore fruit with a ³⁄₁₀-mile clay oval sprouting up in time for their first race in 1954.[8]

The speedway was so remote that water had to be hauled by truck 15 miles to the track to keep it from becoming a cloud of dust during each race. It was years until the owners could pay to dig a well for water at the site. It was decades until electricity was run to the track so they could hold night races. The track evolved from featuring stock cars to supermodifieds—cut down and hopped-up street cars—and eventually to feature sprint cars in the mid-1970s. Skagit Speedway still had classes for stock cars and supermodifieds by 1980, but the top division was sprint cars, and they were the highest-paid and highest-regarded cars competing there. Regardless of what class anyone raced, every driver at the track wanted to race in the sprint car main event on Saturday night.[9]

"I think it was an era when there was so much money around, every logging outfit had one," said Guy Mossington, a nine-year-old sprint car fan at Skagit in 1980.[10]

As a Black woman in sprint car racing, Cheryl would be an outsider no matter where she raced.

It didn't help that her preparation for racing a sprint car for the first time was minimal. Prior to the opening race of the 1980 season at Skagit Speedway, she never been to the track. Most dirt track drivers train for years before thinking about racing a sprint car. After a few years, they finally dare move up to race a sprint car. In 1980, there were no driving schools or professional instructors from whom to learn the art of driving a sprint car.

Cheryl Glass was sure she could be good at driving one immediately. She figured out how to become a winner in quarter midgets in an extraordinarily short period of time, she reasoned, so she must be able to figure out a sprint car just as quickly.

But driving a sprint car is unlike driving anything else. Sprint cars need to be driven hard and fast, aggressively being thrown into the corners and sliding beyond any known limits. One slight mistake and a sprint car will flip violently.

Cheryl Glass didn't know she wasn't supposed to succeed in one.

The pits at Skagit Speedway were inside the oval, putting the cars and drivers on full display of the fans at all times. Regular drivers at the speedway adopted a pit spot and remained in it for the duration of their careers. At some tracks, pit placement could be a random process, relying on which spot was available when they arrived. At other tracks, it could be like a lunchroom at an elementary school where placement is determined by popularity or is the result of it.

For a woman to be allowed in the pits for Skagit Speedway for the first time in 1976 was a monumental feat. Lori Walker, the wife of popular sprint car driver Cecil Walker, spearheaded the change by becoming involved in the operations of the track. From her position with the group, she pioneered the revolutionary idea of a woman being in the pits at Skagit so she could work on her husband's car. The first time Cheryl Glass came to race at Skagit Speedway in 1980, she chose a pit spot next to Cecil Walker and the only other woman in the pits.

"It's hard when you're a woman," Lori Walker said.[11]

There was no licensing for drivers at Skagit Speedway. The only qualification was for a driver to pay their entry fee and have a car that was legal, or close enough. Practicing a race car is vital for young drivers, but Cheryl Glass never drove her sprint car before she raced it the first time. At age 18, she had more confidence than experience.

Most of the fans didn't know what to make of it when they saw Cheryl Glass arrive for her first race on May 3, 1980. Cheryl's accomplishments in quarter midgets were known by a select few at Skagit and didn't matter to anyone. Many who saw Cheryl enter the track for the first time assumed she would quickly fail and never be seen again.

"She came in and it was 'Who's that?' She was shy. Her being Black, you know, and there was none there. None at all. There wasn't any in the sport at that time," said Garey Fauver, a regular sprint car driver at Skagit Speedway at the time. "It would be natural to feel a little strange."[12]

The first time Cheryl slid into the cockpit to drive number 28, she maneuvered her way past the lime green steel bars and into the seat, strapping herself in tightly. When she snugged up the belts, they constricted her breathing slightly. After her car was pushed out onto the oval by a pickup, Cheryl did her best in her first tentative laps around Skagit. This brute of a car had over 600 horsepower and more downforce and traction than she could have known what to do with. The track was rough in the early season from the prior months of rain, and Cheryl was tossed around trying to maneuver her way around the oval.

Cheryl Glass learned how to drive a sprint car quickly at Skagit Speedway in 1980.
GEORGE HESPE

She loved it immediately.

Driving quarter midgets on asphalt for half of her life had not prepared her for racing at Skagit Speedway, no matter what she had believed. On the tight confines of a ½0-mile asphalt oval in a quarter midget, every driver fights for the bottom few inches of the inside of the turns. The only way to pass is when the leading driver messes up and slips up the track in the corners, giving the driver behind the chance to pass on the straightaway.

On a dirt track, drivers are expected to stay in their unmarked lanes. The bottom of a track such as the ³⁄10-mile at Skagit is the shortest way around, but is used by so many drivers it becomes slick. The outside line is purposely treated with more moisture so it becomes tackier, making it better to hook the tires into. Up against the wall, cars can carry more momentum onto the straightaways despite it being the longer way around. Drivers are expected to find a lane around the turns and remain in it, only occasionally sliding from the bottom to the top to pass someone.

Despite being eager to mash the throttle pedal in her first laps in a sprint car, she was far off the pace. Cheryl placed a distant 13th in the first main event of the Skagit Speedway season and was often in the way of the faster veteran drivers. Racers like Keith Jensen, Vern Church, Don Spoon, and Fred Brownfield showed Cheryl how far she had to go. Cheryl earned $28.39 for her finish, the first time in her life she won money by racing.

She was, in her mind, now a professional racer.

Other racers could guess with a great degree of accuracy how much Cheryl's family had spent to launch her racing career. While some of the sprint cars were funded by wealthy businesspeople, other cars were operating on a shoestring budget. A number of drivers sacrificed everything they could so they could afford to race. For a bullet like a RAM sprint car to be handed to an unknown 18-year-old girl to race made them jealous. Meanwhile, she had money, but faced plenty of other barriers.

"Guys who worked out in the woods like Cecil (Walker), guys like me who worked in an industrial environment, just a whole different world of people. Here she is, a young, good-looking girl," said Steve Royce, a fellow sprint car driver. "They didn't expect her to do squat. She had two things: the desire, because that was obviously there, and the equipment."[13]

In most cases, the drivers and car owners don't earn enough money to pay their expenses—or even a fraction—for the night of racing. The funding from a sponsor like a business is necessary to afford to race. Top drivers at the local level barely make enough money to break even on their prize winnings. The start-up costs for Cheryl's sprint car racing were so high that it was nearly impossible for her and her family to make money at it.

Skagit Speedway promoter and co-owner Jim Raper made a deal with the drivers to pay their prize winnings based on a formula that included the number of people who paid to watch the weekly races. It gave incentive for the drivers to help draw paying fans and otherwise help to promote the races. Once Cheryl started racing at Skagit and curious fans found out, attendance increased and the purses went up. But the other drivers still resented her.

The local media latched onto the narrative of Cheryl being a fish-out-of-water from a well-to-do background coming to compete in the rough-and-tumble world of sprint car racing. It made for a compelling storyline. Television stations sent reporters to capture her story. The publicity Cheryl received, in turn, made many of her competitors jealous, despite the fact that they were them earning more money as a result.[14]

The problem when Cheryl started racing a sprint car, however, was she had no opportunities to practice. Her schedule was tight between her classes at Seattle University and other activities.

For as much time, energy, and money as drivers must put into each race night, they don't spend much time behind the wheel. The class of sprint cars earned their name from the short nature of their races.

Seeing how much Cheryl struggled in her first outing, Raper offered Cheryl a deal: return to the track the following day and she could practice on the track all by herself. Cheryl had never driven a car by intentionally sliding it sideways previously, which is the required method when racing on dirt. Raper wanted the track's budding star to be more competitive, while the other drivers wanted her to get faster so she would stay out of their way.

On that dusty Sunday afternoon, Cheryl learned to slide the car sideways. Never afraid to stand on the gas, Cheryl quickly figured out how to finesse the car around the oval with some coaching from a few experts on hand (including Raper, himself a former champion driver). Sprint cars must be driven aggressively to be fast. She had driven scared in the first few races. That day she learned how these sprint cars needed to be driven, being thrown into the turns. It was tougher than she imagined it would be. In the span of one practice session, Cheryl picked up a lot of speed.

"Once she did that, the next race she finished third in," Jim Grantham said.[15]

So Cheryl was noticeably faster at the May 10 race at Skagit, placing third in the semi-main event to transfer into the main event. But in the main event, she was caught up in a five-car crash on the fifth lap—she didn't have the experience to avoid it. She and fellow driver Darrell Radder were sent to the hospital where Cheryl was found to have injured both knees. It was bad.[16]

"I just happened to be the one at the end of the line. It was a chain reaction sort of thing. There was nowhere to go," Cheryl said.[17]

Cheryl wasn't used to the bumping and banging of racing a sprint car. This crash was violent and she paid the price physically. Sprint cars are a tight fit of components wrapped around the driver. The driver's feet straddle the driveshaft or a tube that surrounds it. Their knees straddle the steering box. If the driver's arms are not otherwise restrained, they will go flying out of the car and inevitably hit the roll cage during a crash. The driver's helmet is located inches from exposed metal tubing. Though there are ways to pad some of the components, many drivers and car owners thought adding it would give the driver a false sense of security or slow the car due to the added weight of the few ounces of padding.

After a few days in the hospital after the crash, doctors diagnosed Cheryl with torn ligaments in both knees. It should have necessitated surgery, but that would have taken her out of racing for months. She wanted to get back fast.

Crashes are an inevitability of racing. Any driver who races more than a few times will crash. Some will be minor crashes. Some crashes cause permanent injuries. And the faster the car, the harder the crashes will be. Skagit Speedway was a fast track. Most crashes there are painful.

"They destroyed a lot of shit back in those days. They wrecked shit in hot laps," said Guy Mossington, a 9-year-old sprint car fan at Skagit in 1980.

To keep the number 28 car in the hunt for the track championship, Jerry Day took Cheryl's place for the May 17 race and won the heat race and trophy dash. He proved Cheryl's car was capable of more than she was doing in it as she watched from the pits, leaning on crutches.

"I was running the fence so hard I got into wall and white walled the tires a couple times," Jerry Day said. "Marvin was there practically shaking. He said, 'You'll never drive my car for me again. I can't take it.' I said, 'If I drive for you a few more times, you'll be a white man.'"

The competition at Skagit Speedway was fierce. With one night of racing each week—occasionally less when that week's race rained out—the drivers at the track were not racing to make a living, but for the passion for the sport. Losing to a woman, especially a Black one, was their worst fear. In their macho world, being beat by a girl, even for 12th place in the main event, meant they were somehow less worthy.

"You had these male egos," said Dave Griffith, a friend of the Glass family who worked with Marvin at Pacific Northwest Bell and an occasional crew member for Cheryl. "The last thing they wanted was to lose a race to a woman. I don't remember anything blatantly racist, but you could kind of feel things under the surface. And then there were all these little instances when she would be bumped when she shouldn't have been bumped."[18]

Cheryl insisted the wrecks she was involved in were caused by the other drivers. She claimed other drivers were retaliating out of jealousy for the attention she received.

She wasn't wrong.

But the attention she was receiving from outside the track was growing.

The promoters of the ⅝-mile asphalt oval at Evergreen Speedway in Monroe, an hour northeast of Seattle, wanted Cheryl to race at their track so badly they gave her a set of slick tires. Those tires normally cost over $400, but they were willing to do anything they could to get her to race in the June 15 Governor's Cup Challenge race. She had only driven a sprint car on dirt, but they felt she could draw curious onlookers to their big asphalt oval. The Washington Racing Association, which raced exclusively on asphalt, had regional stars including Jan Sneva, Blaine Sneva, and Ken Hamilton competing in their series. But it was Cheryl who the promoters advertised was racing on that particular night.

At a track like Evergreen, sprint car drivers hit a top speed of 120 miles per hour at the end of the straightaways. The track was faster than anything Cheryl had raced on, but she also was never afraid of speed. When her name was used in the promotion of a race, the grandstands were packed full of fans who watched Ross Fontes win in the "crab" car—a car with giant crabs painted on it.[19]

By the late 1970s, the sprint car world morphed into its own monster. While classes like midgets became springboards for a driver to climb up the ladder in the racing world just as in the Indianapolis 500, sprint car racing had become a self-contained universe. Some of the biggest sprint car races in the United States paid so well—$10,000 or more to win—that the country's best drivers would hop from high-paying race to high-paying race around the hundreds of dirt short tracks that dotted the country. It was a fiercely competitive world, but one in which a top driver could make a living.

Once every summer, Skagit Speedway put on the Dirt Cup, its biggest sprint car race of the year. The race would pay well enough—a purse of $43,000 was offered in 1980—that drivers would come from all over the West Coast as well as from other corners of the nation. That much money was not unheard of for a big race, but it was enough to draw 50 or more sprint car drivers to the outpost in the far-off corner of the country where they would fight to determine who the best racer that weekend.

Because the Dirt Cup was the crown jewel race of Skagit Speedway, it also drew the biggest audience of the year. Skagit Speedway had grandstands that sat 7,000 before the 1980 Dirt Cup; that was expanded by 400 for that year's Dirt Cup. Thousands more would sit on the hillsides around the oval to watch the race, knowing full well they would be pelted with dirt for their trouble.[20]

"Back then, everybody was so fucking pumped," Guy Mossington said. "Them places were full to the bottom of the grass. They loaded that place back in them days."

The competition that showed up at the Dirt Cup humbled even the best of Skagit Speedway's regular drivers. And the quality of drivers who came for the biggest race of the year was better than those competing on any other race night.

On the opening night of the 1980 Dirt Cup, June 19, Cheryl qualified poorly and spun out early in the race.[21] After the next night's races were cancelled on account of rain, she placed 11th in the C-Main event—the third lowest race of that night—on June 21.[22] Much like the Grand Nationals in quarter midgets, the Dirt Cup offered better competition and showed Cheryl she still had a long way to go. Drivers like Jimmy Sills of California, who beat Cheryl in the C-Main and won the A-Main, still took notice.[23]

"I guess the most unusual part of it was there were hardly any women driving then," Jimmy Sills said. "And then there wasn't very many Black people that were even interested in racing, much less involved. To be Black and female, it was pretty rare."[24]

Once each summer, a handful of regular Skagit racers took off on a tour of dirt tracks in Montana. It was as close to a vacation as some of them got. After a day's travel to Billings for a race at Belaro Speedway on June 27, Cheryl created a buzz.[25] The next night at Thunder Road Speedway in Helena, fans lined up in record numbers to see her race.[26]

Going to Montana was a radically new experience for Cheryl.

The dirt at every track is different with different types of soil and different amounts of pollutants on the racing surface. Some surfaces will accept every drop of moisture applied to them and become so tacky they will pull the shoes off anyone who attempts to walk across them. Some will never accept a bit of moisture, no matter how much is applied. Those tend to become slick as ice after cars start driving on them, developing a glass-like shine that resembles ice. To complicate it more, each track changes drastically throughout a night of racing. Drivers and their crews take educated guesses about what the track's going to be like each time they venture on it, but they never really know. Cheryl had become used to racing at Skagit and what the dirt there was like. She had a hard time adapting to the tracks in Montana.

When Cheryl came out to the flag salute before the second race in Montana, she received such a large reception from the crowd that she blushed.

Steve Royce was an experienced racer from Bremerton, Washington, a shipbuilding hamlet located west of Seattle. He started racing at Elma Fairgrounds Speedway west of Olympia in stock cars and modifieds in the early 1970s before moving up to drive a sprint car owned by his friend Dean Gehring in 1980. On the road in Montana, where pit spots were not regulated by the hierarchy of a track as they were at Skagit, Cheryl parked next to him. Cheryl was struggling in the Treasure State and Royce stepped in to assist. He gave her a few tips on how to set up her car and drive it better. She was immediately faster. In her first year of racing a sprint car, no other driver had treated her like that. Cheryl started calling Royce her "Godfather."[27]

After most races, drivers and crew members who competed against each other all evening, fighting wheel to wheel in heated battle, will gather after the races and tell stories for hours while drinking beer after beer. Those late-night sessions are the key to fitting in. There were few sprint car drivers with whom Cheryl shared much on a personal level. There were a few younger drivers with whom she became familiar, but Cheryl wasn't part of the "in" crowd at racetracks, much as she hadn't been in school, growing up.

"She was so shy. She wouldn't come up to you and start a conversation," fellow driver Garey Fauver said. "That's why everybody thought she just didn't fit in."[28]

After her immediate success in other forms of racing, Cheryl couldn't understand why she wasn't winning races immediately in a sprint car. Her crew decided to make changes to the car to try to make her faster.

The wings on top of a sprint car aid it by producing massive amounts of downforce to push the car into the ground without adding much weight. The side panels of the wings resist the car's desire to turn sideways and help keep it pointing straight when the car is sliding. It takes practice, but the best sprint car drivers use those wings as an aid. And in the case of a crash, the wings also act as a cushion by absorbing energy when a driver flips, which happens frequently. Wings were a relatively new innovation for sprint cars in 1980, and the overall dimensions were limited by a thin rulebook. Of course, the length and width of the wings were limited by the interpretation of the person reading the rule book.

Cheryl's crew theorized that if they changed the design of the wings, it could make her faster by keeping the car straighter on the turns. They experimented with several designs for the top wing and front wing. In some designs, the wings were longer and skinnier. Others used taller sideboards or slightly different shapes. The top wings cost $500 or more, making them prohibitively expensive to experiment with. Most drivers bought a new wing only if an old wing was destroyed beyond repair. Cheryl's family bought wing after wing in an attempt to make her faster.

Her team ended up with so many wings that they didn't always have time to have them painted. Often, she showed up with a new wing with her number 28 drawn on in shoe polish, rather than paint. Eventually, her family and crew found a design that worked for her. The top and front wings had extremely long and tall panels on the left side made of thick aluminum with no braces. They had short sideboards on the right.

"That's what they wanted, and it worked," said Jim Hedblom, who built some wings for Cheryl.[29]

Whether or not the wing made any difference in the performance of her car, Cheryl believed it did.

Cheryl was noticeably faster at the July 5 Mid-Season Championship race at Skagit Speedway. She won the second heat race of the night. It was the first time a woman had won a race of any kind at Skagit Speedway. Then she placed second in the night's trophy dash. In the main event, Irv Westby narrowly beat Cheryl to win, and her second-place finish—also the best by a woman there—marked a rapid ascension in performance.[30]

"I'm finally getting the feel of the track," Cheryl said.[31]

What was making Cheryl faster was that she finally got upset. She was mad she wasn't doing better. She was tired of getting picked on by the male drivers. She wanted to win. So she drove harder, and it worked.

"Who gives a shit what color she is? It mattered what she did when she got going," Steve Royce said. "She had things to deal with things that none of us will."

Cheryl was fast again at the next race at Skagit Speedway, winning another heat race and placing third in the trophy dash. But while running in fourth place in the main event, Cheryl spun in turn two and was hit hard from behind by Art Hillstead. He had been far behind Cheryl in the race. Every other driver easily saw Cheryl's spinning car and easily avoided her car.[32] The 57-year-old Hillstead owned a nearby wrecking yard that supplied cars to drivers in lower divisions to support the track. He could barely see, despite the thick glasses he wore, and was not in physical condition to drive race cars. But he was one of the original investors and builders of Skagit Speedway and still owned a share of it. Nothing was going to keep him from racing.

After the crash, Hillstead unleashed a torrent of racial epithets at Cheryl as they climbed from their cars. Cheryl was still groggy from her helmet hitting the roll cage and didn't comprehend all of what Hillstead was saying, but she got the gist.

"Old cementhead," Jerry Day said. "He crashed a lot. He had one glass eye."

Cheryl was diagnosed with a concussion at Sedro Woolley General Hospital that night. She was later transferred to Swedish Hospital in Seattle where she recovered for a week before being released.[33] Unlike her hard crash earlier in the year, however, Cheryl was running at the front of a race when this one happened.

Just as in that crash, Cheryl's skin color was a constant magnet for racial tension.

"I was known as the blonde nigger," Jim Grantham said. "What I used to do was load the car at night and go stand off behind a tree, and I would watch those drivers come by and just stare at her. It was hilarious. I would say that a lot of people had problems with her up there. When you take a Black girl and you kick a white boy's ass, what do you think happens?"

Tracks other than Skagit Speedway recognized Cheryl was a draw for fans, both those who rooted for and those who rooted against her. Those tracks were willing to go to extraordinary lengths to have her race at them.

She received an offer to race at Riverside Speedway, a dirt track in Cottage Grove, Oregon, on July 25 and 26. The quarter-mile dirt oval was holding the first sprint car races in its 26-year-history, and the organizers wanted her to race. Once more, she had a hard time learning how to drive a new track.[34]

"She hauled it into the corner the first time and the car bicycled and flipped and all it did was crinkle the top of the wing a little bit," Jim Grantham said.

This time when she wrecked, Cheryl was unhurt.

While Cheryl was racing in the big time, younger sister Cherry, then 8 years old, started racing quarter midgets in one of Cheryl's old cars. Cheryl did her best to mentor her little sister. The 10-year age gap between the sisters prevented them from being close at younger ages. When they raced at the same time, even in drastically different classes, was one of the first times they had something in common. In Cherry's first season of racing, she won a regional championship and gained attention. But Cherry never took to the sport as her older sister had. Cherry preferred gymnastics and playing on the monkey bars at school.

"It's not as exciting as racing, but it sure is a lot of fun," Cherry Glass said.[35]

While her little sister was trying to figure out if she liked racing, Cheryl Glass was committed.

Trophy dashes are part of the ceremony of auto racing.

The short races are an excuse to take the fastest cars and have them battle it out for four laps with a cheap piece of plastic as a reward. But it's also a good way for a promoter to draw out a show and add a bit of showmanship.

When Cheryl won the trophy dash at the August 9 race at Skagit Speedway, it meant more than any trophy dash in history.[36] By her beating three other drivers over four laps around the oval, it added another trophy to Cheryl's collection. Much of the crowd was cheering for her, whereas months earlier they had booed. By becoming the first female to win a trophy dash at the track, she smashed a long-held tradition in short-track racing.

Dating back to the 1920s when movie stars would come to races at Legion Ascot Speedway in Los Angeles and the starlets would hand out trophies to winners, trophy girls traditionally congratulated the winning driver by kissing him. By 1980, the position had evolved into its own show at short tracks. An attractive woman, often in a bikini, was selected to hand the winner of each race a trophy. The trophy girl would pose with the winner for photos as he put his arm around her. The male driver would inevitably be a filthy mess, oftentimes unshaven and covered head to toe in dirt and grease, while the trophy girl was the opposite: pristine and gorgeous.

When Cheryl first started racing sprint cars, promoters suggested she should be the track's trophy girl. She assured them she was there to race, not to look pretty.

The problem of Cheryl Glass winning a trophy dash at Skagit Speedway hadn't been contemplated. When she won the trophy dash on August 9, the track officials at Skagit had to improvise.

"All of a sudden she wins a trophy dash and they pull (fellow sprint car driver) Alan Munn out of the pits. He was a young, good-looking guy and they pulled him out of the pits to be the trophy girl," Guy Mossington said.

Cheryl won her heat race that night but was relegated to a 14th place finish in the main event after flipping her car, eliminating her hopes for her first main event win. She still felt she was getting closer.[37] She placed sixth in the next race at Skagit, August 15.[38] Cheryl then placed third in the main event and won her heat race and the trophy dash at the August 23 race.[39]

With her improving results in the second half of the 1980 Skagit Speedway season, she improved to eighth place out of 45 drivers in Skagit's point standings. The points fund paid $5,000, divided among the top 10 drivers.[40] It provided a financial incentive for drivers to compete at the track regularly. Points finishes, and the champions they anoint, also bring prestige.

The world of dirt track racing makes things like cleanliness and appearance difficult to maintain. The crew members of many of the race cars at Skagit Speedway usually wore whatever they wanted: old T-shirts and jeans were standard attire. Cheryl's crew members, by contrast, wore matching team shirts that Shirley designed and sewed. Cheryl wanted to project an appearance. People had never seen a crew as professional in appearance as hers at Skagit Speedway.

The final race of Skagit Speedway's 1980 season would define Cheryl Glass, whether she wanted it to or not.

For years, more racing fans claimed they were at Skagit Speedway August 30, 1980 to bear witness to what she did that night than there were actual seats at the track. It was one night to most people, but it made Cheryl Glass's career.

CHAPTER FOUR

The Biggest Night of Cheryl's Life

August 30, 1980

CHERYL GLASS GAVE UP TRYING TO SLEEP. SHE LAY AWAKE IN BED, until she finally gave up and got up. The pressure she placed on herself that day was immense. Cheryl felt she had to validate her life over the course of one day.

The bed in her room of her family's home overlooking Lake Washington was surrounded by walls lined with reminders of her previous successes. From the start of her racing career, every time Cheryl was given a token of an accomplishment—a trophy, a ribbon, a T-shirt, or an oil can—she installed them on a shelf in her bedroom as proof. The room became a trophy case for her every achievement. As she got out of bed that morning, she saw visualizations of her previous accomplishments. By 1980, she had about 500 awards and showed them off to everyone who came by.[1]

Living up to that wasn't easy. All of those trophies were a constant reminder that she had once been the best at something. From a young age, Cheryl was conditioned that to be successful was of the utmost importance. At times, it felt impossible for her to live up to that standard.

"The problem was she was pushed way too hard," said Jerry Day, who built the race car she was going to drive that day.[2]

Cheryl Glass was only allowed to be a success.

Each night of racing at Skagit Speedway meant a marathon day for Cheryl Glass and her crew.

She and Marvin would arrive at their shop before noon to begin gathering up her car and the significant amount of equipment.

After acquiring a sprint car for Cheryl to race, her family needed a place to keep and maintain it. A sprint car and its massive amount of accompanying equipment requires more space than a two-car garage in a home. The family found a 2,000 square foot shop to rent in an industrial complex south of Boeing Field on 15th Avenue in Seattle. They'd be close to a few other racers, including those who competed in the world of hydroplanes—the area was a center for that form of racing—and drag racing. What was most important to the Glasses was to have a more professional setting to work on their cars in the sizable shop.

Racing a sprint car requires a lot of people. For as simple as the cars are, they require a large amount of manual labor. From loading and unloading the race car to preparing tires to pushing the car by hand to get it in line to be pushed by a truck, sprint cars require a lot of help to get on the track. Though Marvin Glass was a gifted engineer and manager of people, he wasn't a mechanic.

Jim Grantham, Cheryl's crew chief, outfitted the new shop with shelving and carpeting, and he built a wood shop there so he could perform his day job woodworking from the same space. When they needed more help, which was often, the Glasses would pick up friends like Dave Griffith, Robert Carlson, or Kelly Tanner to work as crew members. Like most crew members at the short track level, those men were volunteers and weren't paid. And none of them had experience working on sprint cars.

Grantham joined the Glass family at the shop shortly after noon. They all loaded the car on the trailer and put all the needed equipment into the family's van. When finished, they climbed into the van and drove over an hour north to Alger. It made for a long start to the day.

No matter how good a racing team is, there is always room for improvement. After a long period of time, such as the 1980 season, drivers and crew members become complacent or over-confident with their equipment. They think they've gotten the most out of it. But there is always more speed to be wrung out of a race car. Sometimes a crew needs an infusion of knowledge that only an outsider can bring.

Jim Grantham and Marvin Glass had learned a lot about sprint cars over the 1980 season, but there was more to learn. Some things, such as the amount of stagger of the rear tires and getting the engine to run correctly, can be figured out by trial and error. Items like how much tire pressure is too much and what is the perfect spring rate take years of trial and error to perfect. Only the masters understand the real subtleties of preparing sprint cars.

After Jerry Day walked away from driving and building race cars in 1980, he moved to Alaska for the summer to work and get away from his hectic life in Seattle. Upon his return home late that summer, Day received a call from Marvin Glass saying the team needed help with Cheryl's car. There was one race left in the Skagit season and they needed the expertise that only Day could deliver.

"Something's not right. I'll pay you to go back through the car," Marvin Glass told Jerry Day.[3]

When Day came to the shop south of Boeing's facility, he was astounded. The shop was unlike any he had seen for a sprint car team. He saw Grantham's wood-working equipment and all of the professional cabinets and assumed the family's money was being misspent.

But he also had a soft spot for Cheryl and went to work.

Day went through the RAM sprint car he had built a few years earlier and examined every component. He found the torsion bars in the back of the car had been switched from one side to the other. He knew it wouldn't allow the car to bite its tires in the dirt as they should. He also found a shock that was bent and stuck.

Nothing he found was major, but he found a lot of small things that needed correction.

"I went through the car and put it all back together," Day said. "I worked steady on it for a couple days."

By the time Jerry Day was done, Cheryl's car was capable of anything.

Cheryl Glass and her car were ready to race, but the weather in Seattle didn't look like it would cooperate.

When she and her crew arrived in Alger for the race, the Washington skies were filled with clouds. The rain that those clouds could produce might end the night's races before they started. On dirt tracks, they can't race when it's raining. But Cheryl's optimism this night didn't allow her to get down.

Cheryl had been given every opportunity to succeed due to her family's money. Her competitors could see how the pressure was impacting her. They were growing concerned.

Just before the appointed 6 p.m. start time, the electricity went out at Skagit Speedway.[4] Promoter Jim Raper walked in front of the crowd and asked if the people wanted to wait to see if the power would return. The crowd cheered in response.

The fans came to Alger to watch a race and sensed something special could happen.

At about 9 p.m., with the sun down, the power did return. Time was running short and there was a lot of racing to be completed. Raper opted to condense the racing program to get it completed. He eliminated the trophy dashes and heat races and opted to set the main events by point standings. There wasn't going to be as much racing as a normal night at Skagit.

But there was going to be a race.

As Cheryl Glass prepared to take her car on the track at Skagit Speedway for the first time that night, she had every advantage she could ask for over her competitors. She sat in the aluminum seat of her sprint car, looking around at the other drivers. Jerry Day approached her.

"Go get them girl," Day told her.

When Cheryl went onto the track for a quick hot lap session, she thought her car was working better than it had previously. Her car had been good at other races, but it was only with a season's experience driving that she could understand what a properly prepared race car felt like. Day knew what he was doing when it came to setting up a sprint car, and his changes worked wonders.

Cheryl's confidence skyrocketed after those few laps. But she had to wait to really race.

The stock car and supermodified classes—lower divisions—got to race first and the top sprint car drivers like Fred Brownfield and Marc Huson competed in a match race. And other drivers got to race in trophy dashes and semi-main events.[5]

Cheryl was forced to wait hours.

Cheryl and 18 other sprint cars were finally ready to be pushed out onto the track for the main event, which was the last and most important race of the night. She could tell that the track was going to be challenging, with a rough cushion on the outside and a thin racing line on the bottom near the tire barriers that separate the track from the pits.

Cheryl was starting in the third position for the 35-lap main event, but she had a pair of fast drivers ahead of her in Alan Munn and Keith Jensen, both winners at Skagit during the season. Passing them wasn't going to be easy.

When it came to Cheryl Glass's racing, her parents held distinctly different roles.

They both helped fund her racing and Marvin was active in preparing her race cars, but Shirley Glass had another important role.

Knowing that Cheryl would be photographed any time she was at a racetrack because of all the attention she received, Shirley needed to make sure her daughter looked good. Shirley meticulously designed and sewed each of Cheryl's driver's uniforms. If she had anything to do with it, her daughter was going to be worth watching.

But Shirley only reluctantly came to her daughter's races. She couldn't get past her fear of her daughter crashing the race car. At Skagit Speedway, Shirley found a spot at the top of the grandstands each week and brought a few family members or friends to sit with her. Whenever Cheryl was on the track, Shirley inevitably covered her eyes.

"I would be so scared to be up there with my daughter racing," Shirley Glass said. "I'd have towels and newspapers because I was scared."[6]

That night, Shirley was in her seat, covering her eyes when Cheryl went on the track. She couldn't force herself to watch.

As Cheryl Glass's sprint car was about to be pushed to fire the engine up for the race, she felt a calm she had never felt before.

Strapped tight in the cockpit, she held the brake pedal firmly with her left foot, while the pickup behind her pushed her to 20 miles per hour. The rear tires sliding in the dirt, Cheryl released the brake pedal and the engine turned over. Cheryl flipped the ignition switch and the engine roared to life. She gave the number 28 car a little throttle with her right foot and pulled away from the truck and onto the ³/₁₀-mile dirt oval. It was a procedure she had performed 100 times that year and something that was difficult months earlier had now become second nature.

As Cheryl idled the car around the dirt track, she watched through the visor in her helmet as other cars roared to life from the pits and onto the track. When all 19 cars finally were running, the flagman waited until the last of the pickups went back into the pits. He then twirled the coiled green flag in the air and turned out the yellow caution lights that ringed the track with the flick of a switch for all the drivers to take a warm-up lap.

Cheryl sped away. The car was working well. After battling her self-confidence all season, Cheryl was as prepared as possible for this race.

The flagman aggressively waved the caution flag and turned back on the yellow lights that surrounded the track. It was time to line up.

The cars of Alan Munn and Keith Jensen settled into their spots side by side on the front row. Cheryl caught up to them and lined up behind Munn on the inside of the second row so she could start the race in her assigned third place.

Cheryl Glass had hundreds of horsepower available to the urge of her size 9 right foot. She made so many trips around Skagit Speedway's dirt that season that she knew exactly when to hit the throttle pedal. She was ready to mash it to the floor and send gallons of methanol to its end in the engine.

As soon as she saw the green flag unfurl, Cheryl stomped her right foot and took off. She had two men to pass. Alan Munn sped away with the lead on the first lap. Keith Jensen settled into second place, right on Munn's tail tank. Cheryl dropped slightly behind the two leaders at the start. But she was determined not to let them get away.

A large pack of cars hounded her from behind. They wanted to pass her. But Cheryl ran a consistent line in the opening laps and wouldn't give them an inch to pass her. Cheryl settled into a rhythm, pulled away from the rest of the pack, and tracked down Jensen. On the seventh lap, coming out of turn two, she maneuvered under Jensen and passed him for second place down the backstretch.

Three laps later, the engine in Munn's car blew up in a cloud of smoke, and he pulled his car into the pits in the infield.

Cheryl was leading the race.

The driver, who many people assumed was a novelty, an 18-year-old Black female model and disco dancer, was where no one thought she would ever be: leading every man in the last race of the season at Skagit Speedway.

Cheryl Glass was out front on the awkwardly slick oval, but Keith Jensen wouldn't let her get away. He pressured her in every corner and forced her to drive a perfect line, every lap. Cheryl refused to get off the bottom of the track. She wouldn't give Jensen any opportunity to pass her.

For 25 laps, Cheryl was so fast that she rapidly caught cars in the back of the pack. One after another, she passed each one to put them a lap down. When a car was on the bottom of the track, she effortlessly went high and passed them. Like Jensen, the other drivers following her hoped she would make a mistake, but she never did.

Even her supporters didn't realize that Cheryl possessed this kind of skill as a driver. It had been so recent that Cheryl had been the driver getting lapped, so she understood what those cars were going to do before they did it. She was so good at passing them, that she made those slower cars look like they weren't trying.

Miraculously, the race didn't have any yellow or red flags to tighten the field. If anyone was going to pass Cheryl for the lead they were going to have to earn it.

As Cheryl took the white flag, signifying one lap remaining, Jensen was determined to make one more charge at passing her and winning. He had seen enough of the tail tank of her number 28 car. Jensen sent his car deeper into the first turn than he had all night. Somehow the car stuck to the track. Coming out of turn two, Jensen managed to pull inside Cheryl.

This was his last chance.

Seeing Jensen gave Cheryl the motivation she needed. Going into turn three, Cheryl tossed her car into the corner harder than she had all night. Jensen tried to match her, but got his car too sideways in the process and had to collect it to keep going. By the time he straightened it out, Cheryl was already driving out of turn four. She was heading safely to the checkered flag with no other car around her.

When Cheryl Glass drove under the checkered flag to earn the win, signifying the end of the race and the season, she felt a weight heavier than her car lift off her back.[7]

Cheryl led the final 25 of 35 laps to win her first sprint car main event. It was something every driver, pit crew member, track official, and fan wanted to do. Only a few ever would.

Some of the people in the crowd sat in stunned silence for a few seconds, not realizing the magnitude of what they had witnessed. A woman winning a sprint car race was something that had never been done prior to Cheryl Glass doing it. Before the sound of the cars died at the conclusion of the race, a round of applause erupted from the crowd and drowned out the engines.

When she pulled her car to a stop on the front stretch for the post-race winner's presentation, only Cheryl understood what she had to sacrifice to reach that level. She removed her helmet and climbed out of her car gently. She hadn't fully recovered from her previous injuries, but in that moment, it didn't matter.

Cheryl Glass won the sprint car main event at Skagit Speedway.

Skagit Speedway promoter Jim Raper was the first person to greet Cheryl in the makeshift victory lane on the front stretch, in front of the crowd. He shook her hand and handed her a huge trophy for winning the race. The trophy was nearly as tall as her.

Most of the male race car drivers she had beaten were embarrassed. To many of them, losing to a girl was a fate worse than death.

Cheryl's ascent from being the outsider to a winner occurred in record time. Cheryl did something that rookies—especially ones who had never previously raced on dirt—hadn't done. She was the first female driver to win a main event at Skagit Speedway. But she also was the first woman to win a sprint car race at that level anywhere in the United States.

"I didn't know that women, particularly a Black woman, wasn't supposed to drive a sprint car, wasn't supposed to be 'Rookie of the year' and wasn't supposed to win main events and 'walk' the good ole boys," she later said about the win.[8]

After the race, driver after driver approached Jerry Day and complained about how the race played out. They made excuses about how

Cheryl Glass is photographed with a track official after winning a race at the track in 1980.

Cheryl's win wasn't fair. They argued it wasn't right that she started so far forward in the field. They complained how there had been no heat races to determine the starting positions for the main event. They were frustrated that there weren't any caution flags to help them by tightening the field.

These were excuses made by men frustrated by being beaten by someone they assumed they were better than only because of outward appearances.

"You just got your asses whipped by an 18-year-old Black chick," Jerry Day told them. "So go tell your stories to someone else. I watched it and she kicked your ass."[9]

One by one, they walked away.

Cheryl Glass had a hard time understanding why fans would wait in line after a race to get her autograph. The line of fans wanting a piece of her that night was long. That fateful August night lasted for hours as adults and children sought her signature in victory lane.

Cheryl's underdog status showed fans that if she could succeed, they could, too. Even her detractors—and there were plenty—saw by her performance that a woman could drive a sprint car and win a sprint car race.

Cheryl did what few rookie sprint car drivers had, especially young ones. To win a main event after competing in a dozen races was a stunning accomplishment. And she wasn't a humble winner.

"I've come a long way," she said. "When I first started racing there was no one to pattern myself after. I'd just go out there and wing it."[10]

She received fan mail for weeks after the win. Some fans asked for her autograph and others wanted to congratulate her. She kept each piece of mail.

"Cheryl, I'm writing this for 4 people that watched you last night. You had her hooked up & we wish you luck. Lonnie, Susan, Morella, C.J., Joe."[11]

Cheryl's win also clinched the Skagit Speedway Rookie of the Year award in the sprint car class and fourth place in the sprint car class points. Those were things a woman had never achieved in a sprint car.[12]

Her finish also gave Marvin Glass second place in the car owner standings.[13] Cheryl's finishes in the number 28 car were combined with Jerry Day's for enough points to finish only behind champion Fred Brownfield's number 92 car. That also was something a Black man had never done at that level.

It had taken every bit of effort Cheryl could give and tens of thousands of dollars of her family's money, but she had proven that she was a success. And she was rewarded for it.

That win made her special to the dozens of people who sought her autograph that night.

"You don't understand when you're making history," Shirley Glass said. "You just don't think about that. You just think about whatever your goal is."[14]

Cheryl Glass's success came at a significant personal cost. But the pressure she had placed on herself—as well as the pressure from her parents—didn't go away completely with the win at Skagit Speedway. The few other sprint car drivers who had got to know her were concerned that her success was coming at too high a price.

She had a hard time doing things for the sake of having fun. She only allowed herself to compete if she could prove to people she was the best at it.

"Cheryl has considerable potential, but is being pushed too hard," sprint car driver Fred Brownfield said in 1981. "She doesn't have enough laps yet. She drives a good line and is a smooth driver, but she still has a lot to prove. Her family certainly wants to see her succeed, and I think from my vantage point that they have a tendency to keep on her."[15]

Cheryl couldn't accept her win as an accomplishment. She only saw it as a step toward more success. Even after her biggest triumph, Cheryl struggled to let go of the pressure she and others had been placing on her. Her friends didn't understand that one win was the start of a burden that would follow her for years.

The story of an 18-year-old Black model who won a sprint car race was too much for the mainstream media to pass up. In a flash, she went from being written about in local newspapers and niche publications to fielding interviews for stories from the *Associated Press*, *The Weekly World News*, and *National Speed Sport News*. This was a national spotlight she had never known. The publicity she received led to offers from car owners at higher levels of racing who wanted her to drive for their race cars. Track promoters also wanted her to come and race for them after that night and were willing to pay for the honor of her coming to their tracks.

Many saw Cheryl's win as a step forward for women racers. Some saw it as proof that Black people could win races. That one win meant a lot to more people than Cheryl would ever know.

"It really pleases me to realize that it is finally happening. Keep up the good work. I've never been to Washington, but if you travel with the World of Outlaws on the East Coast, I'll meet up with you some day. Until then, I send my best wishes for your continued success on the ovals," *National Speed Sport News* staff member Linda Mansfield wrote to her.[16]

That one win became the defining moment in her story.

Most nights after a race, Cheryl Glass, her family, and friends arrived home late.

When the Glass family finally left Skagit Speedway that night, Cheryl and her family had a lot of work left to do. After the race ended, they loaded the number 28 car back on the trailer and stopped at a car wash to wash the dirt off everything for a few hours. They hosed everything off with water in the cool late-night air, the mud flowing off in a chocolate brown river. It's a task no one savors. Yet no one could stop smiling that night after the win.

They reached the south Seattle shop where they unloaded Cheryl's car and all the pit equipment and stored it. It was the middle of the night before the Glass family and their friends went home.

As the Glass family pulled the van into the driveway of their Seattle home, the first rays of sun were coming from the East. Cheryl carried her life-size trophy for winning the main event inside the house and placed it in her bedroom. It was only one of the hundreds of trophies, but it meant more than any of the hundreds of other trophies did. She took a shower and went to bed.

Cheryl knew that every night driving a race car was not going to be as sweet as that August evening. She wanted to enjoy it. She had gone through a lot to become a winner and had learned from the difficulty of accomplishing the task. Cheryl's win came after such hard times that it made the victory feel more significant.

"You have to take your hard knocks with the winning, too," Cheryl Glass said.[17]

After taking a shower, Cheryl laid in bed and couldn't sleep. This time, it was for a different reason. She stared at her new trophy and imagined filling the room with more trophies from sprint car and Indy Car races. That thought made her happy.

CHAPTER FIVE

From the Backwoods to the Big Time

September 1980 to February 1981

CALIFORNIA CALLS TO RACE CAR DRIVERS THROUGH THE PACIFIC Northwest.

In Washington, the rain is so overwhelming in some years that races can only take place is in June, July, and August. And there are still rainouts in those months. Rainouts are so commonplace that racers often have their favorite bar to go to when the races are canceled. Before most races, they scan the schedules of every racetrack within a three-hour radius to see whether, if their race gets rained out if there could be another race they could compete in that night. Blue-collar workers turn themselves into expert meteorologists, reading clouds with remarkable accuracy to figure out when and where the rain might come from.

Meanwhile in sunny California, races take place from February through November. It makes the drivers from the North jealous. No matter how much effort the drivers from the Northwest put in, it is hard for them to compete with the Californians because the southerners get to race much more.

"They didn't have near the seat time we did from California," said Jimmy Sills, a Californian from Placerville and one of the best sprint car racers in the nation in the 1980s.[1]

In the fall of 1980, 18-year-old Cheryl Glass decided that California, and the racing it offered, was the inevitable next step in what was becoming a remarkable career as a professional race car driver.

Even as Cheryl had been finding success at Washington's Skagit Speedway and earning national acclaim for how she, as an 18-year-old Black female rookie, had overcome the odds to defeat every white man racing sprint cars to win the track's final main event of the year, she desired more. She could never turn off that desire. She had one win and she needed more.

Drivers from the Northwest often hear about how great racing is in California and Arizona, and it makes them jealous. There were multiple showcase dirt tracks that specialized in sprint cars in 1980 in the Southwest. Tracks like Ascot Park in Los Angeles, Calistoga Speedway in the Napa Valley, Silver Dollar Speedway in the farming hamlet of Chico, and Manzanita Speedway in the desert that surrounds Phoenix would draw 100 cars for some of their big races. Many of the best drivers in the nation, and thousands of fans, regularly come to some of the high-paying shows at those tracks. Dozens of other dirt tracks littered the Southwestern states and ran sprint cars on a regular basis throughout the year, providing opportunities to race multiple times per week. For the drivers of the Northwest who grow frustrated by the weather, California and Arizona sound like paradise.

When the racing season in the Northwest concludes in late August or early September, the top drivers head south like snowbirds. After Cheryl's strong conclusion to the 1980 season at Skagit Speedway, she was determined to prove she belonged with the best drivers that California and the rest of the country had to offer.

The Glass family had befriended Duke McMillen, one of the top sprint car owners of the time, who based his operation from his shop in Sacramento. McMillen, a gregarious man, offered up space in his shop for Cheryl's sprint car and equipment so that her family team could be based in a central location for the extended fall sprint car season.[2]

She was willing to sacrifice to be a competitive race car driver. Even with as much value as Cheryl had placed on academics—and how successful she had been in them—she decided to drop out of Seattle University after completing three years of college so she could focus entirely on racing. She had one year left to graduate, but she said she could go back to school someday.[3] Her time to race was now.

Cheryl set an aggressive schedule for the fall of 1980. Despite few commitments back home, Cheryl decided she would fly back and forth from Washington each week to California with her father so she could race each weekend. Jim Grantham, a family friend who had served as Cheryl's crew chief that year, dedicated himself to working on Cheryl's car for the fall slate of races in California. He left his family, including his young son, and business to move to California for the fall to assist Cheryl full-time. But she wasn't ready to make the same commitment.

One of the crown jewel races of California's fall season is the Gold Cup. Starting in 1959, the annual multi-day race had moved between a few tracks in and around Sacramento over the years. It evolved into a race for the fire-spitting sprint cars. For 1980, it had been moved to a new home at Silver Dollar Speedway in Chico, California. The high-banked ¼-mile dirt bullring at the Silver Dollar Fairgrounds sat on the edge of the city. By 1980, the track had been around for three decades. It had slowly evolved into the state's hub for winged sprint car racing, complete with competitive, high-paying races.

For 1980, the Gold Cup featured the year's most intimidating field yet. The World of Outlaws touring series, the most prestigious sprint car sanctioning body in the world, made the race part of its vast schedule of races across the United States and brought with it some of the best drivers in the nation like Steve Kinser, Doug Wolfgang, Sammy Swindell, Jack Hewitt, and Rick Ferkel. Some of the top West Coast sprint car drivers like Lealand McSpadden and Jimmy Sills signed up to vie for the winner's $5,000 share of the $45,000 purse at the Gold Cup, too. Despite all the biggest names in American sprint car racing coming to compete at the race, Cheryl received a disproportionate amount of the pre-race publicity with obvious headlines like "Black girl races sprinter"[4] and "Sex, race no barriers for driver."[5] She continued to attract the interest of the press. After her one thrilling win at Skagit Speedway weeks before, the media considered her a contender to win at Chico.

"I'll just try and qualify well," Cheryl said before the race. "With $5,000 for the winner of Saturday's 50-lap main event, the competition is going to be fierce. I'll just try and do well, and not worry about anyone else."[6]

Cheryl was one of 17 drivers from the Northwest among the 90 elite entries for the Gold Cup. What drew people's interest was Cheryl was the first woman and the first Black person to compete in the race. Each time she would compete in another race that fall, she held that same distinction. She enjoyed that attention and often played up her differences. The media labeled her with stories titled, "Woman vs. the Outlaws." Cheryl figured that being unique would help fund her passion for racing by attracting sponsorship and more money to fund her racing. But beating the white male drivers who made up the rest of the field is what drove her to want to compete.

Adapting to new tracks wasn't something Cheryl Glass was good at. Cheryl struggled early at Chico. She slowly improved night after night, but for the final night of the Gold Cup, September 27, she was scheduled to start far back in the C-Main event. At 11th place, she was so far back that earning a transfer spot—the top four cars in each main event were given the option to move up to the next faster race—and eventually into the A-Main event was a distant hope.[7]

Early in the C-Main, a red flag came out for a flipping car and Cheryl coasted to a stop on the track. Her crew hustled over to check on her and recognized that a bolt had come out from where the left rear radius rod connected to the chassis. Star driver Doug Wolfgang, already locked into the A-Main event, walked onto the track under the red flag to check the track conditions. Wolfgang recognized Cheryl's predicament and helped the crew make a quick repair to get her car fixed. After the track was cleared and the race got underway again, Cheryl was much faster and moved forward to place third in the 15-lap race to transfer into the B-Main event.

She had a short two-minute break before the next race. While her crew attempted to make quick adjustments and refill her car with fuel, Wolfgang again stepped in and helped the novice driver and crew get the car ready so she could continue on. Starting 19th of 20 cars in the B-Main event, Cheryl displayed some of the best driving of her life. She passed cars on the high side of the banked track and down low. She passed them two at a time. The track's condition and shape was playing to her strength of mashing the gas pedal and driving flat out. She was showing these men that she was legitimate.

"She didn't shy away from competition," Sills said. "She felt that she would rise to the competition."

But the laps ran out. She placed sixth, two spots out of the transfer position for the A-Main event.[8] While local driver Johnny Anderson pulled off the surprise win in the A-Main event that night at the Gold Cup, Cheryl's performance was the bright spot of the night for most observers. Cheryl Glass was now a legitimate threat to the California elite.

While most of the Skagit Speedway regulars headed home to Washington, calling it a season after Chico, Cheryl moved on to compete in a four-race series, the Golden State Challenge Series. It stretched over two weekends between San Jose Speedway and Watsonville Speedway south of San Francisco.

San Jose Speedway promoter Ken Clapp was so taken with Cheryl that he arranged for her to stay with his secretary while she was racing in the series. That way she could be more easily accessible to the media.[9] Newspapers wrote stories about her with headlines like, "Cheryl making tracks in racing"[10] and "A woman in auto racing? Well, why not?"[11]

From the first race of the series, Cheryl showed that she belonged with all the other drivers. After qualifying 20th of 70 cars in the October 3 first race at the ¼-mile oval at Watsonville, Cheryl got faster. Early in that night's A-Main event, she was leading the race.[12] Even those who had seen her performance at the Gold Cup and at Skagit were impressed.

"She had Watsonville won until she cut a tire down," Jim Grantham said. "Watsonville was a little flat bullring. Where she would really shine was in the bullrings. If anything, she was kind of fearless, and that's what caused her to lose the race at Watsonville. She got out front and was gone at Watsonville. She banged into somebody."[13]

The following night at San Jose, Cheryl qualified 10th out of 80 cars and placed eighth in the main event. Even when the men complimented her, they threw in an insult as they assumed any woman couldn't be as physically capable as they were.[14]

Cheryl Glass (28) races to the outside of Lealand McSpadden (01) at San Jose Speedway in 1981.
SHIRLEY GLASS COLLECTION

"It takes a lot out of me to run a night of practice, qualifying, heat races and a sprint-car main event," sprint car driver Tim Green said, "and I'm over six feet and 200 pounds. Then I look at this little very lady-like woman, who drives a lot faster and smoother than some top male drivers, and I'm a little lost for words."[15]

After flights back and forth between her home in Seattle, Cheryl seemed a little out of sorts at the next race. At Watsonville on Friday October 10, Cheryl didn't have the pace she previously carried.[16] It could have been that she was gun shy after crashing out of the race the week before at that or that she was feeling the jet lag from all the frequent flights. But the next night at San Jose, she settled in and finished eighth in the main event. Against sprint car drivers who were making their living by racing, Cheryl placing eighth in the Golden State Challenge Series standings was proof that she wasn't a sideshow.[17]

"When she started running pretty decent it was a big draw for the media," said Lealand McSpadden, the Arizona driver who won all four races in the series and its championship. "She was different. We didn't have very many women to begin with at that time. She was one of the few women at that time. Then to be Black, that just made it bigger for the media."[18]

A week later, on October 19, Cheryl came back to California for a race with the Northern Auto Racing Club at Thunder Park Speedway in Sacramento. The big, half-mile dirt oval was longer than any dirt track on which she had ever previously driven. To the uninitiated, a longer track may not seem like a big challenge. After all, it means the drivers get to go faster. It sounds like fun in that light. But it's a whole different beast to drive. While surveying the big oval of Thunder Park, Cheryl decided she could drive it without ever lifting off the gas.

She was wrong.

In her first qualifying lap that night, she didn't lift off the throttle pedal coming into turn one and slid her black and green car into the outer wall of tires filled with dirt on the outside of the turn. Cheryl's sprint car bounced high in the air, and miraculously landed upright on its tires. The engine in her car stalled when it landed. Cheryl was slightly dazed by the short flight, but she was not willing to give up. Entire fields of hostile white men and track workers never stopped her, so why would getting airborne? When she came to a stop, she motioned to the track workers to push her off so she could continue in qualifying. The accident didn't slow her, and she posted the sixth fastest time of the night. She then placed fourth in the fast heat race and 10th in the main event. Cheryl never let little problems like hitting walls impact her desire to drive fast.[19]

Cheryl was earning a reputation for being fast, even among the California elite.

On one of the trips to the Sacramento Airport to drop the Glasses off to return to Seattle, Jim Grantham ran into McSpadden. The "Tempe Tornado" was already a sage in racing and was well respected for his unique ability as a race car driver. McSpadden recognized Grantham as Cheryl's mechanic from seeing him on the track and stopped him to pass on some advice.

"You can tell that young lady that she doesn't need to drive it in five feet further than anyone else," McSpadden told Grantham.

He didn't relay the advice to Cheryl.

The more time Cheryl and her crew spent working out of Duke McMillen's Sacramento shop, McMillen's influence became more pronounced. He was a mentor and someone who had been around sprint cars and knew the world she was trying to make her mark in. He also had his opinions about what Cheryl needed to do to move up to achieve her ultimate desire: becoming a professional race car driver. McMillen's words carried more weight than those of any other person in the sprint car world to Cheryl. McMillen encouraged Cheryl to race as much as possible, even at races she wasn't ready for.

The fabled Manzanita Raceway in Phoenix was the premier dirt track in all of Arizona. Every fall, Manzanita hosted the Western World Championships for sprint cars on its sweeping half mile dirt oval. To some, it was another big-paying race. But to many drivers, it was the biggest race of the fall.

The catch, however, was the race was for non-wing sprint cars.

In some parts of the country, such as Indiana and Arizona, they prefer their sprint cars without wings. Entire sects of fans and drivers are convinced that a sprint car without a wing is a better gauge of the skill of the drivers than when the wings are on. When the wings are taken off a sprint car, they lose the majority of downforce and require a completely different driving style. Without the wing, drivers can't be aggressive in the same manner. They are compelled to finesse the cars into the corner, backing it in and letting the car slide around more. That loss of aerodynamic grip forces the drivers to seek out more mechanical grip from the chassis and tires from any inch of track where it remains.

Cheryl Glass had never tried to race a sprint car without the downforce producing wings. Other drivers tried to tell her this was going to be different than what she was used to, but Cheryl refused to be held back.[20]

Manzanita wasn't an easy track—even for drivers who regularly raced there. The oval often slicked over with a fine layer of smooth rubber over the dirt, ringed by a cushion of tacky, fluffy dirt that built up next to the retaining wall on the outside.

"Most people who came to Manzanita really hated it," said Lealand McSpadden, a Manzanita regular who won the Western World Championships in 1978.

Despite the difficult situation Cheryl faced in racing at Manzanita for the first time, McMillen convinced her to race the October 22 through October 25 Western World Championships. The media in Arizona ate it up. The story of the first woman to enter the race, especially one with a rapidly expanding resume, was interspersed with the story of yet another promising 18-year-old. A third-generation driver out of New Mexico, Al Unser Jr. was the son and nephew of two Indy 500 winners. Some in the racing world saw sprint cars as a pit stop on what would surely be a career ascent to Indianapolis for "Little Al."[21] Like many young male drivers Cheryl raced against, Unser was struck by her.

"Quite honestly, I thought she was really cute," Al Unser Jr. said. "She was quiet, super-polite, and you know it was all good. Everything about my whole thing with her was really good."[22]

While Al Unser Jr. thought she belonged, others thought differently. Cheryl Glass was convinced she could do anything she wanted in a race car, but Manzanita had a way of humbling drivers. Her lack of experience in racing without a wing put her and other drivers in danger.

"She had no business even being there," said Jerry Day, who built her car.[23]

The competition at Manzanita was fierce. Between local aces like Ron Shuman and his brother, Billy; nationally renowned drivers like Bobby Davis Jr., Jeff Swindell, and Rick Ferkel; and some of Cheryl's fellow Skagit Speedway racers like Fred Brownfield, every position was valuable throughout the week's races. At a race like the Western World Championships, the 60 cars that entered would be whittled down to the final 18 for the final main event on the final night. That's where the lion's share of the $60,000 waited to be won. Many great drivers would not make it to the final race.

Cheryl had a respectable showing on the race's first night, October 22, placing sixth in the semi-main event. It was a start, but she knew she had to drive faster to make Saturday night's big race. The next day, Cheryl placed ninth in the non-qualifiers race.[24] She still had a long way to go.

For the final night's races, Cheryl was slated to start fifth place in the consolation main event, also known as the C-Main event. The race was inverted, meaning she was one of the slowest cars and a bunch of faster cars were starting behind her. Promoters liked to invert fields to encourage more passing. For Cheryl to have a chance at making it to the main event, she was going to make a quick charge to the front and stay there.

Earlier in the day, the track workers put too much water on the dirt in an ill-fated attempt to keep it from getting dusty later in the night's races. As Cheryl and the rest of the field were about to start the race, the track was still greasy, a sensation she wasn't used to. When the green flag flew to start the race, Cheryl was driving faster than she ever had. Then on the second lap, she sailed her car into turn one and tried to catch the berm of fluffy, wet dirt up against the wall. But in the attempt, she drove her car too far into the corner and slid the right rear tire over the cushion.[25] Her car slid into the wall, hitting it with the right rear tire and launched into the air. The car began to flip. Cheryl went end over end, disbursing energy into her body each time the car came down and impacted the track. The only thing that kept her car from flying out of the track was the 12-foot tall signs above the crash wall.[26]

After 13 flips, Cheryl landed hard on the track with the tires miraculously on the ground. She had traveled hundreds of feet from where she first started flipping in turn one.

Doug Wolfgang and Jimmy Sills were watching the race together from inside of turn two. When they saw Cheryl's flip, Wolfgang turned to Sills and proclaimed, "Well, that just added about a second-and-a-half to my lap times," out of fear of the track.[27]

Jim Grantham was standing in the infield in turn two near where Cheryl's car mercifully came to a halt. He rushed to her as the other cars on the track were attempting to come to a stop. When Grantham reached her, Cheryl was drifting in and out of consciousness. The race was halted by a red flag and cars behind her had to take evasive moves to avoid hitting her. A siege of track workers and medics rushed to her aid and her car was quickly surrounded. It was a laborious 20 minutes to get her out of the crumpled wreckage of her sprint car and into an ambulance to take her the five miles to Memorial Hospital.

"When you crashed at Manzanita, you didn't crash easy," McSpadden said. "First of all, high speed. Second of all, you're so close to the wall. Third of all, the grove was very narrow. When you crash there, you crash."[28]

The wreck was one of the most violent a person could take and still survive. When Cheryl made it to the hospital, it took doctors hours to figure out the extent of her injuries. The heavy impacts she absorbed were so violent that she had injuries to her face, neck, right shoulder, back, both hips, both knees, and one ankle. The impacts were so violent that the blood vessels in her eyes were damaged. For several hours, Cheryl couldn't see.

"And other than that, I was just fine," she later said with a laugh.[29]

After she regained her vision, Cheryl insisted the staff turn on the television in the hospital. Television broadcasts were replaying her spectacular crash. Even for a wreck at Manzanita Speedway, which produced many serious crashes, Cheryl's was one that people couldn't stop watching.

The crash destroyed Cheryl's car. The front and back were pointed in different directions, and sheet metal was torn off and scattered around the car. The tires were flat and the steel wheels on the car were smooshed in the final impact.

"It wasn't her fault," Jerry Day said. "It was the fact that she didn't belong there."[30]

Cheryl was credited with a 16th place finish and paid $50. It wasn't enough to pay for the little food she would be able to eat at the hospital over the next few weeks, let alone the medical bills she racked up. Fortunately, she had parents with insurance policies and money.

The Phoenix neighborhood where Manzanita Speedway was located was considered the bad part of town. The track was ringed by wrecking yards and industrial businesses. McSpadden, who may have made more laps at the track than any other person, said it wasn't the type of neighborhood a person would want to hang around.

While the rest of the drivers continued racing for the Western World Championship, Cheryl's crew managed to load the remnants of her car onto the trailer and left to meet her at the hospital. In the dark of night, Grantham was driving the van with the trailer behind it in the unfamiliar setting to an unfamiliar hospital. He had to rely on vague directions from others about how to get there. A few miles from the speedway, Grantham turned the van left onto a road as instructed. As soon as he did, a car with its headlights off struck the trailer carrying Cheryl's wounded car.

"A woman ran into the trailer and flipped the car off the trailer," Jim Grantham said. "The woman, it was dusk, at the time, and I mean it was dark enough. And she didn't have her headlights on. The officer walked up and said, 'Oh my God, it's her again.'"

It took Grantham and Marvin nearly an hour to repair the trailer and load the already severely damaged race car onto the trailer. After a long delay, they eventually headed to the hospital.

"I thought, 'Wow, that is a bad night at the races,'" Sills said.

When Marvin and Grantham arrived at the hospital, they learned the extent of Cheryl's injuries from the crash. Cheryl hoped to leave the hospital that night and go back to the hotel they stayed at the night before, but the doctors told her she was going to remain in the hospital for an extended stay.

Since Cheryl wasn't going anywhere, Marvin and Grantham started the 1,500-mile drive back home to Seattle while Cheryl recovered. It was over a week until Cheryl would be released from Memorial Hospital so she could fly home to Seattle. When her flight landed at SeaTac Airport, she was on crutches and looked worse than she had the night of the crash. Of all the crashes Cheryl had been in so far that season—and there had been plenty—this one was the worst.

"I just remember going to pick her up from the plane after her big wreck down there, just how beat up she was," said James Grantham, at the time eight years old.[31]

Cheryl was entered in several more sprint car races in California that fall for a schedule stretching well into November, including one at vaunted Ascot Speedway. Even if she had a car capable of racing, Cheryl was in no shape to be walking around. She definitely wasn't going to be racing.

When they got her race car back to Seattle, Marvin and Grantham surveyed the damage. It was a complete loss. Little of it was usable, and even the engine needed significant repairs. Even with Cheryl hobbled from her injuries, Marvin Glass was already committed to replacing that sprint car so she could race again. Cheryl hadn't let racers and track

Cheryl Glass is on crutches after her crash at Manzanita Speedway at her family's Christmas party at their Seattle home in 1980.
SHIRLEY GLASS COLLECTION

workers who disliked her for her skin color and gender stop her from competing. She certainly wasn't going to let a few injuries, either.

Jerry Day didn't have time to build a new car for the family. He recommended they purchase a new one from Chuck Delu, a race car builder in California. When Duke McMillen seconded the recommendation, they agreed and decided to buy a car from Delu. They sold the remains of the RAM chassis back to Jerry Day. The Glass family also ordered a couple more engines from Jack Conner, anticipating Cheryl's full physical recovery. The investment for Cheryl to go racing again was more than they had spent to get Cheryl into racing a sprint car the first time.

Even after the worst injuries of Cheryl's life, her family was spending more money than made sense on her racing career. This was, they believed, her shot at the big time. Her uniqueness in the field of race car driving made her special, and she let the avocation define her. Cheryl had committed herself to making race car driving a career. Her parents were willing to do anything they could to keep her racing.

Marvin estimated he spent about $50,000 in 1980 to finance Cheryl's racing—Cheryl estimated $90,000[32]—and she earned less than $5,000 in prize winnings. She had proven she had talent and the ability to be a successful race car driver. But for her to race at higher levels, it was going to cost a lot more.

"I recognize there is some risk, but it's something she's very good at, and she enjoys it," Marvin Glass said. "We're going to do everything we can to make sure the car she's in is as safe as possible. I've told her that I would try to have the equipment ready when she was ready."[33]

Cheryl had been dating her disco dancing partner, 22-year-old Darryl Jenkins, but her injuries were so severe that she couldn't compete with him that winter. Those same injuries, however, weren't going to stop her from getting back into a race car.

Months before her crash, Cheryl booked a four-day road racing school at the Bob Bondurant School of High Performance at Sears Point International Raceway in Sonoma, California, for December. The noted sports car and Formula One driver, Bondurant, opened the school in 1968, a Who's Who of race car drivers. Celebrities like Paul Newman and James Garner used the school's courses as a springboard into the world of professional racing.[34] Though the school likely would have refunded her tuition or postponed her courses had they known the extent of her injuries, Cheryl didn't want to wait.

Cheryl felt she had the hang of dirt track racing. But if she was going to race Indy Cars one day, she would have to learn to road race. It's a vastly different discipline and takes significant training. Cheryl was willing to put in the work, even if she wasn't physically capable.

Cheryl caught a flight for California and over four days, she completed the rigorous course. She drove Datsun sedans that appeared stock and a Formula Vee, an incredibly underpowered open wheel single seat race car that was regularly used as a steppingstone to professional open wheel racing. Her ability to walk was limited, but Cheryl performed well enough in the school to earn a license to race in the International Motor Sports Association, the biggest and most prestigious professional sports car road racing sanctioning body in North America.

To help Cheryl recover from her injuries, Jim Grantham built an exercise apparatus that resembled the cockpit of a sprint car, using a seat from a chair, tables, and weights. The steering wheel simulated the motion of steering a sprint car and gave her the feel of what it would be like to physically drive a sprint car again. It was rudimentary, but it gave her a tool to help her recover from her injuries. She worked out on the apparatus when people were watching or photographing her, but not regularly enough to help her physically.

But Cheryl was healing. Then a letter gave her a boost.

In the sprint car world, the best drivers race cars owned by someone else. To drive someone else's race car—at least someone outside of their family—gives a driver freedom. Not restrained by the financial obligations of owning and operating his or her car lets the driver concentrate solely on driving. They can focus on winning races and championships. By tradition, the car owner pays the driver a share of any prize money they win, usually 40 percent. But the drivers are rarely under contract, meaning they have the freedom to quit a ride at any time. And it also means they are under threat of being fired at any time.

The national attention Cheryl Glass received in 1980 piqued the interest of car owners, including some of the most prominent in the nation.

A motorcycle and roadster racer in his youth, "Speedy" Bill Smith founded Speedway Motors, a speed shop in Nebraska in 1952.[35] Speed shops were dealers for performance racing equipment. They are considered gurus in their communities among the car guys. The speed shop was so vital to car guys in the 1950s and 1960s that every hot-rodder and race car driver would go to a speed shop to purchase the best new equipment to make their cars go faster. Bill Smith got into sprint cars in the mid-1960s, entering a car for one of the original outlaw sprint car drivers, Jan Opperman. Smith's business grew at an epic pace when he launched a mail order component with extensive, slick catalogs. Suddenly, items like front axels for sprint cars could be mass-manufactured and distributed through a centralized purveyor like Speedway Motors. No longer did such things have to be made one at a time by one of the dozens of fabricators in the nation.

Bill Smith was a self-made power player in the racing world. By 1980, he was well-established as one of the top sprint car owners in the nation. His cars were always fast, largely because the equipment he fielded was the best that money could buy. And he put the best drivers he could find in his cars. Smith had high expectations for his drivers, and he was often rewarded for the faith he placed in them.

After learning about Cheryl Glass through her exploits in *National Speed Sport News* and other racing publications, Smith was intrigued. He saw the potential for her to win races and bring attention to his team as well as to the sport. In his first letter to her, Smith offered Cheryl a job as a driver, sight unseen.[36]

"Cheryl had an awful lot of talent," Bill Smith said. "Pretty girl, like I say, very bright. A lot of talent."[37]

Race car teams were exclusively solo ventures, the team fielding one car for one driver. Many car owners thought that was the way because only one car could fit in victory lane at a time, so one car was all they needed. But Smith had the idea of a multi-car team. In his mind, multiple drivers could learn from each other and make each other faster. In sprint car racing, it was a revolutionary idea.

Bill Smith's first letter to Cheryl Glass in December 1980 proposed that she join the multi-car team he was launching. She didn't know who he was. The nuances of the larger racing world were still unknown to the 18-year-old.

Smith hired veteran Ron Shuman to drive a new sprint car he was having built and wanted to put Cheryl in the car that had been driven successfully the year before by Doug Wolfgang. The car Smith was offering Cheryl to drive was the best that money could buy. It had been constructed at Smith's Nebraska facility at a cost he estimated at $100,000. He offered Cheryl a deal she wouldn't get elsewhere: she would receive 30 percent of the winnings she earned; if she won a race, her cut would rise to 40 percent. She would also receive 10 percent of any sponsorship money and 20 percent of money earned at personal appearances. That would give her a monthly salary, something unheard-of for sprint car drivers at the time. Not only would she be a professional race car driver, but she would also be well-kept. Smith said he would supply two full-time, experienced mechanics with the two-car team and a full-time team manager to oversee operations.[38]

And Cheryl would run the full World of Outlaws schedule in 1981.

Sprint car drivers are an itinerant bunch. There are few major series in sprint car racing because only a few pay well enough that drivers can earn a living racing in them. The few sprint car series that last more than a few years hold the power over scheduling and control the biggest races. When AAA promoted races, it decreed that drivers racing for its championships could only race at its specified races. If they raced at any race AAA didn't sanction, they were labeled "Outlaws." The drivers who ventured from town to town across America, competing in only the highest-paying races proudly embraced the "Outlaw" label as their identity.

Ted Johnson, a former midget racer from Wisconsin, formed the World of Outlaws in 1978 as a loose amalgamation of high-paying races in 1978. In the first year of its existence, any sprint car race in the United States paying more than $2,000 to win was considered a World of Outlaws race, including Skagit Speedway's Dirt Cup. With Johnson's arrangement, there was more than one race for the series on the same date on opposite sides of the country. Drivers would earn points based on how much money they earned and a champion would be crowned at the end of the season. This was a departure from how most racing series handed out championships. For the second year of the series, 1979, a more traditional schedule of races was devised and many of the nation's top drivers committed to race in the series. The sanctioning body took a monetary fee in exchange for bringing its series to the tracks. In a few years, the World of Outlaws schedule grew to nearly 100 races per year, snaking across the United States over the course of 10 months. It was a grueling but lucrative journey for those who stuck it out.[39]

The World of Outlaws tour became the goal for almost all sprint car drivers. A ride in that series was considered the pinnacle of that form of racing. Between the prestige and money it offered to competitors, it quickly became the priority for drivers who wanted to race on dirt. To many people, the upstart series had already overtaken the more historically significant sprint car series of the United States Auto Club as the top sprint car series in the nation.

Cheryl Glass learned what the World of Outlaws was and what it could mean for her career. She could compete in more races in one year with the tour than she could in five years racing at Skagit Speedway.

Though her father was funding a new car for her race in Washington for the 1981 season, the deal Smith was offering was too good to pass up. She accepted his offer after a series of phone calls.

"And Cheryl came back to Lincoln (Nebraska) before we left to go to Florida on the first of February," Bill Smith said. "She came into Lincoln and spent almost a week there getting fitted and learning who we were and what we were. I have four sons who were about the same age as Cheryl at that time. I know they, in the evenings after we got through working in the day, they did the bar scenes."[40]

Bill Smith knew that hiring Cheryl would bring publicity to his sprint car team. That kind of thing was important to him. A promoter who wanted to build his Speedway Motors brand, Smith sought out any attention he could get. Cheryl was used to doing interviews, but she wasn't prepared for the onslaught of attention she received when the season started in Florida.

As soon as the Speedway Motors team arrived in the Sunshine State for the start of the World of Outlaws season, the media ate up the story about the now 19-year-old Black female model who was coming to take on the best sprint car drivers on the planet. Cheryl was going to be the first woman to compete in the series. It was easy for track promoters of the publicity people for the World of Outlaws or track promoters to get newspapers and television stations to send reporters to capture her story. She was inundated from attention from media outlets in Florida and from throughout the nation with stories titled, "Glass Pursues Lofty Racing Goal."[41] Cheryl was so inundated with requests that she had a scant amount of time to concentrate on driving her race car. That frustrated her.

"That's got to be a plus for any sponsor that I have," Cheryl said. "But I can drive a race car, too. I'm not just a woman putting around out there filling out the field."[42]

When a race car driver is put up against the best competition on a regular basis, they either sink or swim immediately. For most drivers coming to compete against the World of Outlaws for the first time, it will take months or years to be competitive. Cheryl's self-image and hubris often got in the way of reality.

She had been suffering from the flu when she arrived for her first race of the season at East Bay Raceway Park, a third mile dirt oval in Tampa, on February 4, 1981. That day, in the first non-qualifier's race, Cheryl led two laps, spun on the third lap and placed sixth. She didn't qualify for the night's main event. She also tangled with several other cars during the race. It wasn't a good debut.

The drivers Cheryl was competing against were at the top of their ability. Many already had valuable experience and had earned their place as the elite of the sprint car world. Steve Kinser, who won the first three World of Outlaws series championships, saw Cheryl's impossible situation and approached her to offer advice. Bobby "Scruffy" Allen, one of the winningest independent, low-buck sprint car drivers in the nation, saw that some other drivers were being stand-offish with Cheryl. He made a point to talk with her before the next race.[43]

"Drive within your means and learn how to drive it slowly," Allen told her. "Keep going better and better and better. If you go out there and you crash all the time, you're not going to learn anything but how to put the car back together."[44]

After four straight nights of racing were rained out by the Florida weather, the World of Outlaws made its way to Volusia County Speedway, a half-mile dirt track in Barberville. In hot laps, Cheryl spun her car in front of Lee Osborne, a veteran driver from New York. Osborne couldn't avoid her, clipped her car and flipped, significantly damaged his car. Cheryl's car was only slightly damaged.[45]

"I ran into the liberated woman," Osborne told fellow driver Jimmy Sills.

Cheryl pulled her car into the pits, got out and quit Bill Smith's team on the spot. She didn't say why.

What sounded like a wonderful deal in her correspondence and phone calls with Smith had become a nightmare. When she raced at home in Washington, she had an attentive crew to tend to her car. But in Florida, the only mechanic with the team mostly ignored her and wouldn't make changes to the car when she suggested them.

Though she wouldn't admit it, Cheryl had not fully healed from the injuries she had suffered at Manzanita three months earlier and wouldn't admit that her confidence as a driver had been shaken.

"I think she felt a little let down on our end because I spent so much time trying to get Ronnie (Shuman's) car running," said Mark Todd, the lone mechanic for the team. "But she had the car (Doug Wolfgang) drove the year before and it was ready for as fast as she was going. . . . But the car owner wouldn't even talk to her and obviously she felt a little left out. She just wouldn't stand on the gas, but I think she was scared to death. And the press wouldn't leave her alone either."[46]

Cheryl boarded a plane for Seattle and went home. For all the determination, skill, and fortitude Cheryl possessed, she had failed in her first shot at the big time.

CHAPTER SIX

A Humbling Return Home

March 1981 to December 1981

FAILURE WAS NOT SOMETHING CHERYL GLASS DEALT WITH WELL.

Cheryl's brief tenure with the World of Outlaws tour was a failure. In some cases, drivers who are moving up in the racing world like Cheryl sell off the equipment they competed with at lower levels. That way they have no fallback option and force themselves to commit to their new venture.

Cheryl had her back-up plan at home. Jim Grantham had been completing the finishing touches in building her new Delu Chassis sprint car.[1] Had she had no other options for where to race, she might have opted to stick it out with Bill Smith's team. But she chose to return to Washington.

She decided to try out a new activity: cheerleading. She tried out for the team of the Seattle Seahawks football team in April 1981, the Sea Gals. The team wanted her to perform difficult stunts, which she wasn't physically capable of, given her knee injuries. She didn't make it past the first round of tryouts.[2]

One of the top hydroplane owners in the Seattle area, Al Curtis, tracked Cheryl down and asked her to test his boat, Gladiator. The test went fine, especially for her first time in the water, but Curtis hired another pilot.

Hydroplane racing was huge in Seattle. With the abundant calm waterways surrounding the city, it became a hub of boat racing in the

United States. Seafair, the week-long festival that included hydroplane racing in Lake Washington, took place each year not far from her house. She had been a Seafair princess and the thought of her racing in it was intriguing.

She was then asked to drive the MISS KYYX Hydroplane.

"In fact, my understanding is she could have been the first woman driver at Seafair," said Skip Young, a family friend and hydroplane enthusiast. "The one who became the first woman driver was Brenda Jones. Cheryl could have been, but she said the reason she didn't do it was they weren't willing to pay her any money."[3]

Where most hydroplane drivers were willing to drive for the honor of driving, Cheryl considered herself a professional.

Jim Grantham said that when Cheryl went to race with the World of Outlaws, he decided to move on from his volunteer position as the crew chief of her sprint car team. His son, James, was still racing quarter midgets, and Jim Grantham and a partner made a deal to take over promotion of Harbor Speedway in Elma starting with the 1981 season.

The dirt track was located at the Grays Harbor Fairgrounds, 90 miles southeast of Seattle, but wasn't in operation in 1980. The economy of the area was heavily tied to logging, much like Alger, but it was decidedly less progressive socially than Skagit County. The dirt speedway in Elma, located inside a one-mile oval solely reserved for horse racing, had been a half-mile dirt oval. To be suitable to host auto races again, it needed a lot of work including new grandstands, guardrails, and concession stands. Grantham carved out a new ¼-mile dirt oval that would be more manageable for his track preparation crew and easier on the cars.[4]

Jim Grantham decided that for races at Grays Harbor to be successful, he needed sprint cars to be the featured class.

Though there were many sprint cars throughout Seattle and the northwest, many had a connection with Skagit Speedway. Some of the Skagit Speedway racers were such loyalists, they said they wouldn't go across the street to race. There were so many sprint cars in the northwest that the class splintered into factions.

Skagit Speedway and Harbor Speedway gave out their own championships for the sprint cars. While Skagit Speedway had its races on

Saturday nights, Harbor Speedway raced on Friday nights, meaning drivers could race at both tracks. Then there was the Northwest Sprint Cars Inc. tour and Gordy Adams, Jerry Fanger's car owner, started the Washington State Sprint Car Series for the 1981 season. In that series, drivers would accumulate points between Skagit and Grays Harbor to crown a champion.

"When both groups would get together, we'd have about 20, 25 cars," Fanger said.[5]

The splintered factions could leave some sprint car races with five or six cars, especially the races at Grays Harbor. The one car Jim Grantham knew he could get for his races was the one Cheryl Glass was driving.

Cheryl wasn't happy to lose her crew chief, but Grantham worked a deal that would fund some of her racing for 1981. He procured sponsorship for her from Olympia Beer, which had previously sponsored such race car drivers as Hershel McGriff and Ray Elder. The brewery, located not far away in Tumwater, wanted its beer exclusively sold at the track. It sponsored the track for thousands of dollars and Grantham talked them into sponsoring Cheryl for $8,000 for the season, a huge sum for a driver like Cheryl.[6]

Her new car was painted in the white and gold Olympia Beer colors and given number 28, the same as her prior car. There was a complication with the sponsorship: the 19-year-old Cheryl wasn't old enough to drink Olympia Beer.

The Glass family also decided to make a major upgrade for the rest of Cheryl's racing operation. They purchased an enclosed trailer in which to haul Cheryl's race car, something unheard of at the time. Sprint cars were regularly towed to the tracks on open trailers behind pickups or vans. After seeing the enclosed trailers that the World of Outlaws teams were using, the Glass family had to have one.

That enclosed trailer was the first anyone in the northwest had seen a local racer use. It was practical as it meant not having to load and unload the ancillary equipment needed for a night at the races. And it provided shelter from rain, something that was inevitable in the Pacific Northwest. Many drivers against whom she competed saw that trailer as her family's oversized spending, sending a message that they thought they were better than the other local teams. It was showing off in a way, but the Glass family also wanted to give Cheryl anything she needed to succeed.

Grantham had nearly completed Cheryl's new sprint car before moving to rebuilding Harbor Speedway, but Cheryl didn't have any crew members without him. Marvin convinced 18-year-old Kelly Tanner, against whom Cheryl had raced in quarter midgets, to help frequently. But without mechanics with experience working on sprint cars, she would be at a constant disadvantage throughout the season.

In the first race of the year at the newly christened Harbor Speedway on May 29, Grantham's new design for the track played to Cheryl's advantage. She led early in the main event and pulled out such a lead in front of second place Alan Munn that it appeared no one could catch her.[7] But the lack of experience in Cheryl's crew cost her.

Cheryl Glass races at Grays Harbor Raceway in Elma, Washington in 1981.
SHIRLEY GLASS COLLECTION

"I think there was one or two laps to go and she ran out of fuel. She had it won, driving away," Jim Grantham said.[8]

Though racing had become Cheryl's identity, working on her own race car was not something that interested her. She would take on minor projects, like mounting the seat or keeping the car clean. But when it came to things like installing an engine or replacing a rear end, Cheryl rarely helped. The drivers she raced against assumed she was acting as if she was too good for those kinds of tasks.

"She was not there to mechanic or build and work on the car as far as I ever saw," said Billy Kennelly, her childhood admirer who was rebuilding a midget in the Glass's shop south of Boeing that year. "She was there quite a bit, which was a lot of fun."[9]

The work on the car somehow got accomplished, but her Delu Chassis car was not as good as her previous car was. Cheryl won a semi-main event at Skagit Speedway on June 6,[10] then placed third in the main event a week later.[11]

"She was running tall," Guy Mossington said. "I remember when she came out with that Olympia car, that was serious business."[12]

After a mediocre 14th place C-Main finish in the Dirt Cup at Skagit Speedway,[13] Cheryl put together a string of solid finishes including second place at Harbor Speedway,[14] a trophy dash win at Skagit,[15] and fourth place finishes at Harbor[16] and Skagit.[17]

But Cheryl's aggressive driving cost money. She crashed frequently. Sprint cars are designed with components that can be easily replaced, but they all cost money. Her family spent money so that she could have spares on hand for her inevitable crashes. Destroying components such as wings and wheels became a regular occurrence on Cheryl's cars.

"I built them a wing and my shop was at home then," Jerry Day said. "(Marvin) came to my shop real late at night. He's packing it out the driveway. Marvin called the next day and said, 'I picked up that wing yesterday.' I said, 'It was so dark all I could see was your teeth.' He said, 'Oh, you people.'"[18]

No matter how well or poorly Cheryl did, she received a large amount of attention from the media. The *Seattle Times* published a seven-page feature story documenting her racing.[19] Days later, a Seattle television station aired a special program about her.[20] Fellow drivers grew resentful about the attention lavished on her.

She told the interviewers that she considered sprint car racing a steppingstone. Most of the drivers against whom she raced saw it as the pinnacle for their careers. She made it known in every interview that she planned to be racing in the Indianapolis 500 in a few years—she usually said three years—and then would race Formula One. She proclaimed she would be the first Black person to do either.

"I won two major championships and seldom does a reporter come around and talk to me. I guess you're dealing with a man's ego, and that can be kinda touchy," said Fred Brownfield, the 1980 Skagit Speedway champion. "But I've paid my dues and proven my ability in this sport. She has helped attract women to the races. But there are a number of people that enjoy seeing her get beat, too. But the increased attendance last season helped boost my winnings about 10 percent."[21]

Even with a hectic schedule in 1981, Cheryl resumed interests outside of racing. She entered a few beauty pageants and found more success in those than she did in some races. Cheryl was named Miss Rainier,[22] placed fourth in the Miss Lake City beauty contest and was the runner-up and a princess in the Miss Seafair Pageant,[23] the same boat race she opted not to compete in because she wouldn't be paid.

She didn't have a job and had free time. She thrived on the attention she received from those pursuits.

Cheryl did something she had said she never would: At the August 1 race at Skagit Speedway, she was the trophy girl for the modified trophy dash, giving a kiss to winner Shawn Becker. In the sprint car main event, she was fighting with Lloyd Armey for the win, but made contact with Steve Royce and crashed both out of the race, finishing 14th.[24]

"She couldn't get around (Armey) and I could get past her," Steve Royce said. "I finally saw a hole that I tried to get to, and Cheryl got over and hit me. It took me out of the race. I can remember going over and having a talk with her. 'The guy you're trying to get around, you're about equal in the corners because you're trying to get around. Use that motor to get down the straightaway.' I hope she got something out of that. Maybe it started her thinking, get in there, stab and steer."[25]

Cheryl's presence in racing at Skagit Speedway opened doors for other female drivers. Debbie Kracke was a 16-year-old who had been racing quarter midgets on the same circuits as Cheryl years before. After Cheryl's immediate success, Debbie followed by racing a sprint car at Skagit Speedway. Cheryl was the first and only woman to compete in every race in which she competed in 1980. Then Cheryl raced against Kracke in a heat race on August 1, 1981 at Skagit Speedway, and Kracke beat her.[26]

"I was one of the first women to ever run, and so they didn't know what to expect," Cheryl said. "They gave me a hard time. They ribbed me, they called me names. They made it as difficult as possible for me to be successful."[27]

Cheryl had some decent finishes the rest of the season in Washington, including leading laps in a main event at Skagit Speedway,[28] placing fourth August 22, and placed fifth in the final points standings in the Washington State Sprint Car Series.[29] She returned to California to race again that fall and wasn't competitive at the Gold Cup at Silver Dollar Speedway. She grew irritated by her competitors.

"She was behind me and she'd stick her nose up, back up. Stick her nose up, back up," fellow driver Denny Smith said. "Finally, she put her nose in there and I wiped it off (and crashed her). So she's walking back past the pit seating, and she flipped me off. And because racers are notoriously nice people and not racist and that type of stuff, they started some bad comments. Well, then she flipped them off. It got to be a pretty ugly deal."[30]

Cheryl had a solid run in the opening night of the Golden State Series at Watsonville Speedway on October 2, coming back from a mid-race spin to place fourth.[31] But she was a non-factor at the rest of the four-race tour.

After Cheryl's promising rookie year as a sprint car driver, her sophomore season didn't live up to her expectations. Her few top five finishes—and lack of wins—didn't offset her many crashes. The pressure she put on herself didn't help, either.

"For the equipment that she had, she should have done a lot better," Jim Grantham said. "Your second year can be the worst year you ever ran."

Cheryl's lack of success in her second year drew criticism.

In *Open Wheel* magazine, a national sprint car racing magazine, a columnist noted she was attractive, but criticized her for leaving her ride with Bill Smith after her crash with Lee Osborne.[32] In *Racing Wheels*, a west coast racing newspaper, columnist Jim Simmons took potshots at her despite never seeing her race. Simmons took offense at the large amount of media attention she received. He opined that Cheryl was a sure thing to make it to the Indianapolis 500 because she was a Black female driver. He wrote that the money she could bring in sponsorship would make up for her lack of success as a sprint car driver.

"My own feelings are that she receives a lot more publicity than her ability warrants," Simmons wrote.[33]

Cheryl was stung by the criticism after being widely feted in all the other media. What that criticism accomplished was to make her reconsider racing in the small pond that was Washington dirt tracks.

CHAPTER SEVEN

A Shot at the National Spotlight

1982

AFTER CHERYL GLASS MADE A SPLASH IN 1980, RACE CAR OWNERS FROM across the nation took note and tried to hire her to drive their cars. They recognized that the attention she could bring would lead to sponsorship that would bring them the finances to keep their operations going.

Cheryl was forced to learn the hard way that driving race cars for someone other than her family team could be a disaster.

So many offers came Cheryl's way that she didn't know about them all.

Cheryl said she had an offer from a team to drive in the Indianapolis 500 in 1982, though she declined to name the team. In the early 1980s, upstart Indy Car teams came on the scene every year to field a car in the Indy 500. Beyond the traditional 33 cars that made the race that year, there were 49 other drivers—including sprint car drivers Ken Hamilton, Jan Sneva, and Sammy Swindell—who failed to make the field in 1982. Even Cheryl knew she had nowhere near the experience necessary to race at the 2.5-mile quad oval and would have struggled at the temple of motor sports in the United States in a lesser organization and could have embarrassed herself.

"But I turned it down," she told a reporter from *Avenues* magazine. "When I compete at Indianapolis, I want everything to be just right. I want the right car, the right crew, the right sponsor, everything. Everything wasn't right for this year. I don't want to be an also-ran when I get to Indy. I want to finish at the top."[1]

93

Cheryl needed experience on asphalt ovals if she was ever going to race Indy Cars and was willing to take what opportunities she could to get in that form of racing.

Jack Conner, who built the engines for her dirt sprint cars, owned a sprint car he occasionally fielded for drivers at tracks around the Northwest. Jerry Day had built the car in the early 1970s and later sold it to Dick Wilskey. Conner purchased it and usually employed Ross Fontes to drive it. Fontes had some success and won races in the car. It had been competitive at one point. But by 1982, it was inadequate.

For the first big sprint car race in the nation in 1982, the Copper World Classic, Conner offered to field Cheryl on the mile asphalt oval at Phoenix International Raceway. A race at that level was far above anything that Cheryl had done. Competing in Conner's archaic car wasn't as great an opportunity as she hoped it would be. But she accepted the ride. It would be the first time she raced a sprint car without a wing since her disastrous 1980 race at Manzanita.

"The car was a piece of shit," Jerry Day said. "It wasn't a fast car to start with. Still, what the hell is she doing on a mile?"[2]

Starting in 1977, Phoenix International Raceway hosted the Copper World Classic every January or early February on its oddly shaped oval. Much of the rest of the country was still socked in by snow or heavy rain, but it was always sunny and warm in Arizona. The national television broadcast of the race gave the race prestige. Cheryl had one asphalt race in her life before attempting to race at Phoenix. She wasn't prepared.[3]

Jack Conner earned his reputation as an expert engine builder after years of producing engines for some of the best sprint car racers in the northwest. He bought a house in the Ballard neighborhood of Seattle and built a garage for his huge amount of machine equipment. Conner was a meticulous engine builder. He wouldn't let anyone else do even minor bits of the work and took a long time to complete anything. The engines he built produced more horsepower than seemed possible, but many of his customers grew frustrated at his lethargic pace and opted to go elsewhere.

Conner's sprint car would sit idle for months until the mood stuck him, and he would recruit a driver to race it. In a sprint car, every ounce matters. But Conner's car outweighed every other car entered at Phoenix by hundreds of pounds. People called the car "a tank."

It didn't help that Conner's car had a Chrysler hemi engine that was originally built in the 1950s. Conner extolled the virtues of the big hemi, claiming he could make more horsepower than a small block Chevrolet, which was in every other sprint car. The ancient hemi, however, weighed at least 300 more pounds than any Chevy, negating any power advantage.

Conner said he was put off by Cheryl's lack of humility. But he also could see her potential as a driver and thought she could be competitive in his car. The reality was no one was going to be fast in his hulk of a car.

He wanted Cheryl to succeed, but Conner didn't take the usual step of putting Cheryl in the car to test it before her first race in it. In her first laps in the car at Phoenix, Cheryl qualified a respectable 19th out of 31 sprint cars on January 30 at an average of 117.263 miles per hour. Going faster than she had before, Cheryl was to start up the grid for the February 1 40-lap main event. But her fastest lap was an eternity behind the 129.078 mile per hour lap put down by sprint car champion and Indy 500 veteran Gary Bettenhausen.[4]

"She did shit, but she didn't have a good car," Steve Royce said. "You can run the short tracks, a half mile and below; you get on that mile, that's a whole 'nother ballgame. Anyhow she was all over the place. The car wasn't very good."[5]

Ken Hamilton, in the "Pink Lady" big block Chevy engine sprint car with a pink paint scheme, was the class of the field in the Copper World Classic. Attrition also played a huge factor. Drivers dropped out at a staggering rate, allowing Cheryl to improve her position. Cheryl was running in the top 10 with four laps to go. She bumped wheels with Colorado driver Buz Tapply coming onto the front straight and smacked into the outside guard rail.[6] The impact crushed the right front wheel of the car, and she slid against the wall nearly a quarter mile into turn one before mercifully coming to a stop.

Hamilton had been leading the race by a large margin. As Cheryl's car slid down the track, Hamilton tried to avoid her. But he failed, and it cost him the win.

"I was going underneath her, trying to miss her," Hamilton said. "I climbed over her left front with my right rear and broke a brake line. Shoulda, woulda, coulda—but we should have won that day."[7]

Cheryl accused Tapply of taking her out on purpose because she was a woman. Cheryl was still credited with a 10th-place finish.

"I don't care what anybody thinks," Cheryl said. "All I want to do is race, to be judged as a race car driver. They can leave all that other stuff at home."[8]

Cheryl's rancor wasn't reserved for Tapply; she was also upset with Hamilton about how he raced her. Hamilton's crash dropped him to a seventh-place finish and handed the win to Bob Frey.

"She was mad at Kenny Hamilton about something, and it pissed me off that she was because Kenny Hamilton has won that race. I don't know how many times they lapped her," Steve Royce said. "Kenny would not do anything on purpose. I thought man, she's kind of full of herself now."

She wouldn't race for Conner again, but other opportunities appeared.

Charlie Patterson grew up on a farm outside Indianapolis. At an early age, he began working on cars in the Indianapolis 500 for owners Bob Sowie and Rolla Vollstedt. Patterson started a driveshaft manufacturing business in 1972, then fielded cars in the USAC Silver Crown series. The cars were similar to sprint cars, but were slightly larger and heavier, and raced in longer, well-paying races. Without wings, the cars were a challenge to drive. Patterson had fielded race cars for drivers including Jim McElreath, Emmett Hahn, Jim Hurtubise, and Junior Knepper. His cars were good, but never good enough to win a Silver Crown race.

After reading about Cheryl in *National Speed Sport News*, Patterson decided she had the potential to attract sponsorship money that could keep his self-funded team going. That was only if he could get her to call him back. He called the Glass family home in Seattle multiple times and talked with her parents so many times that they were getting sick of him. Then Cheryl finally called him back. Patterson told Cheryl he wanted to put her in his car in USAC races at Eldora Speedway in Ohio, the Indiana State Fairgrounds and Flemington Speedway in New Jersey, some of the most prestigious dirt tracks in the country. It was a promising arrangement that Patterson offered, and Cheryl agreed.[9]

Patterson arranged for Cheryl to fly to Indianapolis from Seattle in April 1982 and put her up in a spare bedroom at his house outside the city for a week. He needed to fit her in his race car and introduce her to potential sponsors. He knew some Black business leaders around Indianapolis from his driveshaft business. They liked Patterson enough that they agreed to invite her to attend meetings of the Indianapolis chapter of the NAACP. Patterson dropped Cheryl off at one of their meetings so they could meet her. When he came to pick her up, one of the leaders told him, "Charlie, I applaud what you're trying to do. I don't care for her."

Patterson talked to everyone he could think of to try to get sponsorship so Cheryl could race. None of it worked.

"He was going around touting her. You could see his peers were like, 'Why are you messing with this Black girl?'" said Rod Reid, who worked with Indy Car teams in Indianapolis. "She wasn't particularly outgoing."[10]

Patterson had the pull to call a press conference at Indianapolis Motor Speedway to announce that Cheryl would drive for him in another attempt to draw attention. Curious reporters from major publications around the area arrived at the speedway on April 7, 1982, to see this new driver. Indy Cars were testing on the speedway in the background. When Tom Binford, chief steward for the Indianapolis 500, heard Cheryl was coming to the track, he took an interest. At the press conference, Patterson introduced Binford to Cheryl.

"She just walked up to him with a real nasty look on her face," Charlie Patterson said. "She just stuck her hand out and said, 'Hi.' He was very interested in helping get her to the speedway. Finally, Tom looked at me and looked at her and shrugged his shoulders. He said later, 'How do you put up with her attitude?' I said, 'I never really saw her act that bad.'"[11]

Patterson went to such effort to find sponsorship so he could run Cheryl in multiple races that he sent out 200 letters to every Black actor, athlete, and business owner he could think of. None were interested in sponsoring her.[12]

Cheryl grew tired of Patterson's constant pursuit of money.

Short of funds, Patterson gave up on Cheryl's planned debut at Eldora. Cheryl flew home to Seattle for nearly a month before returning to Indiana for the Hulman 100 at the Indianapolis State Fairgrounds for the May 8, 1982, race on the dirt mile oval. It was close enough to home that Patterson could afford to have her race. Other than being fit in his car at the shop, Cheryl had no experience in the car and was not prepared to race in it.

Patterson did the best he could with what equipment he had and things like new tires were considered luxuries beyond his means. Cheryl said she paid $600 out of her pocket so she could have a new set of tires on the car for the race.

Cheryl qualified well enough to start on the pole position for her 15-lap qualifying heat. But the officials informed her that because she was a rookie she would have to start in the back of the pack. She took offense to it. On the second lap of the race, she spun coming out of turn four. But she came back to finish ninth and qualify for the feature race.[13]

Cheryl was convinced she was sent to the back to start the race because she was Black.

When it came time for the race, Cheryl struggled.

Nine laps into the race, the car got out of shape and jumped the cushion in turn four, nearly hitting the wall.[14] She muscled the car into the infield with the engine still running. Patterson ran down and asked her what was wrong. She told him the car wasn't handling well enough and she was done. Patterson reached into the control panel and flipped the ignition switch to shut the engine off. Cheryl told Patterson she wasn't going to drive the car again.

As she climbed from the car, a reporter from a radio station approached her and asked if she had a comment and she said, "No."

It was one of the few times Cheryl turned down an interview.

"I parked it," she later said. "The car wasn't set up to race. I just had a problem with the crew setting it up the way I wanted it. I had every problem—pushing, the rear end coming around, biting. I came prepared to race and I'm not sure the crew did. The crew, because I'm a girl, doesn't think I know what I'm talking about. I'm a racer. I'm a front-runner, not a back marker."

Patterson said he was tired of her attitude and was done with her.

His deal with drivers he hired to drive his cars was they received 40 percent of winnings unless they won when they would receive 50 percent. Though Cheryl placed 21st in the race, she insisted she deserved 50 percent of the $400 in prize winnings because she had paid for tires for the car. After an argument at his shop the next day, Patterson eventually gave up and paid her the $200. He wanted rid of her.

"We intended to run more, but after she pulled what she did there, why, that was it," Patterson said.

It was reported in *National Speed Sport News* that she was fired from her ride with Patterson and that she refused an interview after the race. Marvin Glass took exception with those reports.

"It will serve no purpose to get into all of the unpleasant details leading up to the incidents but attempts to exploit Cheryl continue and no one wins in any of these situations," Marvin Glass wrote in a letter that was printed in the paper.[15]

Cheryl Glass found out the hard way that driving race cars for others had its own drawbacks. "The opportunities she got weren't as great as she may have thought," said Steve Beitler, who raced against her at Skagit Speedway.[16]

While no longer attending college, Cheryl decided she could still learn something. She enrolled in the John Robert Powers modeling course in Philadelphia. It was an expensive effort, and she was no longer drawing much interest to work as a model.[17]

The family still had Cheryl's sprint car, but if she went home and raced in Washington, it would be an admission that she failed at the national level. There were high profile sprint car races in the Midwest where she could get the competition she desired.

The Knoxville Nationals was the biggest and most prestigious sprint car race in the world. Held on the half-mile dirt oval at Knoxville Raceway in Iowa starting in 1961, the race earned its nickname "The Granddaddy of Them All" because it drew the best drivers in the country and paid better than any other sprint car race in the world. For the 1982 race, the Knoxville Nationals was scheduled to pay $10,000 to win and total purse of $100,500, far more than any other race. Over the course of four days, over 100 entrants from around the world whittled themselves down to a select group of 28 for the ultimate main event.

Cheryl learned that at midwestern tracks like Knoxville Raceway, there were no bathrooms in the infield for women. The men's bathrooms weren't much to see either, but they existed. The male drivers often changed into their driver's suits out in the open or on the front seat of the pickup they towed into the pits. Cheryl thought that was unfair. She made it known that she thought there should be separate areas for women, including a women's only bathroom with a place for her to change, even if it was outside the track.

She was the first woman to compete in the Knoxville Nationals and the second woman to ever race at the track. Tracks often spent as little as possible on facilities like restrooms for fans. Though it would have encouraged more women to compete, the track did nothing.[18]

"You got to have it spruced up a little bit," Cheryl told track officials.[19]

To prepare to race at Knoxville, Cheryl needed to get back behind the wheel of her sprint car. She decided she would try to drive in the August 7 World of Outlaws race at Eldora Speedway.

The race was intended to start at 8 p.m., but rain pounded the Ohio dirt, making it impossible to get going. The rain didn't relent until 11 p.m. Car after car was pushed onto the track in an attempt to work the moist dirt into racing shape. Cheryl was push-started from the pits and onto the track. But it was so wet she struggled to make her way around. The surface was as slick as ice, and controlling the car in conditions like that were difficult for the best drivers. Wheel packing a track was not something Cheryl had done often. A truck tried to push Jimmy Sills onto the track, but his car wouldn't start immediately in the slippery dirt. The truck started sliding sideways and Sills' car came to a halt on the inside of the track. The truck left him and drove away with the intention of returning to get him going later.

"And Cheryl came around and plowed right into him. Drove right into him. He was just sitting there," said Jim Hedblom, who had built wings for Cheryl's cars. "She didn't know what to do because of the banking. She didn't know to pick the throttle up and go above or go below."[20]

The cars of Cheryl and Sills weren't seriously damaged, but her confidence was shaken and she didn't race that night.

The Knoxville Nationals was what mattered.

There were 126 cars registered for the 1982 race. The best sprint car drivers in the nation were in the field. Knoxville is a flat half-mile oval with no room for error. Drivers sling themselves around the top or the bottom of the track at ridiculous speeds and somehow make it stick through the wide corners. Those who screw up pay for their mistakes.

Cheryl Glass stands next to her sprint car in the pits before the 1982 Knoxville Nationals.
SHIRLEY GLASS COLLECTION

Cheryl didn't back down from the challenging speedway, qualifying with a time of 19.213 seconds on opening night, August 11. She performed admirably, placing 11th in the B-Main event.[21]

To spice up racing programs, promoters love to dream up unique races that might draw the attention of the crowd, if only for a few moments. For 1982, Knoxville promoter Ralph Capitani envisioned a Race of States. The format would be to pit the best driver in attendance from each state for an all-star field. Cheryl was the only driver from Washington who was competing, thus giving her a spot in the race. A handful of drivers like Bobby Marshall, Jeff Swindell, and Shane Carson decided to race it, but not all top drivers there did. Cheryl was out of her league, but managed to place a respectable 11th, one lap down to the leaders.

Cheryl Glass had played alphabet soup—where drivers start in a lower main event like the C-Main and place well enough to transfer into higher races until they reach the A-Main—a few times in her life. This wasn't one of them. On the final night of the Knoxville Nationals on August 15, Cheryl placed 21st in the C-Main event won by Mick Pickney. She hadn't done as well as she hoped.

Like most every race she had competed in, Cheryl was the first woman to drive in the Knoxville Nationals.

"I don't know what she's doing racing because she is so smart," driver Tim Green said. "She can do almost anything. She won't ever be a superstar, but she's a good driver. She really likes racing."[22]

Cheryl felt she wasn't getting closer to her dream of racing in the Indianapolis 500 by racing sprint cars at dirt tracks.

After the season, Marvin sold her sprint car to a buyer in Australia, a deal brokered by Duke McMillen. Marvin soon sold their trailer for $1,200 and the rest of their sprint car specific equipment.[23] Cheryl Glass's time in sprint cars, the discipline of racing that made her name, was over.

She never reached the heights she believed she was capable of in the category, but she established herself in the racing world.

"To watch her go into sprint cars and see what she did in sprint cars back then in a real aggressive man's sport back then . . . it was pretty unheard of," Billy Kennelly said. "I honestly think she was one of the best female drivers that ever hit the dirt. I would say that in any crowd."[24]

But Cheryl needed a break from racing.

CHAPTER EIGHT

The Wedding of the Year

1983

CHERYL GLASS'S DREAM OF RACING INDY CARS WAS WELL KNOWN BY 1982. What she needed was to be seen by the men who could make her dreams come true. When she wasn't racing, she attended as many Indy Car races as she could.

But it was at a dirt track race where Cheryl met a young mechanic, Richard Lindwall. She was dating another man but left her boyfriend for him. A quiet, white 25-year-old man originally from Illinois and living in Lakeside, California, Lindwall came from an opposite background to Cheryl. Between his good guy personality and his ability to support Cheryl's racing as a mechanic, he gained the acceptance of her family. The pair went on long hikes and shared a love of animals. They had different personalities and backgrounds but seemed to complement each other. Lindwall assumed the role of her crew chief. Months after they met, Lindwall proposed marriage, and the 20-year-old Cheryl accepted.

Cheryl first considered eloping with him, but she changed her mind. If she was going to get married, Cheryl Glass was going to go all out.

"I wanted the most formal, elaborate wedding I could possibly conceive of because most of my life I've wanted to go for broke, to put all my effort into something and have it be the best there is," Cheryl Glass said.[1]

She wasn't racing much in 1982 and had plenty of time to design the biggest wedding she could dream up. Cheryl spent six months preparing for her February 19, 1983, wedding. She wanted everything to be lavish. She wanted the biggest venue and to have the most people possible in the wedding party and at the ceremony.

And, of course, she had to have the most elaborate wedding dress ever designed.

At first, Shirley wanted Cheryl to wear her wedding dress, the one she spent so much time creating and sewing. After Shirley was married, her sister, Dorothy, wore the dress in her wedding. But at Dorothy's wedding, the guests had thrown colored rice as she was leaving the chapel with Waymon Whiting II. It was raining that day and some of the rice stuck to the dress. The dye bled into the fabric.[2] Cheryl opted to create her own.

She started with yards of peau de soie, a satin fabric, and antique lace. Despite never sewing a bead in her life, Cheryl and helpers sewed 40,000 pearls, 6,000 seed pearls, 7,000 crystals, and 25,000 iridescent sequins into the dress. She created a matching 15-foot train with 100 large lace flowers trimmed with 5,000 pearls, 1,000 seed pearls, 3,000 crystals, and 30,000 sequins. Then she created a shoulder-length lace mantilla—a head cover similar to a veil—that was beaded with 10,000 pearls, 1,000 seed pearls, 4,000 crystals, and 8,000 sequins. When the size eight dress was finished, it cost about $3,000, including $1,000 in beads. It was so ornately decorated, the dress and regalia weighed 40 pounds, more than any of her racing outfits. And Cheryl's bouquet, nearly as tall as her, was made up of handsewn silk flowers.

A few months before the wedding, a fire broke out in the Glass family house. Marvin grabbed only Cheryl's dress and escaped. The house was fine, but his choice demonstrated how important that dress was.

She estimated it took 1,000 hours of labor to complete the dress and accompanying pieces. Once it was completed, the dress was appraised at $18,000.

The gown was so labor intensive, she recruited every woman she knew who could help to finish it, and it wasn't done until days before the wedding.

"Her dress, Carol McMillen (Duke McMillen's wife) was up [all night] sewing beads on it, trying to get it finished," Lori Walker said.[3]

Cheryl Glass poses in her wedding dress in 1983. The dress took months for her and her family to make and was appraised at $18,000.
SHIRLEY GLASS COLLECTION

Cheryl designed coral pink taffeta dresses for her bridesmaids, each requiring hand beading of 300 pearls and shoes dyed to match the dresses. The makeup for each of her bridesmaids was professionally applied.

"My father said he wanted to send me off in style, and I could have anything I wanted," Cheryl said.[4]

The Sheraton chain of hotels completed construction of an opulent hotel in downtown Seattle at 6th and Pike.[5] It had a massive room that would serve as the site for Cheryl's wedding reception, the first event to be held there.

Even before the wedding, people spread rumors about how much money the family was spending. Sums that seemed implausible were floated.

"I'm hearing things at the time, they spent $50,000, which is quite a bit of money at that time, probably enough to buy another racing car," said Dave Griffith, who worked with Marvin at Pacific Northwest Bell.[6]

After attending Mt. Zion Baptist Church with her family for most of her life, Cheryl was attending St. Mark's Episcopal Cathedral in downtown Seattle.[7] She opted to hold the wedding at St. Mark's and over 600 guests descended on the church. Each person was given a five-page program and welcomed with pipe organ music, followed by the Northwest Symphony String Quartet.

The bridal party had 24 attendants. When Cheryl was walked down the aisle by her father, she was the center of attention, something she always wanted to be. But when she reached the altar, Marvin didn't know what to do. Cheryl's dress was so long, he couldn't figure out how to get around it to make his way to his seat. The scene brought a moment of needed levity to the ceremony.

"It was really funny," Shirley Glass said.[8]

The person who seemed the most subdued was Richard Lindwall. Being photographed repeatedly was something that happened often in Cheryl's life. Lindwall wasn't used to the attention. In all the photos of the ceremony, Lindwall put on a happy face. But he was more comfortable in greasy work clothes he wore to work on cars than the tuxedo he wore to the wedding.

From St. Mark's, the hundreds of guests traveled two miles to the expansive ballroom of the Sheraton for the reception. While a symphony orchestra played, the guests were treated to a seven-course meal followed by hours of dancing and celebrating. It was the biggest wedding ever for a Black person in Seattle.

"It was a really, really, really nice affair," said Skip Young, a childhood friend who attended the wedding. "I was shocked, but I wasn't shocked. Cheryl had a tendency to do things with kind of a flourish. It wasn't gaudy or braggadocious or anything."[9]

Her wedding became the social event of the year in Seattle.

"There were a lot of people just standing outside," Shirley Glass said.[10]

Cheryl accomplished her goal as her wedding dress entered the Guinness Book of World Records as the most expensive wedding dress.[11]

The story of Cheryl's lavish wedding was carried by newspapers around the country. Some people thought the idea of someone spending

$50,000 on a wedding was unconscionable. There were some concerned about the "mindless, gluttonous extravaganza."

"If she is the achieving highly creative person her father and fiancé say she is, it would seem to me that she could come up with something pretty wonderful without spending $50,000. The very least she could have done is pared it down to $40,000 and donated $10,000 to a local food bank, and created some real happiness," Mikayla Morgan wrote in a letter published in the *Seattle Times*.[12]

Others argued that her wedding had successfully employed dozens of people, keeping them out of food banks in the first place.

"It is certainly nobody's business how the parents choose to use their money," wrote Margaret Lyles, who attended the wedding, to the *Seattle Times*. "The Glass family wanted something big, elegant, tasteful and memorable for their daughter."[13]

Cheryl and Lindwall purchased a small house on Lago Place in Seattle, a few miles north of her parents' house. It was tucked away from neighbors, on a flag lot behind a sleepy street in north Seattle. More than a house, though, it gave Cheryl a break from the bedroom that housed her many trophies. And it gave her space from her parents for the first time in her life.

Cheryl didn't have a job, but she had plenty of free time. Without a car to race, she still chased every opportunity she could find.

The Kelly American Challenge Series was a stock car road racing series sponsored by the temporary employment agency known for its "Kelly Girls."[14] The series paid its competitors well and offered cash bonuses to the top finishing women in the races. Cheryl tried every car owner she could find to try to get a ride in it, but none would employ her.

Neil DeAtley, a businessman from Idaho involved in road construction and rock crushing, was starting a team for the Trans-Am Series for the 1983 season. He had some financial backing from Chevrolet and intended to field two cars for the season in the top stock car road racing series in the nation. DeAtley signed up veteran British driver David Hobbs to the team's lead driver. Hobbs had an extensive resume driving in Formula One, NASCAR, the 24 Hours of LeMans, and the Indianapolis 500, as well as working as a television commentator on races for CBS.

But for DeAtley to be able to finance his racing team, he needed more money than Chevy was providing. His sponsorship talks with Budweiser were going nowhere so he decided he would do something to get their attention.

"What can we do to be different? Well, let's look around and see what's available in the Black department," DeAtley said of potential drivers.[15]

There were few options. He considered two drivers, Cheryl and a young, unknown open wheel road racer named Willy T. Ribbs. Both had some success in racing, but little experience in that type of car. They both fit DeAtley's criteria and showed promise as drivers.

DeAtley chose Ribbs as his second driver; Ribbs won five races that year for the team. There were rumors about why Ribbs was chosen over Cheryl, but no matter the reason, she felt rejected again.

Marvin Glass (*from left*), Richard Lindwall, and Cheryl Glass talk with a man.
SHIRLEY GLASS COLLECTION

Cheryl's celebrity made her valuable as a public speaker. She practiced and wouldn't settle for being anything else than the best. Cheryl told her story to groups around the nation about how she climbed so high in the racing world. Despite the message of positivity coming from a 21-year-old who had little real-world experience, Cheryl believed herself when she told people they could accomplish anything.

"I didn't know I couldn't. Therefore, I could. So can you," she told audiences.[16]

Though Cheryl wasn't competing, she made up her mind that she was ready to move up to higher levels of the racing world, despite relatively few accomplishments. She and her family had spent truckloads of money on her racing over the prior three years. To justify spending more, they needed her to compete at a professional level.

With Richard Lindwall now a full-time presence in her career, she attended race after race in an effort to secure a ride. She had a confidence that teams would desire a barely-known driver with no credentials at the professional level. Lindwall introduced her at every race to any car owner and mechanic he knew, hoping to entice them. Cheryl attended an Indy Car race one weekend and a sports car race the next. What Cheryl found was that professional road-racing teams didn't want a sprint car driver with no road racing experience.

In 1983, Cheryl attended the Bertil Roos School of Motor Racing at Pocono International Raceway. It was a school put on by the professional racer on the road course in Pennsylvania.[17] After a week of classes, Cheryl graduated with licenses to compete in races sanctioned by the SCCA and IMSA. Roos briefly competed in Formula One but was competing in the Can-Am road racing series in the early 1980s. He suggested that the series would be a good step for Cheryl's racing career.

In an effort to attract sponsors, Cheryl composed slick brochures. Only Bardahl, a Seattle-based oil additive manufacturer, put up money to sponsor Cheryl. It only contributed a few hundred dollars. Other companies looked at Cheryl curiously. They wondered if her representing their company would bring them more business or more attention.

Road racing is far different than circle track racing.

In a sprint car on a dirt track, driving the car is remarkably simple: use the throttle pedal, brake pedal, and steering wheel in combination. Once the engine is started, the driver goes down the straightaway, turns left, drives down another straightaway, and turns left again. It takes talent to go fast in a sprint car. And guts.

But even the simplest road racing car takes a great deal of finesse. The throttle, brake, and clutch pedals; the steering wheel and shifter; and a plethora of switches and other controls must be combined in a perfect sequence while weaving around dozens of corners, both left and right, and all with a different radius and camber. There are thousands of combinations and hundreds of adjustments to be made, both in the mechanics of driving the car and in the driving style, in a single lap.

Where circle track racing is about finding a rhythm, road racing is about precision. Some dirt track racers become decent road racers after years of racing on asphalt ovals; road racers have similar issues with transitioning to dirt tracks. The two disciplines are vastly different and nearly impossible to transition between.

The drivers who made that transition from dirt track racing to road racing like A. J. Foyt, Mario Andretti, and Al Unser Jr. became legends in the sport. Average drivers, however, could not make that transition. Unlike dirt track racing, which takes more guts than brains to be successful at, road racing requires patience.

Cheryl convinced herself that with her schooling, all she needed in order to prove herself as a road racer was to get in a race. After that she would excel at the discipline as quickly as she had figured out how to excel on dirt tracks.

Marvin Glass purchased a used Indy Car, a Penske PC6 chassis that Lindwall located for $10,000.[18] When new, the car was one of the best in the paddock, capable of winning any race in which it was entered. It was the same model that carried Rick Mears to a win in the 1979 Indianapolis 500. By 1983, the car was outdated, impossible to make competitive, and worthy only as a show car. To people involved in racing, purchasing that car was a sign the family was not savvy enough to make wise financial decisions.

The Glass family figured it would be a good first step for Cheryl and serve as a car in which she could practice road racing. It was, after all, a decent representation of what she would be racing when she made it to the Indy Car level. The problem, however, was engines for Indy Cars were not for sale. Manufacturers only allowed their engines to be distributed to teams under expensive lease arrangements of over $100,000 per year. Finding an engine to put in the car for Cheryl to practice was impossible. Still, they had the car painted and applied number 82 on it—her old sprint car number backwards—and Cheryl was fitted in the cockpit. Even though there was no way she would race it, she had a session of photographs taken with the car. She may not have been an Indy Car driver, but she looked like she was one.

By having the car, Cheryl was proclaiming she would one day be an Indy Car driver.

There was one road course in the Seattle area, the nine-turn, 2.25-mile road course Seattle International Raceway (SIR) in Kent. Cheryl hadn't made a lap on the track in a race car, but in 1983, she figured the track could serve as the stage she needed to get attention.

Whenever Cheryl wanted media attention, she got it. She announced to the media she would be having a test session on a Wednesday afternoon at SIR in 1983. Reporters, including *Seattle Times* motor sportswriter Dick Rockne and television camera crews, descended on the track for the event. When they showed up, they were informed the team couldn't get the engine in the Indy Car running. To have any validity of Cheryl as a driver, the photographers and camera operators needed to see her in action.

But the car had no engine.

Marvin and Cheryl devised a plan to give them what they wanted. Cheryl would sit in the car and hold a rope connected to a pickup that would pull the car. When Cheryl got up to speed near the photographers and videographers, she would let go of the rope, the truck would drive away and let the Indy Car continue under the remaining momentum past the cameras. It was the only way she could "drive" the Indy Car to satisfy the photographers.

A photo that ran on the front page of the sports section of the *Seattle Times* showed her appearing to drive on the track. Only a few people knew the chaos that was required to stage the photo.

"Only she would do something like that," Skip Young said.

Cheryl told the media she had a new March chassis and Cosworth engine on order, and Marvin likely had put a down payment on them.[19] She told the media she figured it would cost about $2 million for a season on the CART tour. Her family had money, but that was beyond their means. She needed a sponsor to come up with a lot of money so she could race. Cheryl said she was determined to race an Indy Car. She made them believe her.

"We're going to do this one way or another," Cheryl Glass said. "We've got a driver. We've got a team. We have the promotional expertise. It's going to float."[20]

The next time Cheryl got in a race car, it was farther away from an Indy Car.

CHAPTER NINE

Racing in the Big Time Isn't as Easy as It Looks

1984 to 1985

DRIVING RACE CARS FOR OTHER CAR OWNERS SOUNDED INITIALLY enticing to Cheryl Glass. But the thought of being a driver sounded better than it frequently turned out to be. After trying out the race cars of different owners, Cheryl realized she was being exploited for their gain, not for the advancement of her career. Each time she competed for a race car owner, he never asked her to drive for him again.

Cheryl was an assertive race car driver, which might have rubbed others the wrong way. She would say things like: "I'm a front-runner, not a back marker,"[1] "I am confident of my ability,"[2] and "I had to earn their respect by beating them."[3]

Cheryl did manage to secure a test in another hydroplane. She did reasonably well on the water of the Puget Sound that day. Skipping inches over the water, Cheryl had the bravery few others possessed. Some thought Cheryl had the necessary skill to compete in a hydroplane. Ultimately, however, the ride in the Squire Shop hydroplane went to Mickey Remund.[4]

"She didn't want to get her hair wet," said Skip Young, a friend and hydroplane enthusiast.[5]

Cheryl tried drag racing. On the invitation of a car owner, she was going to test a funny car on a drag strip. She strapped in the car, but as soon as the fiberglass body of the car was lowered over her, she felt claustrophobic. She scrambled to get out. It was a long shot that she could transition to drag racing, and she never made a pass.[6] After years of racing in open cockpit cars, a roof over her head was too much for her psyche.

If Cheryl wasn't going to be paid to drive someone else's race car, she would pay to race one of theirs.

She viewed the dirt-track world as if it were a thing of the past, even though it was her identity in the racing world. In three years of dirt-track racing, Cheryl had conquered the form, in her opinion. Cheryl now needed to learn to road race.

Unlike circle track racing, the idea of paying to drive somebody else's race car was an acceptable practice in road racing. While circle track racing always hinged on the willingness of car owners to pay drivers to race their cars, road racing was considered to be a sportsman's pursuit, something to be done for the joy and prestige. Money was almost a dirty word in circle track racing, but buying a ride in road racing was not considered a sin.

Cheryl had driven small formula cars like the Formula Vee at driving schools she attended and initially wanted to race one. But that path up the racing ladder was a long one with small-bore formula cars. It could take decades to learn the skills necessary to be a competent road racer in that path. Cheryl considered herself a professional race car driver, and she only wanted to race in series that paid prize money, of which there were few.

The Can-Am Series offered that opportunity.

At one time in the 1970s, the United States-based series drew some of the biggest names in North American road racing to compete for huge amounts of money. At one time, it featured some of the best drivers in the United States like Mark Donohue, Mario Andretti, Parnelli Jones, Dan Gurney, Phil Hill, and Bruce McLaren. The series also served as a launching point to great things in the careers of drivers like Jacky Ickx, Keke Rosberg, and Al Unser Jr.[7]

The cars were wild, with open cockpits and radical bodies. They produced massive amounts of downforce, making them stick to the ground better. The cars were so fast and specialized, the series became cost-prohibitive for all but a few car owners by the 1980s.[8]

With the encouragement of driving instructor Bertil Roos, Cheryl had her eyes fixed on competing in Can-Am.

The series was drawing healthy fields of over 20 cars in 1984, but few of them were designed for the series. Most were open wheel cars with fiberglass bodywork added later to conform to the rules of Can-Am.

In the 1980s, the series had difficulty securing races. It was struggling financially and went from being a featured class to supporting role. And the series didn't have a sponsor to ensure it would remain viable.

But the purses the Can-Am Series races paid were significant. If Cheryl drove well enough in the series, she could make money at it even though she was paying to race. Some of the series' races in 1984 paid more than $20,000 to the winner.

Cheryl and Marvin investigated several teams competing in the Can-Am Series with the potential for fielding a car for her. When they found Chicago-based Ausca, they knew it was the right situation for Cheryl.[9] The team was owned by Australian Horst Kwechs and American Eddie Wachs. Ausca had been around since 1967 and fielded cars in major road racing series in the United States, including the Trans-Am Series and the Formula 5000 championship. It found success at some levels, but by 1984 were relying on drivers with financial backing to keep the operation afloat.

There was one crew member on the Ausca team that made the pairing seem predestined.

Hersey Mallory was one of the few Black race car mechanics in the world in the 1980s. Mallory got his first taste of racing as a boy by by attending the 1964 Indianapolis 500 and was immediately determined to become a mechanic for a professional racing team. He started at the bottom rung of teams and learned from mechanics like Ron Barnes and Frank Schultz until he proved his worth and climbed the ranks to become a paid mechanic.

Ausca had a fleet of cars it fielded in the Can-Am Series. Most were former Indy Cars or European Formula cars that were purchased, brought to the Chicago shop, torn down to a bare chassis, and rebuilt.

Then a fiberglass body was added to cover the open wheels. Drivers like Wally Dallenbach Jr., Bill Alsup, and Wachs were competitive nearly every time they got in one of the team's cars.

If Cheryl was going to be competitive, Ausca offered her the best chance.

The rental of a car for the testing and race weekend would cost thousands of dollars. Cheryl tried to find sponsorship to offset the cost, but her attempts were unsuccessful again. The family was able to pay to put her in a Toleman chassis former Formula 2 car that had been driven the year before by Stefan Johansson before his move into Formula One. It was a competitive car. There were more powerful cars in the series, but the under two-liter formula in which she would compete would give her an easier transition into the world of road racing.

Cheryl arrived in Chicago in May 1984 and immediately went to the Ausca shops to be fitted in the car. She was so much smaller than the team's

Cheryl Glass tests a Toleman-chassis Can Am car prior to her only race in the series in 1984. The car had fiberglass bodywork added to cover the wheels before the race.
SHIRLEY GLASS COLLECTION

regular drivers, it took a considerable amount of effort to adjust the pedals to fit her comfortably.

"I know I went through hell trying to fit her in the car," Mallory said. "What I heard was most sprint car drivers got in the fucking thing and would go."[10]

The Ausca team took her for a testing day to nearby Blackhawk Farms, a seven-turn, 1.95-mile road course in South Beloit, Illinois, with the Toleman. The car didn't yet sport the higher downforce bodywork required for the car for the Can-Am races out of fear she would damage it in the practice day. Over the course of the day, she slowly picked up speed until she built up enough confidence that she could race it.

Cheryl Glass thought she was ready to race.

For her first race, Cheryl Glass chose the biggest profile event of the season, a race the Can-Am Series was running in support of the Formula One Dallas Grand Prix on July 8, 1984, in Texas.

"We're here with the Formula One circuit, so pretty much of the entire world will pay attention to what happens," Cheryl said.[11]

The type of venue only made things harder.

Racing on street courses is different than any other form of racing. Where a road course is laid out with permanence in mind and fore-thought about every inch—and is raced on constantly—street circuits are tight, unforgiving circuits over streets or parking lots. Street circuits are assembled in the span of a week or so with temporary concrete walls, fences, and grandstands brought in at the last moment possible. The first time a car goes around such a track is in the race weekend's first practice session, and no one truly knows how the circuit will react until cars compete side by side in the race.

What may seem like a minor bump in the surface when constructing the track can turn into a jump under racing circumstances. A manhole in the wrong place in a corner can make it seem like the car is driving on ice. The surface is designed for passenger cars at slow speeds and not for the strain placed by ground-pounding racing cars going as fast as possible.

And there is no way to practice for a street circuit. While road courses are there every day of the year and often available for testing, the only way to learn how to race on a street circuit was to race on one.

It would have made more sense for Cheryl to have competed on one of the permanent courses on the Can-Am circuit like Mosport, Lime Rock, or Road Atlanta for her first race. But Cheryl's primary consideration was her desire to reach the largest potential audience.

The circuit at the Texas State Fair Grounds in Dallas was hastily and poorly designed. Promoted by Chris Pook, the impresario who ran the successful Long Beach Grand Prix in California, the course had components to be successful. Built in the middle of one of the most populated cities in the United States, it was a perfect match with a state where racing—albeit dirt-track racing—was beloved. The race was to be the first on the circuit. But the design was riddled with flaws. The ridiculously complex 23-turn, 2.424-mile street circuit at Dallas lacked run-off areas, something designed into street circuits to help those who make a mistake approaching a turn. And the weather didn't help.

"You have to remember, this was one of the few events that they came out with a street course, and it came from asphalt to concrete and uneven surfaces," Hersey Mallory said. "We had to go with a stiffer spring because we were bottoming out at certain parts of the track. It was a nightmare. It was kind of janky."

Beyond the 100-degree July Texas heat, the oppressive humidity caused even the most fit person to sweat profusely, even when sitting in the shade. When Cheryl put on her thick, fire-retardant driving suit and helmet and got in the car, it zapped her energy in a few laps. And the heat didn't help the asphalt and concrete surface designed to be a parking lot. During qualifying for Cheryl's Can-Am race, the asphalt started bubbling in places under the strain and soon crumbled. The deteriorating track was described as more like a rallycross course than a Grand Prix circuit.

Everything was stacked against Cheryl in Dallas.

"That would have been insane," said Bill Tempero, one of the Can-Am drivers racing that weekend. "Of course going in, I think the first time on a road course would have been tough anyway, but in that environment it would have been twice as tough."[12]

In qualifying, Cheryl struggled. Coming out of a corner on which the asphalt was breaking up, she locked up the brakes and crashed the Toleman into a wall. The car was damaged beyond what the Ausca team could repair that weekend.

Her fastest lap in qualifying was 4 minutes and 23 seconds; polesitter Michael Roe lapped the track in 1:44. She was the 25th-fastest driver of 26 cars in attendance.[13]

Cheryl faced a steep bill to fix the damaged primary car, but Mallory felt obligated to put her in a car for the race. Ausca had a backup car on hand, though it was an inferior Volkswagen-powered Van Diemen chassis, a car which couldn't have been competitive with the greatest driver on the planet behind the wheel.

Cheryl took it easy in the backup Ausca car, completing six laps before retiring from the race. But she also got off easy. As the race progressed, the track's surface broke apart more, and car after car crashed into the unforgiving concrete walls. Of the 50 laps of the race, 11 were taken up by cautions. The race ended up being one of attrition with Roe the winner.[14]

"I crashed," Bill Tempero said. "I slid off in that blacktop that was coming apart. It happened to a lot of us."

The track fell apart so bad during Cheryl's Can-Am race that Formula One drivers Niki Lauda and Alain Prost tried to boycott the Formula One race the next day. Only last-minute intervention and overnight repairs to the circuit convinced the world's best drivers enough to race. It was so hot that between the heat of the day and the oppressive sun that tire engineers registered track temperatures of 150 degrees, the highest they had ever seen. Keke Rosberg survived a track rougher than any Texas dirt track to win.[15]

Cheryl's plans to run more Can-Am races disintegrated in the Dallas heat. Between the cost of renting the car from Ausca for the race and the cost of repairing it—coupled with not finding sponsorship—she had no way to keep going in the series.

Cheryl estimated she and her parents had spent about $300,000 on her racing from 1980 to 1984.[16] They needed financial help for her to keep racing.

The person who wasn't with Cheryl in Dallas was her husband, Richard Lindwall. They had separated and on August 31, 1984, he filed for divorce. He suspected she was having an affair; she suspected he was having an affair, too. They agreed on a quick settlement in which Cheryl kept the house—partially by putting it in the name of her parents—and the divorce was finalized on November 30, 1984.[17]

She would later tell people he was an alcoholic, and that's why she wanted rid of him. The concerns of those who thought Cheryl and Richard were not a good fit were confirmed.

It had been so long since Cheryl had success in racing that she left herself open to more criticism. Robin Miller, then a veteran racing journalist for the *Indianapolis Star*, compared her with *Car and Driver* writer Patrick Bedard—who crashed in his two Indianapolis 500 starts—and Arlene Hiss, a former SCCA driver who struggled in her only Indy Car start at Phoenix, while feting teenage sprint car driver Richard "Sport" Allen.

"But this young man isn't some public relations gimmick. He doesn't belong in the 'Racing Side Show' alongside Patrick Bedard, Arlene Hiss and Cheryl Glass," Miller wrote.[18]

But then something went right in her racing career.

After a controversial 1984 interview given by Bill Coors, the Coors Brewing Company needed Cheryl Glass. Bill Coors said Black people didn't have the "intellectual capacity to succeed."[19] The company already faced boycotts from labor unions including the AFL-CIO, and this was one more struggle than it could handle. One distributor in Seattle said 30 percent of the 1,500 bars they serviced refused to carry the brand after Coors' comments. It hit the pocketbook of the company hard. Peter Coors, also a company executive, approached the NAACP and Reverend Jesse Jackson's Operation PUSH in an effort to hire more minorities in the company and bring in more Black distributors. The money paid by Black people was as green as the money paid by white people. The company couldn't risk losing that share of the market. Coors committed to invest $650 million in minority neighborhoods where its beer was sold.

Cheryl was a beneficiary of that initiative.[20]

Coors committed to sponsoring multiple Black athletes, actors, and entertainers. The company would pay the notable people to appear in advertisements, wear their branded clothing, and give speeches at conventions, events, schools, and clubs.

At the same time, the U.S. Department of Transportation also engaged Cheryl to act as its spokesperson, though it was more for prestige than money.[21] She committed to give speeches at high schools across the country to teenagers about the dangers of drinking and driving. The feds overlooked her being sponsored by a liquor company for the second time in her life.

"Kids, especially, seem to like me a lot. Most of them have never seen anybody who's a race car driver and Black, too, and, on top of that a girl," Cheryl said.[22]

The money Coors offered Cheryl put her former one-year deal with Olympia Beer to shame. She would receive $5,000 per year as a personal services retainer. She would be paid a fee as high as $3,000 for each appearance. And Coors agreed to be an associate sponsor with her in the CART Series, paying $40,000 for races in markets where Coors wanted an increased presence like Detroit. The cost of racing in that series, even in that few races, would run well over $100,000. Cheryl had been searching for sponsorship for so long that signing the Coors deal seemed a watershed moment in her career.[23]

Coors already had significant investments in sponsoring race cars at the time. It was sponsoring NASCAR's Million Dollar Man, Bill Elliott. It sponsored Geoff Brabham in the Indy Car Series. And it sponsored the NASCAR North Series, a regional tour in New England and Canada. And Coors had a sponsorship presence at short tracks across the nation. But, like so many times in her career, she was the first Black driver and the first female driver the company had sponsored.

Cheryl earned an income from Coors, but she also decided she had the skills to start another high-profile, potentially lucrative enterprise.

After the attention Cheryl received for her awe-inspiring wedding dress, women contacted her to design and sew similar wedding dresses for them. She considered herself a race car driver, but with her racing career sporadic, she needed something to do and saw the potential for a business of her own. From her home on Lago Place, she dreamed up designs for wedding dresses. She had imagination and creativity and could come up with something unique. Her dress-making enterprise was an instant hit and expanded so fast that she realized she needed a formal space from which to sell them.

The start-up costs weren't high for the business, but it took every dollar she had—and money from her parents—to get off the ground. She found her perfect location on the ground-floor corner of a building in Pioneer Square in downtown Seattle. The space needed work, but Cheryl was willing to invest her time. Friends and family members eager to see her succeed volunteered their time and effort to work on the building and in the business. Remodeling the space took months. She kept it simple and uncluttered. An exposed brick wall was retained, but the rest of the walls were repainted and some were dressed with lattice. On one wall, she hung framed photos of her driving race cars from throughout her history and a plaque she received for her racing accomplishments.

Cheryl threw a grand-opening party at the new studio and attracted the attention she craved. Throughout the party, Cheryl wore a wedding dress of her design. She always liked a party, especially one in which she could be the center of attention. For potential brides, it made an impression.

Cheryl kept sketchpads of designs for when inspiration struck or a customer asked her. She consulted with a designer who could take her drawings and turn them into plans. And her mother, Shirley, could sew the dresses and make them look attractive. Cheryl couldn't sew, or at least sew well. Shirley had retired from her job at Boeing as her eyesight was failing and would help out at the shop either by working at the reception desk or by sewing dresses. Other employees came and went through the shop with regularity.

The shop gained wide acclaim from the start. Her dresses sold for between $1,000 and $25,000, and women lined up to buy them. Cheryl had so many initial orders that she had a hard time filling them in time, a fault that stuck with her for years. Cheryl didn't just want to make dresses. She wanted to turn weddings into events for the brides, just as she had done for her own wedding. She developed a network of caterers, musicians, florists, and other wedding-related purveyors. She imagined herself becoming the wedding impresario of Seattle.

"I'm the eternal romantic," she said. "I love lace and frilly things and going back to the days when people put a lot of pride and love into their work."[24]

The showpiece of her studio was her own wedding dress. It hung on a mannequin in the middle of the showroom and drew attention. Initially appraised at $18,000, it was re-appraised at $105,000 a few years later. It was worth more than her house.[25]

At 23 years old, Cheryl Glass was a small business owner.

With the Coors money, Cheryl developed a plan to finally launch her Indy Car career. It would take a year to prepare everything, including finding a team for whom she could drive. She also needed to prepare herself physically for the rigors of the highest level of racing in the United States. Though she wouldn't be racing an Indy Car with the Coors logo on it in 1985, it didn't mean she couldn't race a car sponsored by the company in the meantime.

Beyond its investment in star drivers and series sponsorships, Coors was heavily invested as an associate sponsor on Cal Wells' Precision Preparation Incorporated team. His operation fielded two Toyota trucks in off-road competitions and in the Mickey Thompson Stadium Series. Coors wanted to be a player in the market for Black consumers in Los Angeles, and it seemed a logical venue for Cheryl's debut. Coors offered to fund a third truck for Cheryl to race in the series' race on July 20, 1985, at the Los Angeles Coliseum.[26]

Based on her racing resume, Cal Wells decided to give Cheryl a shot.

Mickey Thompson was a California born and bred race car driver, builder, and promoter. After starting his driving career in drag racing, he moved to land-speed racing, to the Indianapolis 500, and then to off-road racing. Being a consummate promoter, he recognized the need to bring the product to the masses. Thompson started a sanctioning body where he would bring off-road trucks and other vehicles to stadiums like the Coliseum. Thompson would haul in thousands of pounds of dirt and pile it on top of immaculate baseball and football fields. He would set up intricate tracks to replicate the most challenging parts of desert courses so that tens of thousands of people would pay to watch the organized mayhem.[27]

Like most of the forms of racing that Cheryl had competed in, women hadn't competed in the series before she arrived.

Cheryl Glass had never seen an off-road race, but Coors was offering enough money to make it worth her time. They offered her $3,000 in appearance fees along with paying for travel, lodging, and meal expenses along with 55 percent of all prize winnings and contingency money of up to $2,000. It was the most lucrative deal she had been offered to race. And it was with a professional team that was fielding a vehicle capable of winning.

For a few days' work, it was too good to pass up.

She arrived in Los Angeles the week before the July 20 race and received lots of media attention. For three days, she was paraded around the city from one media outlet to another. At radio stations, in front of television cameras, and to print reporters, she gave interview after interview. She weaved the story of her life into a grandiose tale of talent and perseverance. Instead of being able to concentrate on the upcoming race, she was forced to spend hours with the media.[28]

"I think we, I say we, we focused on doing a little bit of public relations, media relations with her regarding the fact that she was going to race," said Les Unger, then Toyota's Motorsports Manager. "African American female, come on, that didn't exist, particularly in trucks. I don't think it still has happened. African American and female, she was an intriguing personality, and obviously talented."[29]

A major flaw was exposed immediately.

Cheryl hadn't raced anything in a year and was rusty. And racing a truck in an off-road competition was far different than anything she had ever driven before. Besides going left and right on dirt, the jumps were purposely placed to make the track more difficult. The only similarity between the Toyota truck she would race to anything she had driven before was it had a steering wheel and tires.

When Steve Millen joined PPI in the early 1980s with his background in racing in hill climbs, dirt tracks, and rally racing in his native New Zealand, it took several days of practice in the truck to learn the skills to race an off-road truck. Cheryl was never given the chance to sit in the truck ahead of the race weekend, let alone test it.

The track Thompson built at the Coliseum was diabolical, which didn't help Cheryl. Many drivers gently work their way up to the challenge of driving an entirely new type of vehicle. When Cheryl got in the truck for her first practice session, she wanted to be up to speed immediately. On her first lap, she came upon a tall, sharp jump on the front stretch. Instead of hitting the gas to fly off the jump, she hit the brakes. The truck took a nose dive and landed front first into the following jump, jamming it against the retaining wall.

When paramedics reached Cheryl, she couldn't get out of the truck. Afraid she might be paralyzed, they placed her neck in a brace. Her right foot was wedged between the gas and brake pedals. The track safety workers had to disassemble the pedals and use the Jaws of Life to cut the roll cage to free her. In the impact of the crash, Cheryl's body slammed forward into the steering wheel. She hit it with such force that the steering wheel folded and the steering column hit her in the chest. And Cheryl took yet another hard hit to her head, though she remained conscious this time.[30]

"She landed really super hard," Millen said.[31]

This concussion was one too many for Cheryl. She had more than she could count in her lifetime, but this one stayed with her for the rest of her life.

There was another problem, however; Cheryl wasn't alone in the truck. She had Jim Biroff in a passenger seat along for the practice session. Accounts vary on whether he was a mechanic or a radio personality, but his injuries were worse than Cheryl's. Word spread that Biroff was paralyzed in the crash.

Cheryl was in a hospital when Ivan "Ironman" Stewart, who was supposed to be one of her teammates, won the race in front of 47,000 fans.[32]

"Here's the problem. Cheryl, I don't think any of us really expected her to do great things the first time out," Steve Millen said. "The pressure that was on her was all self-induced. We knew how difficult it was. She put pressure on herself. She was a driven gal. She did bloody well at some stuff."

The injuries from the previous five years as a race car driver had caught up with Cheryl.

CHAPTER TEN

Sponsor Dollars Can't Buy
a Clean Bill of Health

1986 to 1989

CHERYL GLASS CRASHED RACE CARS A LOT.

In her first years of racing full-size cars, she shook off crashes that looked like they would have killed a normal driver. Young race car drivers like Cheryl assume they are indestructible. A few days or weeks after a crash, she would get back in a car and race again. Frequently she was not physically capable of the tasks she was forcing herself to do. She viewed crashes as small distractions on her path to stardom as a race car driver.

But the crash at the Los Angeles Coliseum in 1985 hung with her like none before.

Physical injuries like her broken ankle were easy to diagnose; a few trips to a doctor and a few weeks of getting around on crutches was what she needed to heal.[1] However, the rest of the injuries she suffered in the truck weren't known for years. Cheryl had been dealing with back problems after all of those hard flips in sprint cars, and they were exacerbated when her sternum hit the steering wheel in the Los Angeles crash.

Then the migraine headaches hit.

In her first year of driving sprint cars at age 18, Cheryl suffered at least three concussions while racing, including one that was so bad she was temporarily blinded. On most of those occasions, she got back in the car before she should have. Each subsequent concussion compounded. She claimed the concussions she suffered while driving sprint cars were caused by fuel tanks hitting her in the head. With the lack of safety equipment available in the early 1980s, she was lucky to survive many of the crashes. The concussion she suffered in the Mickey Thompson series crash was the tipping point.

"She had some injuries, especially from that Coliseum debacle that she wasn't able to overcome," mechanic Hersey Mallory said. "She had some severe migraines that knocked the wind out of her sails."[2]

Cheryl's plan for racing an Indy Car in 1986 unraveled.

The migraines hit her with increasing frequency, and her doctors in Seattle refused to give her medical clearance to drive a race car no matter how much she pleaded with them. If her personal doctors weren't going to give her permission to race, there was no way the medical doctors of any racing circuit would.

Once the extent of her injuries became clear, Cheryl's plans changed. In her original contract with Coors, she would compete in three CART Series races in 1986.[3] After striking out in trying to find a ride she could rent with an established racing team, she and Marvin agreed to purchase a March chassis Indy Car that Roberto Guerrero drove for Bignotti-Cotter Racing in 1985.[4] She estimated it would cost $200,000 to run the three races required in the Coors contract: the season opener at Phoenix International Raceway and two races at Michigan International Speedway's high-banked, two-mile oval. Even with the $40,000 from Coors and all the other money she received as a spokesperson for the company, she was still short of the amount she needed to run those races. Prior to the Los Angeles crash, she planned to run a test session at Phoenix International Raceway in February 1986, but she lost her $1,500 deposit on that test day when her health deteriorated.[5] They never purchased the March automobile they had arranged to buy.

Cheryl's injuries didn't stop her from making personal appearances for Coors. She made appearances at the Bill Pickett Invitational Rodeo in Denver,[6] the Congressional Black Caucus in Washington,[7] and at the Colorado Black Women for Political Action in Denver in 1986. Cheryl and other Coors-backed celebrities, including actors Danny Glover and Howard Rollins and singers Jeffrey Osborne and Joyce Kennedy, made speeches at events and would linger for hours after to sign autographs.[8]

For the next few years, Cheryl was constantly on the move, flying from one appearance to another on behalf of Coors or other organizations. She did her best to hide her headaches in public.

Cheryl didn't tailor her speeches to the different audiences she addressed. She kept the message simple, encouraging people to not accept the limitations placed on them by others. She preached a message of empowerment.

"One—I have more to say about what happens to me than anyone else, and so do you. Two—I have to pay my dues. There is no short-cut to getting to where I want to go, and so will you. Three—I do not modify my goals and aspirations based on what other people think of me, but what I think of me. So should you. Last—I didn't know I couldn't. Therefore, I could, so can you," she told them.[9]

But Cheryl was growing skeptical of the message she was delivering to the groups, especially when the audience was made up primarily of Black youth. Though she was given every advantage possible by her family, many of the children she spoke to didn't have the same advantages. She knew many of the organizations she was representing wanted to play up her minority status.

"She had a script that she was supposed to recite. She was saying, 'But you can.' It was not true," said Jim Galasyn, who would later befriend her. "The vast lot of these children were already consigned to the military jail complex. She was very pessimistic about the prospect for Black youth in America."[10]

When Cheryl finally admitted she wouldn't be racing in 1986, Coors canceled its sponsorship of her racing, but kept her on as a spokesperson. Her story had value to the company.[11]

Cheryl Glass still received mainstream media attention in the years when she wasn't actively competing. She still thought the attention would help her find more sponsors to fund her expensive racing dreams. It rarely did. But she was willing to take on any tasks Coors asked of her. The Coors company was her primary source of income.

Cheryl Glass poses for a publicity photo.
SHIRLEY GLASS COLLECTION

Coors paid her to undertake another media tour in Los Angeles in April 1986, this one coming the week prior to the Grand Prix of Long Beach. Where Coors' other race car drivers made appearances with mainstream media outlets, Cheryl made appearances at media outlets like radio and television stations aimed at the Black audience. But she was well paid for the easy work.[12]

"She was supposed to come out for, I think it was five days for $7,000 or seven days for $5,000," Skip Young said. "She says 'Skip, [I'll] amend this.' She put it to a day and sent it back in. $5,000 became $35,000 and the legal department was stuck. She said, 'They're not even going to read this.' I laughed, I laughed, I laughed. That's a good day."[13]

Cheryl was feted as if she were an all-conquering hero even though the closest she was going to get to racing in L.A. was looking at a car.

Washington's state superintendent of schools chose her as one of 100 Outstanding Women in Washington State. Her image would appear in a set of baseball-type trading cards distributed to elementary schools.[14] She spoke at an Alpha Kappa Alpha event in Detroit alongside Coretta Scott King, widow of civil rights icon Martin Luther King Jr.[15] She was awarded the Candace Award from the National Coalition of 100 Black Women, an award presented at the Metropolitan Museum of Art in New York City.[16]

She was given the Wendell Scott "Greased Lightning" Pioneer Award during the 65th birthday party for the pioneering NASCAR driver in Atlanta in 1986. During the party, she had long conversations with Leonard W. Miller, the founder of the Black American Racing Association, and Scott. She told them she was working on a deal to go to Florida to drive sprint cars. She said that in one of her crashes that she had been hurt so bad she couldn't have children. They advised her not to race anything. They recognized that she needed to recover physically more than she did.

"She was interested in going anywhere anybody had any money to get in a car. If you had a car, a three-quarter midget, she'll try it. If you had a NASCAR late model, she would just try it. If you have a sprint car, she'll try it," Miller said. "She was wanting to try to race. And then, too, the last time I saw her at that event, she had a limp. She had a bad limp. When I said limp, she was dragging her leg. She dragged her foot. My wife (Rose) said, 'Hey, why does Cheryl want to keep doing this?'"[17]

With notable people like CNN staff member Wes Montgomery and state legislator and NAACP chairman Julian Bond at Wendell Scott's birthday party, Cheryl was making connections.

She received so many awards that she believed she still mattered.

Who Cheryl really needed to speak with was business owners or representatives of corporations who could contribute money to her racing. Or race car owners. Where the attention she received crossing the nation to speak at events would have had many sponsors clamoring to pay to have their name on the car of many race car drivers, it did little for Cheryl Glass.

After two years of not turning a lap in competition, Coors dropped her from her personal services contract in 1987.[18]

Cheryl paid marketing companies to locate sponsorship to fund her racing. She produced a massive amount of professional-appearing sponsorship proposal material. She printed out sheets of racing accomplishments to distribute to each possibility. They were based on fact, but exaggerated. She claimed she placed in the top 10 in 90 percent of her races. She sent out hundreds of slick proposals. They looked great but didn't bring in any money.

Cheryl's time on the road and effort to keep her racing career going took a toll on her wedding dress business. When she made a dress for Kelly Tanner's fiancée, Leanne—who also was from a racing family—Cheryl took so long to complete it she had to show up at the wedding with the dress. She ended up making alterations in the minutes before Leanne walked down the aisle.[19] Tanner wasn't the only person who had complaints. Cheryl churned through low-paid assistants who were doing the physical work of building the dresses that Cheryl didn't have the ability to. Shirley Glass became the de facto dressmaker while Cheryl remained the face of the business.

Not long after her divorce, Cheryl started dating an older man, 37-year-old Jimmie Tharpe, in 1985. He moved into her house on Lago Place and the relationship went well for a time. But not long after they started dating, according to Cheryl, Tharpe physically abused her. She never told her friends or family about what happened. In 1988, Tharpe was facing charges of insurance fraud, and Cheryl was called to testify against him. She didn't intend to, but when Tharpe found out she had been called to testify, he was enraged. He beat her, made her sign blank checks, and left her on the side of the road to be found by a passerby and taken to a hospital for treatment from the injuries. Tharpe was arrested, but Cheryl said she was so terrified of how he would react that she refused to press charges. Eventually, Cheryl had a change of heart, testified against Tharpe, and he was convicted. In her telling of the events,

Tharpe swore to get his revenge by killing her. He told her he would hire a hitman from Gary, Indiana, the man would fly to Seattle and shoot Cheryl while she slept. He said the hitman would then fly to San Francisco for two weeks before returning to Indiana. Cheryl was so terrified of Tharpe's threats, she obtained a restraining order against him.[20]

Cheryl continued to apply for racing licenses, despite her lingering physical problems and lack of medical clearance. She was rejected enough times in the open wheel world that she started to think about racing in other avenues. She considered racing in the NASCAR Winston West Series.[21] The series was significantly less expensive to run than the CART Series as it was contained to stock car races solely on the West Coast. It fit her background as most of the races were held on oval tracks with a few road courses mixed in. But racing a stock car is as far from the Indianapolis 500 as racing gets. The last driver to make the jump from that series to Indy Cars was Parnelli Jones in the 1960s. But she still talked about it as it could be her next great career move.

"It was mentioned, and it was just mentioned as far as I was concerned in passing," Hersey Mallory said.

In NASCAR, Cheryl wouldn't be the first at everything. Black drivers raced in NASCAR as far back as 1955 when Elias Bowie raced in a Cadillac stock car and women had been racing with the sanctioning body as far back as its first race in 1949. But Cheryl Glass could fill a niche. And she could have raced.

"That's why I think there was so much potential for her to go further in the sport, like higher up. (Indy Cars were) the wrong direction," Billy Kennelly said. "I should have went to NASCAR. Cheryl had the same mindset as me. No, we're open wheelers, we want to go to Indy. Back then, it was a much more serious thing for us that we wanted to go to Indy. Right then, they were pulling in all of those drivers from Europe."[22]

Even three years after the crash in Los Angeles, Cheryl was not physically capable of racing. The migraine headaches became increasingly debilitating. She was bouncing between doctors and spending multiple days each week in hospitals. Doctors tried every treatment and medication they could think of. None worked as more than short-term solutions.

The pain grew so debilitating that Cheryl would hide in dark rooms for hours and try to sleep to escape it.

When Cheryl needed to compose herself together for a media appearance, however, she did so with amazing aptitude.

Turner Broadcasting System produced a special to air during Black History Week in 1988 about prominent Black people to be called "The Achievers." Cheryl was one of the subjects the producers needed. Cheryl was featured along with William Brown, writer and director Billy James Parrott, Navy submarine commander Chancellor "Pete" Tzomes, and dancer Katherine Dunham.

In her segment, Cheryl comes off as braggadocious and erudite, making up facts to better fit her narrative, including making it sound like she drove sprint cars more than she had. She talked about her aspirations for her wedding dress business, saying she would offer a line of dresses and sell them in major shops in New York. She made even minor injuries she suffered racing sound horrific, but left out the repeated head traumas. Cheryl Glass appears happy on camera.

The cameras follow her to a shop where she surveys the old Indy Car with no engine in it and tells the mechanic: "Okay, so I understand we've got a problem with this ignition. It's cutting out between 7,500 and 8,000 RPM and I'm wondering what have you changed on this? Is there anything we can do to prevent that from happening?"[23]

Cheryl attended a private screening of the special after receiving an invitation from TBS owner and magnate Ted Turner at the Beverly Hilton Hotel on January 7, 1988.[24]

Despite not racing, Cheryl still attracted media attention; she paid a service to track and send her all stories about her that appeared in newspapers and magazines around the county. Some of the many articles appeared in remote cities she had never visited. It appeared she was still relevant.

With the sponsorship from Coors gone, Cheryl and Marvin sought out sponsorship from every company they could think of. They took slick sponsorship proposals to McDonald's, Canadian Mist, Crisco, Tide, Folgers, Hanes, Sears, and other major companies. Where many in her circumstances wouldn't get a meeting with company executives, Cheryl often did. She could get her foot in the door, but the companies didn't sponsor her.

And she was feeling pressure elsewhere.

Her race team was sued by a financial services company for $521 for non-payment and she was taken to small claims court in another case. She racked up a large number of traffic and parking tickets—many of which she never paid—and was involved in minor traffic accidents on the street. She often parked either directly in front of her wedding business in downtown Seattle or in a spot in a lot nearby, despite being repeatedly ticketed for it. She racked up dozens of parking tickets for $12 or $15.

Cheryl had time on her hands. She wanted to take on a new hobby. She started working in the medium of stained glass. She spent hours coloring and cutting the glass and fashioning it into things like lampshades. At one store she frequented for supplies in nearby Redmond, Northwest Art Glass, she noticed a 22-year-old white man working in the shipping department in early 1988. Mike Opprecht, who's real first name was Charles, was a junior college dropout working for $6 an hour. He was handsome with dark hair and a mustache. There was something about the young man that caught Cheryl's eye immediately. They talked a few times and there was a mutual attraction. Eventually Cheryl asked him out on a date.

Before their first date, Cheryl went to her parents' house, boxed up all the alcohol they had—they didn't drink much, but kept it for parties—and brought it back to her house. Cheryl didn't drink often, but wanted to see if Opprecht did. After he came over and didn't have a drink, she was more interested. She later told him she was apprehensive because her first husband was an alcoholic.

Opprecht had been dating and living with another woman at the time. When he returned home from his first date with Cheryl, he realized he needed to move out. He needed a place to stay and asked Cheryl if he could move in with her. She told him that he could.

Opprecht was friends with Waymon Whiting III, Cheryl's first cousin. Mike and Waymon grew up not far apart in Bellevue, were on the same soccer teams, and went to school together for many years. But it wasn't until months after Cheryl and Opprecht met that they learned about their connection.

Though he had lived in the Seattle area most of his life, Opprecht had no knowledge of her celebrity status until they became a couple. She informed him she was a famous race car driver, but he couldn't tell she was a race car driver from the looks of her home. She didn't have pictures of race cars on her walls but did have a few pictures of herself with celebrities like singer Cheryl Linn.

The only indication about racing at her house was a 53-foot trailer that was parked next to it that was supposed to be used to haul a race car, an object she didn't have.

"I kept waiting for more driving stuff," Opprecht said. "You tell me you're this famous person who's a driver. What the hell?"[25]

After dating Opprecht for a few months, Cheryl questioned if she was attracted to him. The first time he went to her parents' house for an introductory dinner, they had invited another man they thought Cheryl might be interested in. She wasn't. When Cheryl talked with Marvin about whether Opprecht was her type, he told her, "Maybe he should be."

Six months after they met, July 16, 1988, the 26-year-old Cheryl and the 23-year-old Opprecht were married. Unlike her lavish first marriage ceremony, Cheryl went as small as possible with the second. Opprecht had a friend who owned a property on Guemes Island, one of a chain of islands in Skagit County between mainland Washington State and Victoria, British Columbia. There were no buildings on the land, only a trailer in which the couple would stay as a humble version of a honeymoon suite. Neither Cheryl nor Opprecht invited their families to the wedding. Mike wouldn't tell his parents he was married for years. Pastor Hilary Bitz officiated over the ceremony while Jack Smith, a friend of Opprecht, and Sal Thompson, Cheryl's friend from her modeling days, were the only witnesses.[26]

"I only knew her for like six months when we got married. It was just a very quick thing," Opprecht said. "But let me tell you, the day we got married, life changed dramatically. That's when she told me all about the headaches and we started going to the hospital four or five times a week. She even said, 'If you had known all of this, you married me.'"

Cheryl went to great lengths to conceal the severity of her migraines from her future husband.

She would rank the pain that was caused by each headache between 8 and 9 on a scale of 10. That was from a woman who had been in some of the most violent sprint car crashes of her generation.

Cheryl developed a system to work the large number of hospitals nearby to her benefit. She devised a routine where she went to different hospitals each trip. One day she would go to a hospital in Seattle, the next she would go to one in Everett, and she would go to a different Seattle hospital the third day. Cheryl figured out if she went to four or five different hospitals, she could get any medication she was seeking.

"She played the circuit. We kind of rotated," Opprecht said.

At one point in 1990, physician Stan Schiff said Cheryl was taking Verapamil (to treat high blood pressure), Demerol (a pain-relieving opiate), Darvocet (another opiate), Compazine (an anti-psychotic), and Nubian (another opiate).[27] Schiff didn't know about the drugs she was receiving from other doctors at the same time and how she mixed them. A friend would bring Valium (a benzodiazepine) to Cheryl when she was struggling. Cheryl was so desperate for relief, she would take anything.

Then the disturbing phone calls to Opprecht started.

On two occasions in 1989, Cheryl called Opprecht while he was at work and said she was in such pain that she wanted to jump off the Aurora Bridge to kill herself and end the headaches for good. Both times, he left work immediately, picked her up at their house, and took her to a hospital. He recognized Cheryl was serious.

"It hurt so bad that, what do you do?" Opprecht said. "I would go grab her, pick her up and take her to the doctor. It was always the Aurora Bridge."

Cheryl's condition hurt her struggling wedding dress business.

Cheryl was only a figurehead in the business by the time Opprecht met her. Cheryl would sit at the front desk and consult with the occasional potential customer who came in the Occidental shop, but did little in making the dresses. Cheryl would take the customers ideas and travel to a designer in Marysville, who was paid to sketch the designs. That was given to Shirley, who made the dresses. But Shirley often constructed the dresses with glue, rather than sewing them together. The arrangement, and Cheryl's lack of time management skills, put them frequently behind in finishing orders.

In one instance, Cheryl had been contracted to make a dress for a woman who was getting married in the Central Washington city of Yakima. Cheryl and Shirley were hopelessly behind. To get to Yakima, Opprecht drove a van while Shirley and Cheryl constructed the dress in the back on the 2 ½-hour drive to make it in time for the wedding. During the drive, Cheryl and Shirley worked furiously. When they arrived in Yakima, the dress still wasn't close to being finished. They told Opprecht to drive around on the way to the church to buy more time to finish it.

"We were like an hour and a half late and that lady was bawling. I'm just sitting in the driver's seat of the van. She said, 'Didn't I give you good directions?' The story was we got lost," Opprecht said. "That's exactly what happens every single time."

The business wasn't producing much income for Cheryl, but the fancy showroom downtown remained a status symbol. She rarely had money and Opprecht frequently saw her borrow from her father for basic needs.

Cheryl kept other things from her husband, too. Cheryl's hair was naturally short. Due to her vanity, she felt she needed extensions. Cheryl assumed her appearance mattered to him. Opprecht never knew she had short hair and says he didn't care. She put on a significant amount of weight, much of that coming as a result of the medications she took. She wore low-cut shirts and dresses and provocative clothes in an effort to keep him physically interested. He didn't care about that, either.

Those who knew Cheryl didn't understand what she saw in Opprecht.

"I never got that about her," Lisa Kelsie said. "This one guy, he didn't have any money, her first husband. That didn't last. The next one had no money at all. And I think she basically carried him. I don't think he had any money."[28]

Opprecht was earning $6 an hour, which was frequently more than Cheryl earned.

Cheryl often talked about racing and was consumed with the idea of obtaining funding for it from big companies. She told her husband about how she was negotiating with prominent national corporations for a contract. That potential contract, the one that would resuscitate her driving career, was her most frequent topic of conversation. But by 1989, the racing world had forgotten her.

"The only thing we ever really did that had to do with racing was . . . we were planning on going to Portland for a race, but that didn't work out," Opprecht said. "There was the hydro race that year. I met Bernie Little and Al Muncie's wife and really, the famous drivers and sponsors of the Seafair of the hydros. We sat and got great seats to watch the race. That was the only racing thing we ever did."

For someone who knew as many people as Cheryl did, she didn't have many close friends. On the occasion she had guests over to her house, it was usually her parents. Her mother would bring over cleaning supplies as gifts and clean the house. When Cheryl threw a birthday party for Opprecht, she didn't invite anyone he knew. Instead, she invited her few friends.

Cheryl grew litigious when she thought someone was slighting her.

"That's one of the things that I think drew us apart, little things like that. If something goes wrong, you sue them," Opprecht said. "We'd go somewhere, go on a vacation and we wouldn't get a room. And she said they were just discriminating against her. Maybe I just didn't get it."

Less than a year after they married, Cheryl and Opprecht went to a marriage counselor a couple of times, but it didn't help.

Opprecht's family traditionally spent Christmas Eve together, but that also was Cheryl's birthday. She wanted to celebrate with her family. On Christmas Eve 1989, Opprecht spent some of the day with Cheryl and the rest with his family. The arguments in the following days spelled the end of their coupling.

A few days later, around January 1, 1990, Opprecht decided to move out. He left Cheryl's house for a few days. He came back a couple days later to get his things at a time when he thought she wouldn't be there. When he tried to use his key to open the door, he discovered the locks had been changed. Opprecht climbed through a window and started gathering his few possessions, including his bed, and loaded them into a pickup. He was nearly finished when Cheryl and Marvin arrived.

"She was mad. She throws her keys at me. She was hitting me," Opprecht said. "And then there's a court case over that. I never hit her."

Opprecht filed for divorce on February 22, 1990. She contested the divorce and got a temporary restraining order against him on May 11, 1990, despite his claims that she assaulted him. It dragged out the proceeding. Their divorce was finalized May 12, 1991.[29]

After they separated, Opprecht moved back in with his parents. That's when he finally broke the news that he had been married for over a year. He said that it took him a couple of years to pay off the debt Cheryl and Marvin racked up on his credit card flying to Chicago to unsuccessfully chase sponsorships.

So Cheryl Glass decided to go back to the world where she had been successful.

CHAPTER ELEVEN

A Comeback Turns into a Nightmare

1990 to 1991

EVEN IN THE DEPTHS OF CHERYL GLASS'S MEDICAL PROBLEMS—AND they were severe—what kept her going was her desire to return to racing. When everything else in her life was collapsing—her marriages, her health, her business—she remained resolute in her belief that if she could become a winning race car driver again, everything in her life would be fixed.

She still believed racing in the Indianapolis 500 was her destiny.

"I'd like to be an established Indy driver," Cheryl Glass said. "That's what I'd like to be by the time I finish."[1]

By 1990, the racing world had passed her by.

When drivers compete in races week after week, they get better. When they're out of a race car for a year, their skills deteriorate. Not driving a race car for five years is an eternity. Cheryl assumed she could get right back into racing and be immediately competitive.

At age 28 in 1990, the window of Cheryl racing in the Indianapolis 500 was closing quickly. If she was ever going to achieve her goal of racing in the biggest race in the world—something people once thought was her destiny—she had to make a dramatic move. Since no one else was willing to employ her as a race car driver, Cheryl was going to have to prove herself in a venue where they watched. The opportunity for her talent to be seen by Indianapolis 500 car owners was in the American Racing Series, the support division to the CART series.

In the 1980s, Indy Car owners and open wheel officials recognized they were putting American drivers at a disadvantage. In Europe, open wheel drivers had a distinct path to reaching the top of the sport, Formula One. On the continent, there were multiple versions of formula cars at the lower levels that served as a comprehensive training ground. The lower-class cars had little power, small tires, and no downforce adders like wings. As the drivers progressively rose through the categories, the cars had more power, bigger tires, and more downforce. But every car resembled and drove vaguely like their big brothers at the top of the racing food chain.

In 1985, March chassis founder Robin Herd and Indy Car team owner Pat Patrick approached long-time racing mechanic and British ex-patriot Roger Bailey with an idea: create a "junior" class to Indy Cars. The cars would be slightly smaller than Indy Cars—approximately ⅞ scale—have slightly less power and downforce but would race on most of the same tracks as the Indy Car Series and be aimed at giving younger drivers the necessary experience to one day race an Indy Car. They called it the American Racing Series.[2]

From its inaugural season in 1986, the series proved to be an effective training ground. Drivers like Wally Dallenbach Jr., Juan Manuel Fangio, and Jeff Andretti used it as a springboard to the CART Series and the Indianapolis 500. The rest of the drivers in the series hoped to follow suit. Cheryl Glass saw it as her step if she was to make it to the Indianapolis 500.

It wasn't an Indy Car, but it was close.

At a young age, Cheryl had competed against some drivers who had moved on to find great success in racing, far beyond the initial successes Cheryl experienced. Billy Kennelly won the 1983 Washington Midget Racing Association championship and followed it by winning the 410 sprint car championships at Skagit Speedway the next two seasons. Tobey Butler won the 1987 NASCAR Northwest Tour championship. Kelly Tanner was winning so many asphalt late model races, people couldn't keep track of them all.

As of 1990, the most notable part of Glass's career had been one win 10 years earlier. Cheryl took many medications to deal with the progressively debilitating migraines. As a side effect of the medications she took to help with the headaches, Cheryl weighed over 200 pounds. She had long before abandoned the arduous training regimen of running and lifting weights she once undertook. By 1990, she was not in physical shape to drive a race car. But that wasn't going to stop her.

"She couldn't wait to get back into racing," Mike Opprecht said.[3]

After Cheryl's brief Can-Am stint in 1984, the Glass family kept in close contact with mechanic Hersey Mallory. Over the years, Marvin and Cheryl regularly floated the idea of teaming up with him again to start their own racing team with Cheryl driving. They discussed a number of options of what cars they would field in which series. Those dreams ranged from Cheryl's long-shot Indy Car dreams to her fleeting NASCAR aspirations. Mallory had long since moved on from the Ausca Can-Am team and become one of the top mechanics on Nissan's fledgling, factory-backed Electramotive IMSA team. The Japanese brand wanted to establish itself in performance automobiles after its name change from Datsun. It was spending lavishly to hire drivers like Geoff Brabham to pilot its factory-backed IMSA programs.

In one of their frequent phone conversations, Marvin brought up to Mallory the idea of fielding a car for Cheryl in the American Racing Series. Mallory was busy with the Nissan efforts, but he was willing to make sacrifices to help relaunch Cheryl's career. He had become a trusted family friend and wanted to help.

Every time Cheryl drove for someone else—such as her Silver Crown ride in 1982 and her Can-Am rice in 1984—it turned disastrous. From ill-prepared cars to an ill-prepared driver, the situations always ended quickly and in dramatic fashion. She felt the teams were interested in making money and not making her a race car driver. She was right. In 1990, the owners of those types of cars weren't willing to take a risk on a past-her-prime race car driver with little experience in anything remotely resembling their expensive race cars.

The only way Cheryl Glass was going to race again was to buy a car.

The plan emerged when Marvin Glass found one of the series' spec Wildcat chassis cars for sale by an owner associated with Indy Car driver Danny Sullivan, the 1985 Indianapolis 500 winner, located in North Hollywood, California. Marvin called Mallory, who was living in San Diego at the time, and convinced him to go look at it. The family's initial plan was to buy the car and have Cheryl compete in the final few races of the 1990 season.

"They wanted to do two races. They wanted to do Nazareth and they wanted to do Laguna Seca. Nazareth is a tri-oval. She's used to ovals and turning left, so that would be pretty good for us. For Laguna, that's another can of worms," Hersey Mallory said. "They called me and I went to North Hollywood where the car was at. I go up there and I took a look at it and I give Mr. Glass the results of what I found. I looked at the motor and I saw the run time for the motor and how many spares they were offering."[4]

Mallory decided the package was a value at the asking price and advised Marvin it was what they needed to get Cheryl back in a car.

Marvin wired the money to Mallory to purchase the Wildcat, which Mallory did on August 11, 1990. He picked it up September 11 and took it to his home in San Diego. He didn't have a big garage, but it was big enough to disassemble the car, perform the necessary maintenance, and reassemble it to race-ready condition. Mallory took a month off from his job to work on Cheryl's car.

Racing costs money—a lot of it—even in a support division.

The family had few remaining tools and little basic equipment like jacks from her former racing that could be used to support the aspiring operation. But they had a trailer for an 18-wheeler in the yard of Cheryl's house. They needed a lot of additional equipment to get Cheryl on the track, even with the spares they received in the package from the purchase of the Danny Sullivan car.

In July 1990, Cheryl's attorney reached a settlement to a lawsuit involving a road car accident from 1988 for $35,000. She received $16,000 of that, all of which was almost immediately swallowed up in starting the racing team.[5] The only sponsors willing to take a chance on Cheryl were Elegant Eye, a small glasses company based in Seattle and owned by Cheryl's friend, Sally Kaye, and long-time associate sponsor Bardahl. But that only produced about $500, barely enough to buy the tires needed for one weekend's races.

Marvin was making a significant salary as vice president at Pacific Northwest Bell and invested every dollar he could to get Cheryl back racing again. It was still not enough. Over the summer of 1990, Marvin traveled around Seattle, asking friends and business associates for loans or gifts of money to raise the rest for the team's formation.

"He came around and borrowed some money from us," said Dave Griffith, a family friend who worked with Marvin at Boeing and Pacific Northwest Bell. "And we never got paid back for it. I don't know how many other people he approached. It was in the thousands, but it was less than $10,000. It almost looked to me like it was a million dollar investment, but they had to race someplace."[6]

The costs added up quickly. To knock her rust as a driver Cheryl attended another racing school in 1990 at a cost of $2,606. Though the car came with an engine, they still had to lease an engine at a cost of $7,000. They had to rent a track (Phoenix International Raceway) so Cheryl could test the car at a cost of $15,015. They also had to purchase a truck with which to haul the trailer around at a cost of $27,426.[7]

In total, Cheryl's family spent over $156,000 to get her going again.

Cheryl Glass (18) drives in practice for the American Racing Series race at Laguna Seca Raceway in 1990. Roberto Quintanilla (64) tries to pass her on the outside.
SHIRLEY GLASS COLLECTION

Unlike many of the series in which Cheryl competed, the American Racing Series had an advanced process that included a medical evaluation and a rigorous driving test overseen by series officials.

Before she could drive a lap in competition, Cheryl needed medical clearance to prove she was capable of racing after a five-year layoff.

Cheryl's migraine headaches had become increasingly debilitating. Cheryl was on so many medications that even if she had been physically healthy, she would have had a hard time operating a car on the street, let alone on a racetrack.

"You know how they used to wear those little fanny packs? Those would have pain pills in them. She took a lot of pain pills and tranquilizers and shit," said Lisa Kelsie, her hairdresser.[8]

To pass the medical portion of the test for the American Racing Series, Cheryl lied.

In the required medical forms, she claimed she had never been seriously injured—despite her long and well-documented history of injuries sustained in racing accidents. It was because of that lie that she was given medical clearance to race for the first time since her violent crash in Los Angeles in 1985. But she still had to prove she had the physical ability to drive such a race car.

ARS series officials required newcomers to pass a driving test on an oval track to receive a license to race.

Cheryl's migraine headaches worsened the closer she got to the test. In the short amount of time he was around her in the run-up to her first race, Mallory had to take her to the hospital multiple times when the headaches worsened.

Cheryl chose to do her licensing test at Phoenix International Raceway. It was the only track on the circuit where she had experience. Cheryl passed the licensing test at Phoenix with weeks to spare for the October 7, 1990, race at Pennsylvania International Raceway in Nazareth, a one-mile tri-oval in Andretti country.

Beyond the on-track performance, one of the requirements was that drivers had to demonstrate they could get out of the car in a reasonable amount of time. The exercise was to simulate what they would have to do in case of a fire or catastrophic accident. That proved more difficult than driving. Cheryl weighed around 200 pounds and was trying to quickly bail out of a car designed for a 130-pound man. It took her a few tries, and some finessing, to pass that part of the test.

Mallory recognized Cheryl's physical impediment and encouraged her to go on a training regimen. The weight of a driver plays a key role in racing. Beyond the disadvantage in carrying extra weight by slowing the car, racing under high G-forces for hours at a time is physically taxing on even the most fit athletes. Mallory warned Cheryl that fitness would be vital if she ever raced on a more physically demanding road course, as she intended.

Cheryl didn't do it.

One of the mechanics recruited for the ARS effort was Richard Lindwall, her first ex-husband. He had remarried, but remained friends with Cheryl and the Glass family after divorcing her. When she needed help with a race car, he would drop everything from his new life across the country and rush to her aid. Lindwall joined the family at Phoenix for the test, on the ensuring long tow back to Seattle, and then across the country to Nazareth.

Cheryl had confidence she would do well in Nazareth. Mallory, however, knew many of the drivers against whom she would be competing through his time as a mechanic in professional racing. He knew their skill level and how they were in better equipment—despite it being a series where every car was intended to be the same. He also knew how many of the drivers had large sums of money supporting their racing efforts. They could afford to have their car fixed if they crashed while trying to win. She couldn't.

For one of the few times in her career, Cheryl wasn't going to be the first woman to race in a series. That distinction in ARS was held by French driver Cathy Muller. That happened a year before in 1989.[9]

But after a decade of trying, Cheryl Glass was finally getting her shot at what she considered the big time in the world of auto racing.

Though only 11 cars were to comprise the field for the Nazareth race, including some who had been competing in quarter midgets back when Cheryl was such as Robbie Groff and P.J. Jones, this was a level of competition she had never seen. In the first practice sessions for the race, Cheryl performed well, considering her long layoff. She qualified for the race ninth with an average speed of 130.383 miles per hour. Robbie Buhl won the pole with a speed of 143.426. At that pace, she would be lapped by the leaders every 13 laps.[10]

"I don't know that she was really prepared to race Indy Lights (American Racing Series) at that time as far as having enough seat time," P. J. Jones said. "I don't think she was physically in that great of shape in that time of her life."[11]

As Cheryl exited the car after qualifying, she triggered the fire suppression bottle with her leg. It covered her legs with fire retardant chemicals and resulted in painful chemical burns. Unless forced by series officials, racers and crew members rarely arm their fire suppression bottle for fear of such an event.

"Normally I wouldn't set it, but I was concerned for her well being out there," Mallory said. "This time the fire bottle went off."

Cheryl refused to back out of the race, especially after enduring as much as she had to make it that far.

When the 11-car field lined up under cloudy skies for the October 7 race, Mallory looked over the cars and noticed that the brash, hard-charging P. J. Jones was slated to start behind her due to a mishap in qualifying. After helping Cheryl into her car, he had Lindwall hold the umbrella over her to get her calmed down.

Mallory thought it wasn't a good situation for Cheryl. P. J. was in the cockpit of his car as Mallory approached. Mallory bent down to ask on which side P. J. planned to pass Cheryl on the first lap. He knew the young hard charger was going to be so much faster, he could pass her at will. P. J. said he was going to pass on Cheryl's right.

"We got an issue here," Mallory told Cheryl in the cockpit. "You can go along with it or you can profit by it. I want you to let him go. Cheryl, he's either going to run in the back of your gearbox or you're going to let him go. He's not afraid to tear up some equipment. He's sponsored by the racing rims. He's not in the hurt for money."

Like the veteran drivers who advised Cheryl she wasn't going to learn much by wrecking early in her career, Mallory was trying to teach her that she would learn far more from making laps than getting in a first-lap crash.

But she took Mallory's words as an insult to her ability as a driver. As the field made its slow warm-up laps leading to the green flag, Cheryl heard Mallory's words ring through her head, and she wasn't happy.

When the green flag flew, Cheryl stayed to the inside of the first turn and P. J. easily passed her on the right. She stayed in the low groove as the race went on. Robbie Groff and the rest of the leaders soon lapped her, but she maintained a steady pace. Groff held off Buhl to win the race and the $25,000 winner's prize. Cheryl placed a respectable seventh, largely because other cars crashed or broke, but earned $2,000. After her long layoff from racing, it was a promising finish for her debut race in the series.[12]

Cheryl blamed what she saw as a lackluster performance on the chemical burns from the fire retardant.

There was one race left in the 1990 season. The technical, sweeping 11-turn, 2.238-mile road course in Monterey, California called Laguna Seca Raceway loomed on October 21, 1990. The track was a challenge for the best drivers, and the list of drivers entered jumped to 17 cars for the season finale.

Considering Cheryl's lack of experience in road courses and poor physical fitness, Mallory discouraged her from racing at Laguna Seca. Most of the other drivers had competed in hundreds of road races. Mallory urged Cheryl to stick with oval tracks until she had more experience in the car. He wanted her to have a shot when she competed in a road race. For a reason Mallory never understood, Cheryl was determined to race at Laguna Seca.

Marvin Glass had been in contact with a pair of mechanics who had success with production-based cars and who convinced him that he needed to hire them and get rid of Mallory. After the Nazareth race, Mallory towed the car to the one-room shop of Jeff Kenetech and Edwin Huft near Grayslake, Illinois.[13] Mallory—who had sacrificed so much to help her—wasn't impressed by the pair. Lindwall then towed the car to the road course at Willow Springs International Raceway outside Rosamond, California, where Cheryl would test prior to Laguna Seca. When Mallory arrived, he figured out he was being replaced by these inexperienced mechanics, and he wasn't happy about it. He returned to his day job with Nissan's IMSA championship effort.

"Apparently, they seemed to think they could do a better job than me," Mallory said.

Mallory was never paid for the hundreds of hours of work he put into Cheryl's racing.

After the test session at Willow Springs, Kenetech and Huft trailered Cheryl's race car to Monterrey for the Laguna Seca race. The race would be one of the most well-attended CART races of the 1990 season—outside of the Indianapolis 500.

But Cheryl crashed a few laps into the first practice session of the weekend. The front end of her car was severely damaged. There was no way it could be fixed in time to race that weekend. Though she never turned a lap in the race, she was credited with a 17th-place finish.[14]

Dejected, she sat in the tent watching her mechanics strip her race car down so they could load it in the trailer to take it home. She appeared

Cheryl Glass sits in her American Racing Series car for a media appearance at Seattle International Raceway. She had a hard time fitting in the small car.
SHIRLEY GLASS COLLECTION

dazed as people approached her. Cheryl was noticeably upset. Her great plan for a triumphant road course debut in the series was destroyed before she raced a lap.

Willy T. Ribbs, the first Black driver to reach the highest level of American open wheel racing, was driving a golf cart out of the paddock after a practice session in his Indy Car. Ribbs spotted Cheryl, immediately stopped, and walked over to talk to her. He had read about her many times over the years and wanted to finally meet her. Ribbs, who by then had become a noted road racer including 17 wins in the Trans-Am Series, approached Cheryl and offered to help teach her the finer points of road racing. With so few Black drivers competing in high levels of racing in the country, he wanted to see her succeed. After talking for a few minutes, Cheryl walked away from Ribbs.[15]

A few days later, Ribbs called Mallory and told him what transpired.

"I don't know what to tell you about your girl," Ribbs told him. "I tried to help her."[16]

Ribbs never talked to her again.

Cheryl Glass didn't want instruction about how to drive a race car unless she was paying for it. The American Racing Series was far more competitive than Cheryl realized when she decided to race in it.

"It was competitive as hell," P. J. Jones said. "You had Paul Tracy, you had, shit, Johnny O'Connell. You had (Robbie) Groff, Mark Smith at that. You had some really good race car drivers, it was some good competition. (Eric) Bachelart, too. There was a lot of people in that era who made it to Indy, made it to sports cars, made it to other parts of racing."

Cheryl told people she was considering designing and selling a line of fire suits for women, which was a revolutionary idea. The racing suits of the day were made solely to fit a man's body with no thought of a woman wearing one. For a man, even a heavy one, the fire suits were fine. But for a woman, especially one with a bust like Cheryl's, the chest area was constricting and restricted her arm movement. Cheryl had a hard time turning a steering wheel and breathing with one zipped up.

"These things just weren't made to fit a woman's body," Cheryl said.[17]

Despite having a good idea, so few women drove race cars in 1990 that there was no market for driving suits for women.

Cheryl's plan was to race in the entire 1991 American Racing Series season. It was being rebranded as Indy Lights to better play up the connection with its big brother series.

Her family had gone into debt to finance Cheryl's entry into the series, and it was going to cost hundreds of thousands of more dollars for her to run the full season. They didn't have that kind of money and couldn't attract sponsorship to make up the rest. But after spending so much to get her going, why not go all the way and give her all of the tools she needed to succeed?

"I would really like to get back on the winning track again. It's been too long," Cheryl told a reporter from *Racing for Kids* magazine.[18]

In the off-season, her car had been taken to the Illinois shop of Kenetech and Huft, where it underwent extensive repairs to be returned to racing shape. And it was repainted from its previous red and white livery to a more colorful pink and blue paint scheme.

"Last year we had a red car and there were eight other red cars (in ARS). I got sick of trying to figure out which one was Cheryl," Marvin said.[19]

The opening race of the 1991 Indy Lights season was the star-studded Long Beach Grand Prix in the Southern California sun. The race drew the national spotlight as a celebrity-filled crowd of over 100,000 watched cars speed through the concrete canyons of the 1.67-mile street circuit.

When she entered the registration tent for the race, the track workers didn't recognize her as a race car driver.

"I've heard it all. It has ranged from 'Are you delivering something?' to 'Who are you getting credentials for?' to 'What do you want?' Some people have been very rude," Cheryl told a reporter from the *Long Beach Telegram*.[20]

There was no way to practice for a place like Long Beach, though she did one test on a road course before the season started. Cheryl struggled in the first practice session of the weekend. She spun her car twice and stalled the engine in turn one as the session was coming to an end. In qualifying she didn't improve, timing in 18th of the 18 cars.[21]

"It's funny enough, the oval she went to, Nazareth, she wasn't bad. Road circuits, she was mediocre. But she stunk at street circuits like Long

Beach. I don't know if it was the walls or what," said Roger Bailey, the series director.[22]

Where some racing series are governed by boards made up of car owners and drivers, the Indy Lights series had a comparatively authoritative rule. The series had a rule that all drivers were required to wear baseball caps with series sponsor Firestone on them. The series wanted its sponsors to get maximum visibility. Cheryl's vanity about her hair was well known, and she went to great lengths to make sure it was perfect at all times. She felt her appearance was vital in attracting sponsorship. She wasn't going to ruin her hairstyle with a baseball cap. She found a headband with Firestone on it and wore that instead. The series officials weren't happy about it. But ultimately, they didn't do anything about it.

Driver's meetings are a tradition in racing. Prior to the race, the drivers gathered together in an area at the track and are given the same pre-race instructions by series officials they received at the previous race and all of the ones before that. Driver's meetings are a tedious practice that could be accomplished by instructions printed on a piece of paper. Attendance is required and if a driver misses the session, they are penalized money or by being sent to the back of the pack to start the race.

After her first few races in the Indy Lights series, Cheryl insisted she didn't need to attend the driver's meetings; she sent a crew member with $100 to pay her inevitable fine and to stand in her place. Other drivers resented her not attending the mandatory meeting.

"I've been racing all these years, they're not going to say anything new," Cheryl told Skip Young.[23]

Her experience in Long Beach ended as her car sputtered to a stop due to electrical issues after 14 of 45 laps. She was credited with a 17th-place finish.[24]

A few of Cheryl's competitors complained to the series officials about how she was making it dangerous for them due to how slow she was. The officials opted to do nothing about the complaints, figuring that the ensuing race a week later at Phoenix International Raceway would be more suited to her skill set and be a better gauge of her talent.

But when she found out about the complaints, Cheryl was enraged.

She told anyone who would listen that there were dark forces at work in the world of professional racing.[25] She saw how other teams in the series were better funded and speculated that opposing teams were being funded by illicit drug money.

In the 1980s, drug money was funneled into racing in such quantities that IMSA—the top professional road racing series in North America—received the nickname the International Marijuana Smugglers Association. To be fair, however, many of the drivers and team owners also smuggled cocaine. A number of drivers in IMSA and CART including John Paul Sr., John Paul Jr., Randy Lanier, Bill Wittington, and Don Whittington went to prison for drug smuggling.[26]

The drivers Cheryl was competing against, however, were never found guilty of the same crimes.

"I don't know what kind of evidence she had, but she came to believe the operation was a huge money laundering operation," Jim Galasyn said. "I had never heard that before she presented this idea. That knowledge was not good for her to have. And she went further and said that in fact all of this drug dealing that was occurring was essentially sanctioned by the DEA. She got in trouble when she threatened to expose the DEA involvement."[27]

A team in the Indy Lights Series, Personal Investment Group Racing—also known as P.I.G. Racing—was owned and operated by Norm Turley, a police officer in Long Beach. The team fielded cars for drivers such as P. J. Jones, Ted Prappas, Jon Beehkius, Dean Hall, Jeff Ward, and Mötley Crüe singer Vince Neil. Turley's cars were usually sponsored by the Say No to Drugs Foundation. Cheryl was suspicious that the team was a front for a government agency laundering drug money. No one on the team ever was charged with such crimes.

Cheryl wrote an article detailing the extent of how drug money was intertwined with racing. She tried to get it published, but it never was.

Cheryl wasn't getting better on the track.

In the first laps of the opening practice session for the April 21 race at Phoenix International Raceway, Cheryl crashed in the fourth turn on the mile oval and hit her head. She was woozy and likely had another concussion. But she refused to withdraw from the race.

"The impact cracked my helmet, but I can get a new one," she said.[28]

She had to borrow money for a replacement helmet. Her team worked for eight hours to repair the damage to the car and body so she could qualify 14th of 16 cars.[29] The Phoenix oval was supposed to be the one track on the circuit on which she should have been fast.

Laps into the race, the leaders caught up to Cheryl and went by her to put her a lap down. Then they did it again. And again. She completed 30 of the 75 laps, then crashed again.[30] Several drivers had to dodge her to avoid crashing. They again took their grievances to the series officials about how her racing was dangerous.

"She's always believed that the accident that she had was set up, that the CIA set her up for that," said Stuart Bramhall, who would become her psychiatrist.[31]

Hersey Mallory, then living and working on race cars in England, received a call from a series official he knew from his days of working on cars in the CART series. He was informed the series had suspended Cheryl's competitor's license.

Though it was just a piece of cardboard, that competition license was of vital importance to Cheryl.

A few weeks later, Skip Young, a friend of Cheryl's since childhood, went to Cheryl's bridal shop and saw her for the first time in years. She explained that the Indy Lights series had pulled her license and voiced her displeasure. Young said he reviewed the tape of the broadcast of the race and in his opinion the camera angles of the accident exonerated Cheryl.

She theorized that the real reason her license was revoked was she had threatened to expose the drug money funding teams in the series.

"We were going to find a way to get her license reinstated," Young said. "She was going to call a press conference and have a protest at the Detroit Grand Prix and let this be known. When the word got out to the association, they sent her license back to her, no letter or nothing. Her license came back to her."

She could have pulled off the protest in Detroit, but by Cheryl getting what she wanted, her passion and outrage was deflated.

The drug smuggling that Cheryl alleged was never proven.

After the perceived slight, Cheryl told people she was planning to take the summer off from racing and would return for the 1992 season. Between her latest concussion and increasingly debilitating migraine headaches, Cheryl was still not physically capable of competing at the level she needed.

When later asked about it, however, Cheryl claimed she left racing because of harassing comments.

Getting her license back wasn't enough to get Cheryl racing again. Her family spent over $200,000 so she could race four times and borrowed heavily to do it. The $3,600 she earned in prize winnings didn't make a dent into the debt the family accrued to put her in a race car again.

Cheryl Glass didn't know it, but her racing career was over.

Chapter Twelve

Dreams Come Crashing Down

1991 to 1992

CHERYL GLASS'S HOUSE WAS NOTHING SPECIAL.

Located in north Seattle at 19262 Lago Place, she bought the simple 870 square foot, two-bedroom, one-bathroom home located under power lines in 1982,[1] when she married first husband Richard Lindwall. The house was difficult to find as it was off the beaten path and located on a flag lot. Undeveloped city-owned property bordered it to the north. It was generally peaceful. When she was home, Cheryl could find calm in a chaotic world.

Cheryl was never content with the house. She initiated a series of renovations. She poured more money than she could afford into turning her house into her dream home. Sometimes the work was minor and amounted to little more than repainting of walls. At other times, she took on more ambitious projects. The only work Cheryl did herself was small things like painting trim. She preferred to hire contractors to do the big work.

One of Cheryl's few hobbies was gardening. When she had free time, she spent hours in her yard. She was ambitious with her gardening, planting flowers and shrubs. They were the few tasks of manual labor she enjoyed. She preferred expensive, pretty plants and spent more than she should have to beautify the yard around her house. Cheryl found it relaxing.

When Cheryl was going through her divorce from Richard Lind-wall in 1984, she transferred the title of the house to her parents.[2] But she never moved out of the house, even after her second husband and boyfriends moved in and out. When Cheryl went through difficult times, the house was often the one stable thing left in her life. It was her refuge from the attention and pressures of being Cheryl Glass, the national-ly-famous race car driver. She rarely spoke with her neighbors, and the few she talked with knew her as Cheryl, not as the race car driver.

The neighborhood appeared idyllic. Lined with trees, it was a conservative, middle-class neighborhood that was relatively quiet, the kind of middle-American place where people wanted to raise their children.

One of the few neighbors she ever saw was a man who infrequently visited his property, the one that separated hers from Lago Place.

"He showed up once a year and laid out on the lawn chair," said Mike Opprecht, who lived at her house for a year and a half. "Once a year. And then I never talked to any of the neighbors. Not that they were not nice, you don't run into them."[3]

There was one other family of color in the neighborhood—they lived across the street from her—but Cheryl never met them. The only things that made Cheryl stand out among the middle-class neighbors was the large, 50-foot trailer alongside her house for a few years and her flashy, white Mercedes Benz convertible. The car was originally purchased for her mother, but Shirley didn't like it and the car became Cheryl's.

In 1991, Cheryl was living in the house alone. After her previous improvements to the home, she opted to have an ambitious remodel undertaken on her kitchen. A contractor from nearby Belleview had performed previous renovations and she was generally pleased with their work. She chose the same firm for her kitchen upgrades.

The company started work in late July 1991, ripping out windows on exterior walls and tearing apart the counters of her kitchen. She was often at her bridal shop during the day as they worked, so she didn't pay attention to their comings and goings. What she noticed was the prog-ress, or lack thereof, as she returned home each day. The contractor sent multiple laborers, and they came and went at odd hours. They repeatedly set off her home alarm system. Cheryl grew so frustrated about being forced to return home in the middle of the day and disarming it that she turned the system off.[4]

As the sun was just rising at about 5 a.m. on August 6, 1991, a person took the temporary plasterboard from the exterior bathroom window of Cheryl's house out and climbed in. A few people entered and began pillaging her possessions. They took items like a stereo speaker, cash, a telephone, and tube of red lipstick. They broke several items including the frame of a photo from the 1983 Indy Car test session at Seattle International Raceway. One of the people used her red lipstick to draw a three-foot tall swastika on her living room wall and scrawled "WEISS MACH," a misspelling of Weiss Macht—"White Power" in German.[5]

When Cheryl woke hours later, she found the damage to her home and called the police to report a burglary. Washington State Police officers responded in minutes. She told investigators that she slept through the incident and didn't know what happened.[6]

She told investigators that she had been the victim of several racially motivated incidents perpetrated by neighbors in the prior few years. She said her mailbox was blown up with fireworks and graffiti had been painted on her house. The police were skeptical when she told them she thought the burglary and vandalism of her house were racially motivated.[7]

"I think they were out to steal some stuff, but they wanted to let me know they didn't appreciate who lived here," she said later that day.[8]

Cheryl told police that money was stolen from the nightstand next to her bed while she slept, and the lipstick had been in her purse in her bedroom. The police doubted Cheryl could have slept through the burglary, especially with all the damage done to her house. But she was on so many medications that sleeping soundly even as men pilfered her personal belongings a few feet from her head was plausible.

Later that day, Cheryl posed for a photo next to the "WEISS MACH" script for a newspaper photographer. Her arms crossed in the photo, she had the appearance of someone who was annoyed that something like that would happen to her home than of someone who was intimidated. She talked to newspaper and television reporters later that day about the incident in the same calm manner she did after races.

The contractors from Bellevue returned later that day and cleaned up her house. A couple weeks later, they completed the remodel of her kitchen and left.

Cheryl returned to the police several months later.

She told them she needed to tell them more details about the burglary. Cheryl said there were three men involved in the burglary, and all were skinheads. She said two of the three men had raped her. The police were skeptical of Cheryl after changing her story that long after the incident. The burglary was months earlier and it was too late to gather physical evidence of the rape. Detectives thought something in Cheryl's demeanor was erratic. They asked her to be evaluated by a psychiatrist. She declined.

The police told her that there was nothing more they could do. Stung by the police declining to take action, Cheryl grew distrustful and resentful.

Police spokesperson Rob Barnett said the swastika and writing on her living room wall was likely done to distract from the investigation into the burglary. But he stopped short of discounting the possibility of racial harassment. There had been several incidents of racist messages in vandalism of buildings not far from Cheryl's house in the preceding months. King County Police Lieutenant Harold Hansen said those incidents didn't appear related. Several known hate groups had followings in the Seattle area in the early 1990s and were becoming brazen in spreading their white power messages.

"That's what happened in Germany when the Nazis grew in power in the 1920s. They tell us to ignore these incidents, that these people will go away. Well, history shows that they don't," said Chip Berlet, an activist working for Political Research Associates, a non-profit that studied the political right wing.[9]

Skip Young had been friends with Cheryl for most of their lives. After the rape allegation, Young offered to move in with her. Cheryl accepted. She needed a friend around.

Young's father, Eugene Young Sr., had worked at Boeing with Marvin and Shirley Glass, though in different departments of the vast corporation. Skip Young—the real name of Eugene Young Jr.—and Cheryl grew closer in the late 1980s. He would stop by her shop to talk about racing and life. Skip had raced hydroplanes and was still heavily involved in that type of racing. Though he came and went from Cheryl's life, he always followed her racing career through the media. The pair spoke a common language, though Skip thought Cheryl's passion for racing had diminished by 1991.

Skip started working at Boeing in 1978 after graduating from college. Not long after his father died in 1991, he decided he had enough and quit. He took a series of odd jobs including as a disc jockey, but spent much of his time at her Lago Place house. On any given day, he could be found outside working on projects including gardening. He worked in the yard so much that a few passing neighbors told him that he was making them look bad. He thought they were joking. He didn't realize they weren't.

Shirley Glass encouraged her daughter to date Skip. They became nearly inseparable for the next few years. Cheryl called him her boyfriend while Skip said she was his "companion."

Cheryl was struggling mentally but refused to tell those closest to her. On February 2, 1992, she attempted to kill herself. When the King County Sheriff's office responded to Cheryl's Lago Place house, they found she had attempted to commit suicide by taking a large amount of sleeping pills. She was taken to a nearby hospital where her stomach was pumped.[10] She survived.

For much of their first year as a couple, Cheryl and Skip appeared to be living a relatively normal, quiet life in her secluded house. Cheryl avoided racetracks and hid her inner turmoil from those closest to her. Skip speculated Cheryl's enthusiasm for racing waned because other race car drivers, one of whom was Black and another a woman, had accomplished what she had once set out to. Her goal to be the first Black person to race at the Indianapolis 500 was accomplished by Willy T. Ribbs in 1991.[11] Al Unser Jr., against who Cheryl raced sprint cars in 1980, won the 1992 Indy 500 in his 10th try at the race by a margin of .043 seconds in front of Scott Goodyear.[12] Also in 1992, Lyn St. James, the second woman to race the Indy 500, placed 11th and earned Rookie of the Year honors.[13]

"I don't think she was upset with (Willy T. Ribbs) about him getting to the Indy 500," Hersey Mallory said. "I think the drive had dissipated before that."[14]

Much of what made her special on a racetrack was no longer there for her to pioneer.

"I remember, what was it, '92? The Indy 500 was on (television) and she didn't want to watch it. She didn't want to hear anything about it," Skip Young said. "I was kind of watching it and then she would ask me about some updates. She didn't want to see and hear it. A lot of those guys she had raced against coming up."

Cheryl told people she was again considering racing in the NASCAR Winston West Series in 1992. She still thought that she would one day return to a race car. She complained about how men could be fat and bald and could get sponsors. A woman, she said, had to have a perfect figure, beautiful skin, and perfect hair to attract sponsors.

Marvin sold her Indy Lights car and the remaining racing equipment, including the truck and trailer, at a steep discount.[15] The car was about to lose much of its value as the series was to have a new chassis manufacturer the following year. But the family had gone into debt to finance their family-owned operation and they needed to recoup what they could. They gave up the rental of the race shop south of Boeing, a sign Cheryl was done racing. The remaining boxes of newspaper articles and photos that had accumulated in the shop were moved into Cheryl's old bedroom in Marvin and Shirley's house. Cheryl couldn't bring herself to get rid of even the most trivial records of her accomplishments as a race car driver. She liked being able to prove her successes.

What she did get rid of, however, were her once precious trophies. Those hundreds of trophies residing in her childhood bedroom represented the pinnacle of Cheryl's life. Cheryl had tried hard to live up to those early accomplishments. By ridding herself of those status symbols, she was trying to move past that part of her life.

"She gave those to the young racers coming up," Shirley Glass said.[16]

Cheryl considered other career paths. She talked about going back to college. She had three years of college courses in engineering, but was considering studying forestry or physics.[17]

For the first time in years, Cheryl looked forward to a fresh start.

Then it happened.

On the one-year anniversary of the break-in, August 6, 1992, the event came rushing back. Cheryl was considering having the bathroom of her house remodeled. She contacted the same Bellevue-based contractor who worked on her kitchen the year before. The contractor returned along with a helper to give her a quote on the further renovations.

"I noticed Cheryl was acting a little funny," Skip Young said. "This guy made small talk with me, but there was something real creepy about him. After they left, I said, 'Oh my God, that was one of the guys, wasn't it?' She didn't say nothing.

"I said Cheryl, 'Was that one of the guys?' She nodded her head."

Young convinced Cheryl to report the suspect to the police. She did, but with hesitance. She was already convinced the police wouldn't help her.

"She identified the guy that raped her, and they didn't prosecute him," Shirley Glass said. "It doesn't make sense."[18]

She filed for an anti-harassment order in court against the contractor a month later. She wanted he and his workers to stay away from her home.[19]

Cheryl became single-minded in her pursuit of one of the men she alleged raped her. She tracked him down and found his home an hour's drive away. She staked out his house and looked for clues about who he was and the people he was involved with. Cheryl found a Washington State Police cruiser parked in front of the alleged rapist's house; she learned he was a roommate and nephew of a Washington State trooper. She thought the state police were part of the conspiracy against her. She learned the alleged rapist had ties with local Neo-Nazi and other white supremacist groups.

She took the information to the King County Sheriff's office, and they investigated the man Cheryl alleged was one of the two rapists. Prosecutors contacted the man, and he submitted to a polygraph examination; he passed the test.

They declined to press charges against him.

Cheryl's life then went in a downhill spiral.

Former clients of her wedding dress business sued her, claiming she owed them thousands of dollars. Where she had fought for herself in court before she was raped, she now acted indifferent. On some occasions, she didn't show up for court and was found guilty. She never paid most of the judgments against her.

Cheryl again attempted to commit suicide on August 24, 1992—weeks after seeing her alleged rapist—by overdosing on sleeping pills. Police showed up at her house, revived her, and took her to Providence Hospital to have her stomach pumped.[20]

While in the hospital, Cheryl consented to seeing a psychiatrist. The doctor didn't have her medical records, such as her previous head injuries and the debilitating migraine headaches. She was initially hesitant to the examination, as she had never been to a psychiatrist. She only relented when she decided the psychiatrist could confirm her story and encourage the police to further investigate her alleged rape.

But the psychiatrist diagnosed Cheryl with multiple personality disorder. In the report, they wrote, "she had been raped during the burglary and that several of her multiple personalities had watched the crime occur."[21]

Cheryl, her friends and family refuted the diagnosis of Cheryl having multiple personality disorder. After the diagnosis, the police investigation into her alleged rape ended. The police said there was insufficient evidence of the crime. The King County prosecutor declined to prosecute the alleged rapist in December 1992.

Cheryl was despondent and became convinced a vast police conspiracy was aligned to protect one of her rapists. She also convinced herself of a conspiracy among her neighbors. When she lived on Lago Place with white men, most of the neighbors took little notice of her. When Skip moved in, that changed.

According to Cheryl, having one Black person living on Lago Place was too many for many of the residents.

"I hate to say this, but I don't think they wanted to see anything Black out there other than nighttime," Skip Young said. "It wasn't like we had a lot of people coming out there."

For much of the first decade she lived on Lago Place, Cheryl was frequently travelling to compete in races and for speaking engagements. Before Cheryl was allegedly raped, her neighbors had little idea she lived there. After the incident, the neighbors knew who she was.

CHAPTER THIRTEEN

Repeated Run-ins with the Police Exacerbate Her Mental Illness

1993 to 1994

CHERYL GLASS DISLIKED FEAR.

From the first time she got in a quarter midget in 1971 until the last time she got into an Indy Lights car in 1991, Cheryl was able to push fear out of her mind. Her lack of fear was how she won races. It's what made her who she was.

In confrontations with her neighbors and police in 1993, Cheryl refused to show fear. She was confrontational and assertive in most situations. When someone said a cross word to her, she lobbed one back. Where some people would seek to diffuse potentially confrontational situations, Cheryl's competitive nature didn't allow her to back down. Cheryl needed to win, and she wasn't afraid of the consequences if she didn't.

After the allegations she lobbed against police and their associates after she was raped, run-ins with police became a frequent occurrence. If Cheryl did anything, the police noticed. Police departments near her Lago Place home became more assertive whenever a complaint involving Cheryl came to them. They reacted to her diagnosis of mental illness and treated every incident involving her as a priority.

Between 1986 and 1994, there were 84 instances when officers responded to calls involving Cheryl.[1] The worst year for those encounters was 1993. She had theories about why the police acted increasingly aggressive with her. She speculated that the rape accusation brought more attention from the authorities.

"Why would people want to do this to somebody who had something horrific happen in her house to her?" Skip Young said.[2]

Cheryl thought that the incidents were connected with the accusations she lobbed years before about how government agencies like the CIA and FBI were funneling money through racing. She also became convinced that organized crime played a role.

Her years of peacefully living in the neighborhood were over.

"It was like a war zone," Skip Young said. "I called my mama every day. I wasn't scared of the police, and I wasn't scared of the neighbors. It was just that these folks thought they had a right to do what they wanted to do. One of her neighbors sprayed a water hose on her even though she was on her property line. And they would yell the word, 'Nigger.'"[3]

Cheryl's distrust of police led her to meet with State Representatives James Wineberry and Martin Applewick to air her complaints.[4] The state legislators pressured King County Sheriff James Montgomery to investigate what was happening between her, the Lago Place neighbors, and police. Detective Thad Frampton of the Internal Investigations Unit of the King County Sheriff's office investigated Cheryl's complaints. Frampton determined that Cheryl's claims were unsubstantiated.[5]

After Cheryl's multiple personality diagnosis, she sought mental health help on her own. King County public health staff members referred her to talk with their counselors, but her distrust in that entity was deep. Still, she wanted to disprove the assertion of the hospital psychiatrist. She wanted a different assessment than the one she had received.

In March 1993, Cheryl saw psychiatrist Stuart Bramhall for the first time.[6]

Bramhall was a professor at the University of Washington who specialized in working with people of color, especially those who lacked the financial means to pay for counseling. Despite owning her own business, Cheryl was on Social Security. She was receiving medical coverage from Medicaid, a program that helps with medical costs for people with limited income. For someone who came from means and sold wedding dresses for thousands of dollars, she had financial need.

There was something about Bramhall that made Cheryl trust her immediately. Cheryl felt she could tell Bramhall things she couldn't tell anyone else.

Cheryl unloaded her problems on Bramhall. She told Bramhall the migraines had grown so severe they had become uncontrollable and were causing extreme depression. Cheryl admitted she considered committing suicide. But she didn't go into detail about her two suicide attempts in the prior year or how she had considered killing herself for years.

Cheryl told Bramhall her parents were controlling and taking the profits from her wedding dress business. She said she was getting by on an allowance doled out from her parents. She said her mother had physically assaulted her on several occasions. And she was resentful about financially supporting Skip Young, who was working sparingly in part-time jobs.

Aside from her headaches, Cheryl's multiple physical conditions hindered her further. She had irritable bowel syndrome and frequently suffered from diarrhea. She walked with a limp caused by injuries to her feet and legs from racing. She continued to have chronic knee and ankle pain that kept her from standing for long periods. She had a hiatal hernia, which she knew would require surgery to repair.

"Her life was such that because of her injuries from the past racing accident she had, she didn't really have control of her life," Bramhall said.[7]

When Bramhall dug into the medical records concerning Cheryl's previous multiple personality disorder diagnosis, she found that the doctor who diagnosed her didn't account for large portions of Cheryl's medical history.

Doctors accused Cheryl of seeking opiates unnecessarily, which caused her more anxiety. Bramhall asked Cheryl about Tegretol, a medication typically given to people with seizures. Cheryl said she had tried it, but didn't receive relief when she took it. Bramhall suggested Cheryl give the liquid version of the medication a try, and Cheryl agreed.

"She immediately had relief from the severe migraines. That stopped, and the emergency visits stopped from the migraines," Bramhall said.

Cheryl kept diaries for most of her life, but Bramhall encouraged her to keep detailed notes about every one of the increasing number of encounters with police and neighbors. By keeping track of the incidents,

Bramhall told her, Cheryl could better distinguish what was real and what she perceived. Cheryl and Skip began detailed notetaking about the hundreds of altercations throughout 1993. On some days there were multiple incidents she documented. Many of the entries detailed altercations with the police; the rest were with the neighbors.

An entry by Skip Young said: "On the morning of May 22, 1993, Cheryl Glass was sprayed with water from a garden hose by Richard Underwood, Mrs. Underwood's husband. He sprayed her continually. I called 911. King County Police responded with Officer Seager and Sgt. Swanson. Richard Underwood was not ticketed or arrested for this incident (The previous month—on April 22—when walking past our garden, he told Cheryl, 'kiss my ass!')."[8]

Many of Cheryl's disputes with neighbors centered around the property lines of Cheryl's house at 19262 Lago Place.

Cheryl's house was on the flag lot behind the house recently purchased by Terry and Robin Raymond at 19268 Lago Place. When Cheryl bought her house, there was a gravel driveway that cut through the Raymond's property to the street. It was never part of her property and she didn't have an easement to use the land, but she did anyway. The dirt driveway that was part of Cheryl's right of way was on the edge of the undeveloped land on the edge of Raymond's house and frequently flooded. Cheryl said the dirt path was unpassable in the rainy months, of which there were many in Washington. Cheryl and Skip argued that the only way they could to get in and out of her house was the gravel driveway that cut through the Raymond's property. Cheryl claimed she had documentation including a survey from King County that stated the driveway was part of her property.[9]

When the Raymonds bought the property in June 1993, Cheryl and Skip were initially friendly with the family. Cheryl and Skip built a row of fence posts to separate the properties. The posts cut through the Raymond's property.

"I dug them with no posthole digger," Skip Young said. "They looked real pretty."[10]

Cheryl argued she had an easement to use the gravel road after using it continuously for 10 years; the Raymonds argued she was using it by forcible detainer, and it was a burden on their property. Cheryl argued the Raymond's property was two pieces, the Raymonds argued she had a proper easement to come and go from her house on the edge of the property and not through theirs.

Then the fence posts were torn out. Cheryl and Skip alleged the Raymonds tore the fence posts out, but the Raymonds denied doing so.

"To date, Cheryl has refused to respond to the request to remove 'her fence' from the County right of way. The County plans to remove this fence within the next week or two if Cheryl does not do it voluntarily," a King County officer wrote.[11]

The disputes escalated.

Cheryl had a copy of a book titled *Junkyard Garden* that she read obsessively. The book gave instructions on how to turn found objects into planters. Along the fence line, Cheryl put in a row of found objects like a toilet and shoes that she turned into planters for flowers. She decided if neighbors were going to complain, she would give them something to complain about.

"And then we put lights on it. It was lit up at night. We were very creative," Skip Young said. "They would try to vandalize that, too."

Police followed Cheryl and Skip from their home to a location of the Safeway chain of grocery stores near her home, multiple times in July 1993. On one occasion, Skip went to the store on his own. He pulled into the parking lot and entered the store.

"I came out, a guy said, 'We don't want you niggers in the store. We don't want you in the neighborhood either,'" Skip Young said.

Neighbors thought the behavior of Cheryl and Skip was growing more erratic and irrational. They acknowledged some of the events Cheryl and Skip alleged, such as fence posts being removed and children of neighbors yelling racist remarks at her.

But after dealing with Cheryl's constant complaints and having police show up on their quiet street multiple times per day, neighbors grew frustrated. Cheryl filed lawsuits—three in 1992—and drew their ire.

The neighbors tried to diffuse the situation by bringing in surveyors who were supposed to be neutral to get a determination on the property in question. Each time they did, the surveyors were met with resistance from Cheryl.

A surveyor for the Raymond family, Max Meyring, was trying to determine the property line between Cheryl's house and the Raymond's on July 14, 1993. Meyring was a friend of the Raymond's. He said that while he was going about his work, Cheryl hit him in the arm with a lawn chair she had been sitting in and threatened to hit him with a dog chain. Meyring claimed he received an abrasion on his arm.[12]

Meyring called the police and hours later King County Police officers Sandi Amos-Pitts and K. D. Lange arrived to find Cheryl and Skip working in the garden. Amos-Pitts arrested Cheryl on the charge of fourth degree assault, handcuffed her, and placed her in the back of the police car.

That's where the narrative changes depending on who told it.

Cheryl claimed that when Amos-Pitts and Lange arrested her, they intentionally injured her hands and ankles while she was in the back of the squad car. She said they also injured a valve that had been installed in her esophagus by being so rough.[13]

"One grabbed one hand, the other grabbed the other," said Young, who watched the incident. "There's a quick grab and you twist the hands. It messes with the ligaments. You can't see it on the X-ray. You don't get any broken bones, it's just ligaments are sore. If you're a race car driver, you have to have your hands. The problem they had was with the witness, me. I was there. I saw this."

A neighbor who declined to be identified said that she witnessed Cheryl's arrest from the window of her house.

"She went with them, no problem," the neighbor said.[14]

Cheryl's allegations of police brutality during the incident launched multiple investigations. The officers disputed Cheryl's version of events; investigators sided with the police. Cheryl was convinced the police siding against her was a result of the conspiracy between the police and her neighbors.

"Federal civil rights violation cannot be proven because: Medical evidence inconsistent with allegations; Insufficient evidence to prove subject's criminal intent; Insufficient evidence to prove use of force was excessive," the FBI later found regarding the incident.[15]

For the next six months, Cheryl used a wheelchair to help her get around and wore splints on her hands and ankles. She had surgery on her left ankle on December 23, 1993, and months later had surgery on her

Cheryl Glass sits in a wheelchair in her wedding dress business in downtown Seattle. Her foot is in a boot and both wrists are in braces.
SHIRLEY GLASS COLLECTION

right. She also had surgeries on her hands. Over the next year, she could barely work. Her previous physical ailments were exacerbated, which further caused a decline in her mental health.

The Raymond family grew tired of the constant battles with Cheryl and Skip. They put their house up for sale. On September 21, 1993, they were showing the property to Chan Tak and his family. The Raymonds took the Tak family for a tour through their house, and the Taks told them they were interested in purchasing it. Then they went outside to survey the rest of the property. The Tak family was standing in the gravel driveway and discussed where the property butted up to Cheryl's. When Cheryl saw the Taks, she came out of her house and yelled at them, "Get the fuck off my property. Can't you read the no trespass signs?" She told them any trespassers would be shot on sight.

Robin Raymond told the Taks to ignore Cheryl.

"Fuck you bitch," Cheryl yelled to Robin Raymond.

Cheryl was again arrested and charged with fourth-degree assault. This time the judge issued a "No Contact" order between Cheryl and the neighbors. The Raymonds argued that they were suffering by not being able to sell their home as they desired.[16]

"Each of the defendants is African-American," Cheryl's attorney John Zilvay argued. "There are no other African-Americans living in the neighborhood. The defendants have been the targets and victims of continuous and concerted racially-motivated incidents ever since they purchased and moved to Parcel 2."[17]

The clashes between Cheryl and her neighbors intensified. Terry Raymond spit on Cheryl in one incident. In another, she pulled out an ice pick while having an argument with him. The Raymonds allegedly spray-painted racist graffiti on her house and shrubs. Cheryl allegedly pulled a gun on Terry Raymond.

The rift grew. On one occasion, Terry Raymond played his bass guitar into an amplifier at a deafening level with the speaker pointed at her house and then did the same with the bagpipes. Cheryl responded by pointing her stereo and playing it at maximum volume at the Raymond's house at 6 a.m. and continuing until 11 p.m. Some neighbors claimed Cheryl and Skip were playing country western music, a genre she and Skip abhorred.[18]

"We'd hear all this, what the hell? Okay, you want to play that one," Skip Young said. "He was a big Beatles fan. I got a cassette, it was the Chipmunks playing the Beatles. He was livid."

The noise complaints went back and forth for months.

The police showed up again and again to Cheryl's house. The cases lingered in court for years, long after the Raymonds and Cheryl had moved out of the neighborhood and their former homes were occupied by others. After finding for the Raymond's after a trial, the courts assessed $9,870 in damages to be paid by Cheryl, Marvin, and Skip Young. They never did.

Cheryl was broke.

She was once again reconsidering what she was doing with her life.

"She couldn't define herself," said Lisa Kelsie, her hair stylist.[19]

Cheryl never made much money in racing, and her bridal business was a shell. The business was consistently behind in bills and struggling to make enough money to keep the lights on. Cheryl could hardly work after her surgeries, and she had largely ignored her house in the years after it was broken into. Cheryl got by on money borrowed from her father.

Then she received an unexpected influx of funds.

Seeking to capitalize on the success of sexual thriller movies from the 1990s like *Basic Instinct*, Warner Brothers in 1993 waged a bidding war for film rights for Michael Crichton's upcoming novel, *Disclosure*. Before the book was released in January 1994, Warner Brothers paid $1 million for the movie rights, believing it could be its next blockbuster movie. With a track record of books being made into hugely profitable movies like *Jurassic Park*, *Rising Sun*, and *The Andromeda Strain*, the next movie of a Michael Chrichton book would be a gold mine. The novel focused on a man in Seattle who is sexually harassed by a female superior while working in a computer company. The Seattle area was becoming a hub of tech companies. It was a natural for Crichton to place the fictional company, DigiCom, in the Puget Sound.[20]

The movie was fast tracked into development with Michael Douglas, Donald Sutherland, Dennis Miller, and Demi Moore signing on to star, and Barry Levinson signing up to direct. Like the book, the movie was set in Seattle, and much of the production was to be filmed around the Puget Sound. Though the interior scenes at the DigiCom offices were to be filmed on a sound stage in Los Angeles, the producers wanted an authentic Seattle building for exterior shots of the office building.

There were a few locations in the downtown core that showed some promise from a design standpoint. Something drew them to 102 Occidental Avenue Southwest, Cheryl's wedding studio.

Few Seattle locations had the character of Cheryl's business, and the location scouts were convinced it would look good on motion picture screens. But Cheryl played hard to get. She needed the money more than she would admit, but the first few times studio representatives asked her if they could film there, she put them off. She acted as if she had more important things to concern herself with. When a Warner Brothers location scout approached Cheryl, she replied, "I don't have time."[21]

After being spurned, the production company scouted several other locations in downtown Seattle, but they eventually decided Cheryl's business was the location they had to have. Besides the red brick façade of the building, they were attracted to the ornamental cement over the front door with a lion above the archway of the front doors.

She was days from insolvency. That didn't stop Cheryl from driving a hard bargain for the use of her shop.

"She said they were going to turn the phone off on Friday and on Monday she got a call, they were going to do that movie at her shop," Lisa Kelsie said. "It was like one week before the phone was going to be turned off. She said, 'We're getting $30,000.' It was like $10,000 for three weeks. That was a blessing."

The money was enough to keep her and her financially-strapped business afloat for years. Cheryl moved the dresses and equipment from her showroom into the basement of the building. For the three weeks of filming, Cheryl decided to treat the bonus as a vacation. It was supposed to be the first time in years she could relax at home. She deposited the checks from Warner Brothers and took on a few small gardening projects around her house while they filmed.

The set designers turned her business into the lobby of DigiCom for the movie. They redecorated the space slightly, including repainting some walls, to make it look like their intended purpose. Cheryl had no interest in watching the filming of the movie. She had so much of the spotlight for so much of her life, Cheryl Glass preferred to stay away from attention for once. Her mother and sister, Cherry, were curious about the filming and came to the shop to see what was going on. They stood outside and looked in the windows to watch some of the filming.

"The police told us to move because we were looking in the windows," Shirley Glass said.[22]

After filming on the picture had wrapped, the production team began the arduous task of restoring her shop to its previous condition.

"They come back and they're repainting it," Skip Young said. "She goes, 'Skip, they're painting it the wrong color.' I said, 'Oh, really.' I said, 'Why don't you tell them to stop.' It's in the contract that if they don't paint it the right color, they have to repaint it and pay her $2,500. I just had to laugh at that. That's called fortune without fame."

But Cheryl's brief vacation had made her other problems worse.

CHAPTER FOURTEEN

Home Becomes a Battleground

1993 to 1996

CHERYL GLASS FELT SHE COULD DEAL WITH ADULTS WITH WHOM SHE had problems. When it came to people around her own age, whether the incidents were good or bad, she could deal with them. But she struggled with children.

A group of teenagers who lived in Cheryl's Lago Place neighborhood taunted her repeatedly. She complained to law enforcement about Colby Underwood, Sean Thornburg, and Joshua Piano, saying they harassed her nearly every day. The mother of one of the teenagers alleged Cheryl had hit her with a rake. Cheryl accused the Underwood family of removing the fence posts she and Skip installed along her driveway. Cheryl struggled when the boys were around.[1]

The school bus that brought the boys home from school dropped them off at a stop on Lago Place near Cheryl's house. Whether they saw her or not, they yelled verbal abuses at her and Skip. The boys spray painted "FUCK YOU NIGGER" on a three-foot-by-four-foot sign and placed it in front of her house. She said they blocked her driveway with a Kool-Aid stand repeatedly and stomped her plants. In one instance, one boy yelled, "Why don't you blow me? I'll give you five dollars to suck my dick!"[2]

Cheryl persuaded the school district to move their bus stop 250 feet away so they would no longer be in her vicinity. But when a substitute driver was brought in, he dropped the boys off back in front of her house.

Cheryl and Skip complained to the school district and were issued an apology. In December 1993, Cheryl was granted an order of anti-harassment against 15-year-old Colby Underwood, requiring him to refrain from making derogatory comments about her.

Police came and went from Cheryl's house so often that she and Skip were on a first-name basis with many of them. Cheryl didn't get along with most of the officers. One police officer who responded to a call asked if he could touch her hair.

"Officer (Derrick) McCauley, he just walks right in," to the house, Skip Young said. "He says, 'Your alarm went off.' She says, 'I don't have an alarm.' No hard feelings against him, just bizarre stuff. Some of it, you couldn't even be mad about. Some of it was so ridiculous."[3]

King County Police officer Kevin Johannes was one of the few officers Cheryl and Skip got along with. When Johannes answered a call, he was usually able to diffuse the situation and calm down all the parties. But in early 1993, he was transferred to another detail within the department. The incidents at Cheryl's house so frustrated the police that the department brought Johannes back to the beat that included her house to try to improve the situation.

"He was a guy who really tried to help," Skip Young said. "He come back, he was like, 'What the hell happened?'"

The neighbors had enough of Cheryl. In their view, they were concerned for their safety after what they viewed as erratic behavior of Cheryl and Skip. They also disliked how the frequent police presence disturbed their quiet neighborhood.

Eight neighbors petitioned the King County Department of Public Safety in June 1993, asking police to intervene in the disputes. They wrote to the police about an instance when Cheryl sat in a lawn chair in the rain at 5 a.m., gardening in a gas mask, multiple violent threats she directed at neighbors, death threats, Cheryl and Skip essentially living in a van in the driveway for long periods so they could watch the neighbors, and Cheryl throwing glass into neighbors' driveways. Officers from King County agreed to meet with the neighbors at a police station.

"The police didn't organize the neighbors. We asked for their help," a neighbor who refused to be identified said.[4]

In the letter to the police, the neighbors expressed concern over what they considered hostile behavior on the part of Cheryl and Skip. They detailed how Cheryl threatened neighbors by saying things like "Do you want to be on the hit list with them?" pointing to a neighbor's house. "They're going to be dead in three weeks." They said she threatened to burn down the house of one of her neighbors. They said she explained to a neighbor in detail how she was going to sodomize another neighbor before killing her.

They felt Cheryl's behavior had become increasingly aggressive, and they said they didn't understand why. "Ms. Glass seems to alternate between this very aggressive, calculating, foul-talking person and a mild but recalcitrant 10-year-old. We have not been able to discover the motivation for these wild swings of personality, however, we are concerned that they are growing more extreme and that Ms. Glass is a danger to herself and the community," the neighbors wrote the police.[5]

According to Cheryl's version of the events, however, the authorities had recruited the neighbors, and formed a joint effort to have her prosecuted. She thought the neighbors were jealous of her notoriety and that she maintained her home better than theirs.

After meeting with her neighbors, the police wanted to have a similar meeting with Cheryl and Skip. Cheryl had grown so untrusting that she didn't want to have the meeting in her home. In September 1993, Cheryl agreed to meet with King County Police Major Jackson Beard and Sargent Clem Rusk at a restaurant with Skip and her parents. For an hour, Cheryl gave a detailed description of incidents she was having with her neighbors. She said she was tired of the police department's disrespectful attitude toward her.

Beard said he was impressed with how well spoken and educated Cheryl and her family were. He told Cheryl that her negative opinion of police contributed to the problems between her and officers who responded to her calls. He told them the frequency of disputes led officers to be wary when they responded to one of her calls.

"That's why officers unsnap their guns when approaching you is because they feel threatened," Beard told them. "That one second can make the difference between life and death."

Cheryl and Skip provided the detailed logs they had been keeping of incidents with the neighbors.

"There are over 100,000 Black people living in the neighborhood. I don't think that they would be doing this. Maybe this isn't a Black thing," Rusk told them.

"Then why are we being called niggers, then?" Cheryl asked him.[6]

At about noon on a day in October 1993, Skip Young's mother, Mary, arrived at Cheryl's house in her white Cadillac to take the couple to lunch. A couple hours later, they returned to the house and saw an unmarked brown car in the driveway of her home. A short white man got out, walked to the Cadillac and identified himself as King County Police Detective Warren Myers. Myers only addressed Mary, ignoring Cheryl and Skip, and told her that no one was at the house and she didn't need to go there. The detective got in his car and drove away. Mary continued to drive up to the house and dropped Skip and Cheryl off at their front door. Mary drove away and returned minutes later, telling Skip and Cheryl that the detective pulled her over and wanted to know who she and Skip were.

"They could be robbers," she said Myers told her.[7]

Minutes later, King County and Lake Forest Police arrived at the house after Myers called in a burglary in progress. After Cheryl and Skip showed their identification, the police left.

"I went down to the station and went over to his desk and had a few words with him right at his desk," Skip Young said.

Despite her concerns that the Federal Bureau of Investigation was involved in the conspiracy against her, Cheryl felt she needed to do something and filed a formal complaint with the agency.

The FBI opened a case in September 1993, assigning agent Nori Hamilton to it. Cheryl's initial interview with Hamilton lasted two hours. Cheryl laid out her version of events yet again. It was a relatively easy speech by that point. Cheryl told Hamilton that she wanted officer Sandi Amos-Pitts to be prosecuted for beating her and causing injuries to her ankles. She wanted the rest of the King County Sheriff's Office to be prosecuted for other abuses she suffered. Hamilton interviewed

Cheryl's doctors and surgeons about the medical procedures she had undergone and the ones she had upcoming.

Cheryl told the FBI that she and Skip had been singled out because they were Black.

"The King County Police have created, condoned and endorsed a philosophy of non-assistance to us, fostering a hate-filled climate where people think they can do anything to us, they are active participants in this continued violation of our civil rights," Cheryl wrote.

According to Cheryl, Hamilton told her, "Maybe you shouldn't call the police anymore."[8]

Cheryl criticized King County executive Gary Locke for failing to act on her behalf and wanted him to be removed from his position. She asked for the resignation of King County Sheriff James Montgomery as well.

None of that happened.

The FBI investigated. It went as far as to perform a surveillance of the neighborhood in an effort to uncover the truth.

"They had the undercover guys, they'd be walking the street," Skip Young said. "I said, 'Hi, Mr. Undercover FBI Agents.' They said, 'How'd you know?' I said, 'It was the shoes, those big block shoes.' The thing about not having any sense of humor, that's true. They ain't no fun."

The FBI brought in the U.S. Justice Department's Civil Rights unit due to the nature of Cheryl's racially-based allegations. They went through every police file involving her and dug through the scrupulous notes she and Skip kept about altercations with neighbors.

But after three months, the FBI couldn't substantiate most of Cheryl's allegations.

What the FBI determined in the final reports were the property line disputes and noted Cheryl's erratic behavior. In December 1993, the case was closed.[9]

To Cheryl, her claims being dismissed by another authority was further evidence of a conspiracy against her. She was convinced that law enforcement agencies were scheming to persecute her because of the star she had once been.

"Some neighbors are making statements that Eugene and I have mental problems," Cheryl said. "They need to prove all of us Black people have mental problems."[10]

One of Gary Locke's aides with King County told the media that if the public were to look at the police records, they would see there was no substance to Cheryl's allegations.

By May 1994, four of the eight families on the street had moved; Cheryl said she wasn't going anywhere.

Cheryl was already seeing psychiatrist Stuart Bramhall for help with her mental health issues. But she also wanted proof that her diagnosis of multiple personality disorder, which police and prosecutors repeatedly used against her, was untrue.

"She said, 'Maybe you need to ask me about Ms. Booty, that what Skip likes.' Throw me in the mix here. We had a laugh about that one," Skip Young said.

Cheryl's distrust of the police grew.

She was confined to a wheelchair for months after undergoing another surgery. When John Anderson, the brother-in-law of Cheryl's neighbor, Regina Foucht, came to visit in February 1993, he drove to the Foucht's house to visit. Anderson accused Cheryl of pelting his parked 1993 Nissan Pathfinder with rocks when he parked on the street, according to the police report. Cheryl told him he was trespassing and threatened to call the police. Anderson alleged that Skip picked up a shovel and advanced on him, prompting him to make a hasty retreat back to his car. The next day Anderson returned with his young daughters and parked across the street. Cheryl again threw rocks at his Nissan. Anderson was frustrated and picked up some rocks and threw them back at Cheryl. He called the police on her and a warrant for her arrest was issued.[11]

Skip insisted he and Cheryl didn't throw rocks at Anderson. If he wanted to inflict damage, Skip said, he would have hit the Nissan with a baseball bat.

"People want to act like Cheryl's the villain here when she wanted to live peacefully," Skip Young said.[12]

As authorities weren't doing anything to help her, Cheryl organized a protest on the neighborhood in March 1994. She gathered dozens of friends and led them from her wheelchair through the Lago Place neighborhood. Supporters carried signs saying, "No More Race War," "Racist Police State," and "Justice for Cheryl Glass," as they followed her. Television and newspaper cameras captured the scene.[13]

Between 1993 and 1994, Cheryl was arrested 13 times by police, charged with eight misdemeanors and one felony charge of malicious mischief and reckless endangerment. After meeting with King County prosecutor Norm Maleng in March 1994, he decided it was a no-win situation for the county. Two months later Maleng announced the county was dropping all charges against Cheryl and Skip. Some of the civil lawsuits between Cheryl and her neighbors would linger in courts for years. But King County wanted to avoid Cheryl more than she wanted to avoid them.[14]

Though she harbored deep resentment toward public officials, Cheryl decided the charges being dropped gave her an opportunity to move on.

Cheryl recovered enough from the surgeries that she thought she could put her life back together. To her, that involved returning to driving race cars. With the migraines under control, Cheryl decided she needed to get back in racing shape. She lost over 45 pounds in an effort to regain her prior fitness.

"She really wanted to return to racing, but she was too obese to fit in a car. That was her goal and she did accomplish the weight loss," Stuart Bramhall said.[15]

Nothing came from her desire to return to racing, however.

Cheryl's years of problems with neighbors and police caused her to ignore her wedding dress business for long periods. When she did pay attention to her business, it wasn't with the focus as she once had. She went from being late in paying rent on the Occidental shop to not paying it at all.

When she was at the business, strange things happened.

In one instance, a cross-dressing man came to her store and sat in front of her while she was at her desk. He started to remove his clothes while talking with her. She asked him to leave and he took the rest of his clothes off while walking out the front door.[16]

In another instance, a couple asked for a discount on a wedding dress, but she refused. She said the couple retaliated by throwing her down the stairs and locked her in the bathroom. When police arrived, they again sided against Cheryl.

"One time, I remember this that came up, that she had gone to the bathroom or something," Shirley Glass said. "Cherry wanted to talk to her because one of the customers had said something icky about Blacks or something while my older daughter was out of the room. My younger daughter told my older girl that she wanted to talk to her, and she told her. She said, 'Don't worry about it, Cherry, I'll take care of it.' You know how my daughter took care of problems? Charged them more money."[17]

Lisa Kelsie came into the store one day to see Cheryl and was shocked by her appearance. For much of her life, Cheryl fretted over every stitch of clothing and her hair had to be perfect at all times.

"I do know that a couple of times I went to the shop she was sitting behind the desk. I said, 'You look like a homeless person,'" Kelsie said. "I think she just needed someone to talk to."[18]

Cheryl was repeatedly sued by clients for whom she didn't deliver wedding dresses. She failed to show up for court for some of the cases, and even when she did, the plaintiffs always won.

Cheryl and Skip had lived together as boyfriend and girlfriend for four years. In 1995, Marvin approached Skip and told him it was time for him to move on.

"I kind of looked at that as his way of coming in and saying, 'Okay I got this,'" Skip Young said.

Marvin Glass told Shirley he wanted a divorce. She didn't fight the dissolution of the marriage after 35 years, but fought to keep the family house. Shortly before the divorce was finalized, Marvin took out a loan on the house without her knowledge.

"I've always said, 'Go on. Don't be making everybody's life miserable,'" Shirley Glass said. "That's stupid. Move on. You don't want to be here, move on. But don't try to take everything from me, that's stupid. He tried to take everything. That's what a lot of lawsuits and things were about. He wanted to get everything."

Cheryl had been through a lot and vowed to remain in her house on Lago Place. But she eventually reached a breaking point.

One day in February 1996, Cheryl and members of her family got into her van to leave the Lago Place home. When Cheryl tried to start the engine, it wouldn't turn over. She smelled gasoline and got out. When she inspected the van, she found the fuel line had been cut and gasoline was leaking onto the floorboard. She said that days earlier police had searched her van. When she took the van to a mechanic, he told her the van should have burned and exploded. It was enough of a scare that Cheryl finally decided to leave the neighborhood.[19]

After separating from Shirley, Marvin moved into an apartment in the Bothell neighborhood not far away. Cheryl moved in with him because she didn't want to be alone.

"I know her father lived in the small apartment with her while Cherry and Shirley lived in the big house," Lisa Kelsie said.

While the rest of her life had collapsed, Cheryl found a new purpose.

CHAPTER FIFTEEN

A Descent into Despair

1996 to 1997

CHERYL GLASS HAD BEEN SEARCHING FOR A PURPOSE.

When Cheryl protested how police treated her, she found something that had been missing. In protests, she could be as loud and expressive as she wanted. The more she made noise and gathered attention at a protest, the better. Cheryl decided being a disrupter was better than being a victim.

Much like when she gave speeches to rooms full of executives when she was in her 20s, Cheryl's dynamic voice carried weight with the audiences at protests. She found comfort in being the center of attention again, especially when the people were following her message and not following what she represented.

"For her, that seemed a really good outlet," her psychiatrist Stuart Bramhall said. "She was finally being able to fight back against the harassment she experienced."[1]

When Cheryl found a cause to protest, she took it. Bramhall referred Cheryl to several community groups she had been involved with including Mothers Against Police Harassment. Cheryl joined a group called Refuse & Resist!, which opposed police brutality among other causes. When a group sought to buy a building from the school district in Seattle to turn into a museum about Black history, Cheryl gathered friends to go to the meeting and speak in support of the sale.

Antonio Jackson, a 25-year-old Black man was visiting Washington from Oakland, California, on December 14, 1993. Jackson was at a Safeway in Federal Way, just south of Seattle, and one of the security guards said they thought they saw him steal a pack of cigarettes. Donald Carrick and Scott Elston, two white men, chased Jackson down, wrestled him to the ground and put him in a choke hold. Jackson suffocated and died. Police were slow to call for medical attention for Jackson and stopped a bystander from resuscitating him. A jury found Carrick and Elston negligent in his death, and Safeway settled with Jackson's family a year later.[2]

Cheryl joined in a protest in front of the Federal Way Safeway store where he died in 1996, and television stations filmed the protest and reported on it.

Cheryl tried to enlist support from some of her former racing friends to join her growing number of causes. Many had a hard time recognizing her at first because they hadn't seen her in years. She figured active racing stars could help bring more attention to her causes. But the only thing race car drivers protest is each other when someone is cheating, and that's only to get them disqualified.

Cheryl found a group of protesters with whom she connected, however: the Revolutionary Communist Party. With them, she was no longer the one trying to rally support. The support found her.

The party, formed by Bob Avakian in 1975, was organized to overthrow the capitalism of the United States and replace it with socialism. Cheryl found the group through a connection in one of the party's associated groups, the October 22 Coalition to Stop Police Brutality. The Revolutionary Communist Party became notorious for infiltrating peaceful protests and marches and inciting violence. Several people suspected the group had been infiltrated by the FBI or was started by the FBI for the purpose of identifying and tracking radicals.

Cheryl started taking part in protests with the Seattle chapter of the Revolutionary Communist Party and was immediately struck by their dedication and passion to their cause. One of the Seattle chapter's leaders was a man known as Reid Swick. He was struck by Cheryl's fearlessness, even in the face of authority.

At one protest, a group of people went to Pike Place Market in downtown Seattle after a group had been arrested for stomping on an American flag days earlier.

"There were a lot of cops standing across the street watching us," Reid Swick said. "She said, 'Are we going to do this, or what?' The rest of us were hesitant, but that's how she was. She was brave."[3]

Cheryl had little money, but gave what she could to the Revolutionary Communist Party. She gave speeches about how the American capitalist society enslaved people and makes its own crime by giving people no hope. She spoke of how Pike Place should be renamed Revolution Market.

After her many run-ins with police, Cheryl refused to live alone, and it wasn't long until she moved out of the apartment she shared with her father and into an apartment with Swick—about 100 feet from the Aurora Bridge.

Being involved in causes didn't stop Cheryl's other problems but made them seem like a distraction.

Cheryl stopped paying the $1,200 monthly rent for her wedding dress business at 102 Occidental Avenue in August 1996. The building's owner filed a lawsuit, seeking to evict her. Cheryl's multiple excuses, including arguing that she hadn't been informed of a change in ownership of the property and that she had been sending payments to the prior owner, didn't work. The prior landlord had no record of receiving them. The reality was Cheryl had little money. Even after her parents would pay her back rent, she would inevitably fall behind again.[4]

Cheryl wouldn't let go of her wedding dress business, no matter how bad business was. She also wouldn't let go of her racing career, no matter that the sport had left her behind. And she couldn't let go of the brutality she suffered at the hands of the police.

Seattle civil rights attorney John R. Muenster filed a $1 million lawsuit on Cheryl's behalf in district court against King County, King County Sheriff James Montgomery and officers Sandi Amos-Pitts and K. D. Lange on July 10, 1996. She claimed the police department was propagating a Fascist conspiracy against her.[5]

Cheryl did what she could to draw attention to the case. She tried to get local newspapers interested, but had no success. She tried national television shows like *A Current Affair* and talk shows hosted by Montel Williams, Oprah Winfrey, Maury Povich, and Geraldo Rivera.[6] The producers of some of the shows talked with her and showed interest, but none took up her cause. Cheryl Glass was no longer a prime candidate for attention.

Jim Galasyn was a student in a class that Bramhall was teaching at the University of Washington while working a day job at Boeing in 1996. Galasyn was interested in conspiracy theories involving the U.S. government such as the Iran-Contra Affair. He had a degree in electrical engineering from Massachusetts Institute of Technology and had lived in Seattle most of his life, but had never heard of Cheryl.

Bramhall brought Cheryl's situation to Galasyn's attention and suggested he meet with her. Cheryl wanted to get her story out, and Galasyn was one of the few people Bramhall knew who was proficient in early message boards on the internet. In the fall of 1996, Galasyn set up an appointment to meet with Cheryl in her bridal shop. The first time he entered the business, she was sitting in a wheelchair with both feet in casts. As she laid out her story for nearly two hours, he paid rapt attention and was immediately interested.

Cheryl told him her theories about what happened to her. She explained how, after her threats of exposing the Drug Enforcement Agency when she was racing in Indy Lights, the agency propagated a vast conspiracy that led to her being raped in 1991. This was followed by the ensuing years of repeated abuse by her neighbors and police. She had no skills with computers and needed help connecting with others who might sympathize with her.

Cheryl wrote a two-page narrative of her version of events, including the lawsuit and a *Seattle Times* story from when her house was burglarized.

"Will Cheryl live long enough to see her suit through? This file is Cheryl's insurance policy—please propagate it to interested parties on the net," Galasyn posted.

"It would be her story, by her, by Cheryl Glass," Jim Galasyn said. "If anyone would want to contact her, they would contact her directly. Not as many people had the technical skills to do it. She had other things on her mind rather than learning how to do internet bulletin boards. She had printed up her story and I said, 'Email it to me.' She emailed the story."[7]

Galasyn routed the post through a series of remailers to remain anonymous and keep from being attached to her story for fear of being sucked into the conspiracy. He posted it in multiple places on the internet, including on sites for people concerned with police abuse.

"The thing was she felt like she was under continuous surveillance," Jim Galasyn said. "There were mysterious men hanging around her store. She said all of that stopped for at least a few weeks after that."

Cheryl began telling people if she died, the cause wouldn't be suicide. She was convinced government forces were closing in on her.

After joining the Revolutionary Communist Party, Cheryl was able to funnel her energy into activities like protests and her mood seemed to improve. Some people in Cheryl's life were concerned about Reid Swick. Galasyn said that Reid Swick wasn't the real name of Cheryl's boyfriend.

Cheryl Glass attended many protests around Seattle for a number of causes.
SHIRLEY GLASS COLLECTION

"I was admonishing her about dating Mark Taylor-Canfield," Galasyn said.

At first things were good between Cheryl and Swick, as were the early days of many of Cheryl's relationships. The two had some ideological differences but bonded over their shared activism and views about police abuse. Their relationship declined quickly. Cheryl trusted him less as the days went on. She soon found herself despondent.

"Over a period of two or three months, she had been requesting a lot of emergency appointments because of a lot of conflict with the boyfriend, the RCP boyfriend, his name was Reid," Bramhall said. "When I last saw her, she told me she was convinced he worked for the government. And he was trying to undermine her."

In an attempt to increase her physical fitness, Cheryl started going for walks over the Aurora Bridge.

Cheryl's perceived failures trapped her in an endless spiral. The attention she once received from others, feting her for being a trailblazer and being the best, had dried up. People were forgetting her. Those who did see her were shocked at her appearance.

In the spring of 1997, Cheryl reconnected with Dave Griffith, who she viewed as an uncle figure. He had remained friends with Shirley Glass. He lived close to the apartment Cheryl shared with Swick and visited her frequently. He noticed something was different. He decided he would see her another time.

Galasyn stopped by Cheryl's business for a visit in June 1997 and there was something wrong about her mood. She was restless and unable to relax. Her mind raced with thoughts about how the conspirators were going to kill her.

Not long after, Skip Young was walking past Cheryl's bridal shop. They remained friendly after their breakup. They had been friends since childhood and there was no acrimony. But Young didn't stop that day. Something stopped him.

For much of her life, Cheryl held her hair as a symbol of beauty and power. She wouldn't wear sponsor caps like other race car drivers because she didn't want to disturb her hair. In 1997, Cheryl told stylist Lisa Kelsie she wanted to grow her hair down to the middle of her back, a long mane of hair she hadn't worn in years.

Cheryl had an appointment with Kelsie for a routine haircut in early July 1997. Days before her appointment, Cheryl called Kelsie and left her a voicemail informing her she was calling off the appointment. Cheryl said she had cut off her hair. Kelsie knew something was wrong.

Any physical exertion took its toll on Cheryl.

The injuries sustained over the years while racing—and the many surgeries that followed—added up. The act of going for a walk could be difficult for her even on good days.

In the summer of 1997, several people saw Cheryl on the Aurora Bridge. Some saw her walking from one side of the bridge to the other and others saw her standing in the middle of the span, looking over the railing. The Aurora Bridge had a reputation as the "suicide bridge" of Seattle; most people who knew the city knew what that meant.[8]

Cheryl spent the morning of July 15, 1997, in her apartment on Whitman Avenue. She talked with her father, Marvin, by phone three times that morning. Then she called her sister, Cherry, at 2 p.m. What she spoke about with her family members is unknown.

It was a relatively cool July day, even by Seattle standards, topping out at 67 degrees. Cheryl put on a dark blue shirt and a zip-front gray hooded sweatshirt, a pair of long black pants and a gray wool hat. For so much of her life, fashion was synonymous with Cheryl's identity. On this day she wore non-descript clothing.

Cheryl left the apartment on Whitman Avenue at about 4 p.m., carrying a briefcase. Her walk to the Aurora Bridge took less than 10 minutes. The afternoon traffic on the bridge was significant, but Cheryl didn't stop. Nothing separated her from the cars zipping by as people drove home and she paid them no attention. She walked to the middle of the bridge and felt a slight afternoon breeze as she peered over the short railing. Where she stopped in the middle of the bridge, the water flowed 140 feet below.

Propelling herself over the short railing of the Aurora Bridge would require her to use every bit of strength she could. But it was the one thing that would end her pain.

The dizzying highs of Cheryl Glass's life were no longer relevant.

People who survive suicide attempts by jumping off bridges say that as soon as they get over the railing, they realize their problems aren't as hopeless as they thought. Cheryl Glass might have thought that when she jumped off the railing of the Aurora Bridge. No one will know because Cheryl stood no chance of surviving.

It took about three seconds for her body to hit the water.

Steve Mason was driving north across Aurora Bridge at 4:37 p.m. and saw a person standing next to the railing. After passing the person, Mason looked in the rearview mirror of his car. He didn't see anyone on the bridge anymore and called the police. At the same time, Sean Bull was paddling his kayak in the water beneath the bridge, not far from his home. He heard a loud splash, turned around and saw a body floating face down in the lake. He paddled to where he heard the splash to see what happened. He found a body. Bull then paddled a short distance back home and called the police.

In the 57-degree water, Cheryl Glass's body floated.

At 4:41 p.m., a harbor patrol boat was dispatched. In seconds, the boat reached her body and officers pulled her from the water onto the deck, where they tried CPR. One person piloted the boat back to the nearby station while another continued to try to resuscitate her. By the time they reached dry ground, medics from the Seattle Fire Department had arrived and continued to give Cheryl CPR for a few minutes. The injuries she suffered were so severe the medics gave up. She landed in the water on her right side, causing significant trauma to her torso, breast, and thigh. She also received a cut on her torso. The impact of falling from 140 feet caused lacerations to her spleen, liver, and aorta, and fractures of her left ribs. The impact with the water killed her nearly instantly.

The paramedics declared Cheryl Glass dead at 4:54 p.m. on July 15, 1997. She was 35 years old.[9]

"I had a friend who had a business right under the bridge, Larry Stewart," said Jim Grantham, her former sprint car crew chief. "It wasn't uncommon for somebody to jump off there. Larry Stewart said, 'They ought to put a dumpster there.'"[10]

The only property police found on Cheryl's body was her driver's license in the pocket of her sweatshirt, but it didn't help much. The photo on the license was old and barely resembled the person the authorities found. Cheryl's listed next of kin was her mother, Shirley, and the police initially only had Cheryl's Lago Place address from where to find Shirley. Officers spoke with neighbors of the Lago Place house who informed them the house was in Shirley's name, but it had been rented to others for over a year. Four hours later, at about 9 p.m., officer Dale Amundsen finally made his way to Shirley's house on 42nd Avenue. He informed Shirley and Cherry that Cheryl was dead.

Television stations and newspapers picked up the story of how the one-time star race car driver had killed herself. Skip Young, who days earlier decided he would later return to see her, found out Cheryl had died when a couple of his neighbors told him they saw it on television.

Cheryl had registered as an organ donor. Reluctantly Shirley approved the organ harvest. Cheryl's heart and eyes were removed and donated to others.

When medical examiner Norman Thiersch examined Cheryl's body the next day, he ruled her death a suicide. No suicide note was found. Thiersch found extensive scarring throughout her body, a combination of injuries from driving race cars and surgeries she had after run-ins with police. Cheryl had two scars on her forehead, two on her abdomen, parallel scars on her right knee, one on her right wrist, another on her right hand, one on her right thigh, and another on her left ankle and foot.

A toxicology screening of Cheryl found no evidence of Cheryl abusing illegal drugs, but it did show elevated levels of benzodiazepines, a common class of sedative used to treat anxiety and depression. It didn't find the Tegretol she had taken for years to deal with the migraines.[11]

From the moment she was notified of her daughter's death, Shirley Glass was convinced that Cheryl hadn't killed herself. When police delivered Cheryl's still-wet clothes, she looked them over, placed them in plastic bags and put them in a freezer in her basement. They remained there for decades.

"I looked at her clothes," Shirley Glass said. "If you look at them, you see, this is weird, why would somebody cut the clothes the way that they did? And then there were a pair of panties in there. They were new and they were cheap. My daughter and my other daughter, they were picky about their underwear. She had on brand new clothes. Why would a person who committed suicide put on new clothes?"[12]

After the autopsy, Cheryl's body was cremated. Her ashes were placed in an urn that resembled a trophy and placed on a shelf in her mother's home next to some of Cheryl's remaining racing trophies, including the one she received for rolling over a quarter midget more than any other driver.

Shirley feared Cheryl had been killed by the police, something Cheryl had warned was an inevitability. Cherry, who had graduated from college and had a pilot's license, had always dreamed of traveling abroad. Shirley paid for her to travel to Europe after Cheryl's death.

About a week after Cheryl's death, Shirley received a letter. The writer was a man who said he had been working on a building near Aurora Bridge and saw Cheryl's death. The writer said he saw someone throw her off the bridge. Shirley read the letter closely and thought it seemed legitimate. But she placed it in Cheryl's diary and hid it in her house where no one would find it. She never saw it again. Shirley feared bringing the letter to the police would bring repercussions on her and her family. She didn't mention the letter to anyone for 20 years.

Until she died in 2022, Shirley often proclaimed that Cheryl did not commit suicide. She said there were too many inconsistencies in the evidence.

"And one of the things that bothered me is that the briefcase came, somebody gave it to the police department and they said it was located on the opposite side of where she jumped," Shirley said. "Recently one of my friends told me recently that the briefcase was left on her door."[13]

At the time of her death, Cheryl's financial situation was more dire than anyone knew. She owed $28,696.39 from court cases dating back to 1987 and had other debts that weren't recorded. A few debts were paid by her mother after her death, but most were never paid.

Some people who knew Cheryl thought that she was driven to commit suicide through an intricate psychological attack waged over the prior seven years by the government. Some speculated that her death had something to do with organized crime. They speculated that the year's-long campaign had culminated in Cheryl's giving up and killing herself.

"A lot of us thought that it was a message," Galasyn said.

Some speculated Cheryl had been diagnosed with multiple sclerosis or another debilitating disease, but her autopsy found no signs of any such illness.

Skip Young said he was skeptical about the claims of Cheryl committing suicide by jumping off a bridge because she never wanted to get her hair wet. He knew how physically limited she was and thought she would have had a hard time climbing over even a three-foot tall railing on her own. But he also knew it would be hard to have thrown her off.

"I can't see how someone could pick her up and push her off of there," Young said. "They'd have had a fight on their hands. Her knees were bad, so for her to get up there and do that would have took some effort. Could someone have thrown her off? You know, that's a tough one."[14]

Her friends wondered if there had been more they could have done to prevent her death, as if had they reached out they could have prevented the outcome. Cheryl called for help so many times that there was regret about not doing more to assist her.

But Cheryl's history of mental illness, including depression, and multiple head injuries had compounded. It appeared she had finally accomplished what she had tried to with the previous suicide attempts and threats of killing herself.

"You don't throw somebody off the Aurora Bridge in the middle of the day, in the middle of the day when there's traffic," Lisa Kelsie said.[15]

Cheryl's funeral was held July 22, 1997, at Mt. Zion Baptist Church in Seattle, the church she had grown up attending. A subdued crowd of about 200 people watched Reverend Samuel McKinney officiate a program that focused on her early years. The program read like a resume of her good times, back when Cheryl was accomplishing a first for a Black woman every weekend. Much like the huge bridal party at her first wedding, Cheryl had a large group of honorary pallbearers. Florence Durden, Dave Fisher, Dave Griffith, Karl Holifeld, Kay Omera, Sally Kaye, Lisa Kelsie, Vi Mar, Patsy Taylor, Sally Thomas, and her ex-husband Richard Lindwall all served.[16]

At the funeral, Cheryl's boyfriend, Reid Swick, wanted to distribute political pamphlets to the attendees, informing them of the conspiratorial forces he was sure plotted against her.

"I don't know how, I ended up being the person to take the idea to her mom," Jim Galasyn said. "Her mom was like, 'No.' Why did I have to do that here?"

The divorce of Shirley and Marvin had been finalized, but many in attendance didn't know it. The couple put aside the acrimonious aspects of their divorce and appeared as the proud parents they had once been. It would be the last time many friends saw or heard from Marvin.

Word filtered slowly to some in the racing community of her death. Some didn't hear about Cheryl's death for decades. Many of those who once raced against her had lost track of her. She had been so far removed from racing for so long, many had forgotten about her.

Cheryl was remembered more in the racing community for the barriers she broke than her driving ability and accomplishments.

Cheryl's mother kept all of her possessions for decades, tucking them away in a scattered pile of boxes in Cheryl's childhood bedroom at her house in Seattle. The room that once housed hundreds of trophies of Cheryl's accomplishments became a repository for scattered information about her career.

The National Sprint Car Hall of Fame at Knoxville Speedway in Knoxville, Iowa, included Cheryl in a display in 2013. The car she drove for Charlie Patterson in the USAC Silver Crown race in 1982 is there, though in an earlier form and not with Cheryl's name on it. The sprint car she drove at Phoenix in 1982 for Jack Conner is there with her name on it.

It's one of the few places where Cheryl Glass is remembered.

Afterword

Who Was Cheryl Glass?

CHERYL GLASS WAS A COMPLEX, NUANCED PERSON WHO TOOK GREAT pride in her accomplishments—of which there were plenty—both on racetracks and in other venues of life. But her feats and the status she earned in life contributed to her destruction. She had great success at an early age, and the expectations placed on her due to that success grew exponentially. Cheryl had lofty aspirations, ones that were impossible for her to reach with the path she took.

Cheryl Glass was a pioneer, not just in the racing world, but in the worlds of sports and in society. No one had done what Cheryl did. Black women didn't race sprint cars before her. They still don't.

I admire Cheryl for what she did, but I also think she serves as a cautionary tale. For most of Cheryl's life, people expected her to carry the weight of entire groups: Black people and women. These were small groups in the racing world, but Cheryl Glass was burdened with representing them. From what I can tell, she wanted that responsibility early in her racing career. Cheryl thought that status would lead to more opportunities in the sport of auto racing. In a way, that's what happened. But those same opportunities didn't provide her with success.

Most people I talked with about Cheryl admired her—in the prism of looking back 20 years after she died. Drivers like Al Unser Jr. and Jimmy Sills competed against her. They didn't recognize what she accomplished until later on.

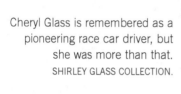

Cheryl Glass is remembered as a pioneering race car driver, but she was more than that.
SHIRLEY GLASS COLLECTION.

For much of Cheryl's life, she was judged on her appearance. In my research about her, I found dozens of references to her being a model. People assumed her appearance mattered. At times it did. But after her looks faded in her late 20s and she gained weight, people assumed she no longer mattered. Looks are how women are judged in our society. It's not the same with men, something Cheryl pointed out.

It is likely that Cheryl suffered from chronic traumatic encephalopathy (CTE). She had the known symptoms: erratic behavior, aggression, depression, problems planning and carrying out tasks, substance use, and suicidal thoughts. Cheryl was never diagnosed with CTE, largely because it was unknown in her time, and no scan was done on her brain after she died. But she suffered repeated head injuries throughout her racing career and never let most of them heal. The earliest head injury I can document of hers was when she was 12 years old, and when she was 18, I know of four more (including the one at Manzanita Speedway where she lost her eyesight momentarily). If Cheryl's concussions had been treated correctly when they occurred, her life may have turned out differently.

In my opinion, Cheryl Glass tried to climb the racing ladder too fast. She thought after three years of racing a dirt sprint car that she was ready to move up. She wasn't. She learned how to drive one type of race car at a decent level. I will never say Skagit Speedway's top sprint car class is anything other than very good. It's not the best, however. But Cheryl never learned how to really race. Her enthusiasm for moving up in racing exceeded her skill. In racing, drivers have to learn how to win. One win usually leads to more. But drivers need to learn how to win at a level consistently before they are truly ready to move up to the next. Cheryl put too much pressure on herself to be the first and the best at everything. It led her to take chances she shouldn't have taken, to move to the next race before she was ready, to push through injuries that needed time to heal. We'll never know what kind of driver she could have been if she had the proper training and support. She could have been great.

That doesn't take away from what Cheryl accomplished. What she did as a driver was impressive. And she gave young girls someone to look up to, someone to admire, and allowed them to dream of racing, just like her.

Acknowledgments

It was 2018 and I was on pit road at a road race in Eastern Oregon. My first book, *The Brown Bullet: Rajo Jack's Drive to Integrate Auto Racing*, had just been sold to a publisher. I was happy that the book I had worked on for years was going to be published. But when I was telling a pit marshal about it, she said, "Why didn't you write a book about a woman?" I didn't have an answer. I brushed off the suggestion. I couldn't think of a female driver that I would want to write a book about.

While reviewing source material for *The Brown Bullet*, I came upon an article by Shav Glick in the *Los Angeles Times* that also mentioned Cheryl Glass. I knew Cheryl's name, but I knew nothing about her. I found that she won a main event at Skagit Speedway. To me, that's legit. A few months later, I decided to write a book about Cheryl.

There was a large amount of newspaper articles about Cheryl, but I also culled much of the information about her life from interviews, court records, police reports, and other public records.

Shirley Glass, Cheryl's mother, was immensely helpful in writing this book. She talked to me repeatedly and let me go through the bedroom full of Cheryl's stuff (and even her wedding dress). Shirley said, "I want my daughter to get her due." Shirley died at age 85 in 2022, before this book was published.

It impressed me how vivid the memory of race car drivers were about Cheryl. I couldn't have written this book without former drivers like Jerry Day, Tobey Butler, Bill Tempero, Steve Royce, Jimmy Sills, Jerry Fanger, Lealand McSpadden, Al Unser Jr., Bobby Allen, Steve Beitler, Steve Millen, P. J. Jones, Garey Fauver, Billy Kennelly, and Denny Smith. I also need to thank auto racing luminaries Dennis Mattish, George Hespe, Ken Clapp, Charlie Patterson, Les Unger, Lori Walker, Leonard Miller,

Roger Bailey, Guy Mossington, Charles Mossington, and Rod Reid for taking the time to talk with me about Cheryl. And people involved in Cheryl's personal life including Mike Opprecht, Jim Galasyn, Stuart Bramhall, Dave Griffith, Lisa Kelsie, Hersey Mallory, Jim Grantham, James Grantham, Eugene (Skip) Young Jr., and Jim Hedblom were invaluable.

Personally, I must credit my mother, Marcia Poehler, for her making sure I learned to read and write and being a constant sounding board for this book. My sister, Margaret Poehler, of course helped with all legal matters, and my other sister, Laura Caulfield, provided her medical expertise in reviewing medical records. My aunt, Patience Jackson, read and gave feedback on every word. Friends who contributed included Robert O'Neill, Mike Shank, Ron Cox, and Chasity McCarthy. I also must credit Claire Withycombe, who helped me mold the manuscript from a rough draft into the finished product.

I also want to thank my agent, Barbara Collins Rosenberg, for finding a home for this book and editor Christen Karniski of Rowman & Littlefield for giving it a chance.

Notes

Introduction

1. Bryn Berose. "Project Transforms Fairgrounds Racetrack." *The Daily World* (Aberdeen, Washington). May 15, 1981. D3.
2. Jim Grantham, interview with the author, June 8, 2020.
3. Jim Grantham, interview with the author, September 20, 2020.
4. Jerry Day, interview with the author, April 7, 2023.

Chapter One

1. Tennessee State Marriages, 1780–2002. Nashville, TN: Tennessee State Library and Archives.
2. Shirley Glass, interview with the author, November 7, 2020.
3. All quotes by Shirley Glass are from interview with the author on July 30, 2020, unless otherwise noted.
4. "Dice Game Said Cause of Killing." *The Tennessean.* July 12, 1942. 40.
5. "Faces 1–20 Year Term in Reformatory." *News Journal* (Mansfield, OH). October 26, 1945. 1.
6. United States, World War I Draft Registration Cards, 1917–1918.
7. United States, Social Security Death Index, 1935–2014.
8. Cook County, Illinois Birth Index, 1916–1935.
9. Jim Grantham, interview with the author, July 12, 2020.
10. "Engineering Graduates Wed Following TSU Commencement." *Nashville Globe and Independent.* June 10, 1959.
11. Jim Kershner. "Boeing and Washington's Aerospace Industry, 1934–2015." https://www.historylink.org/file/11111.
12. "Engineering Graduates Wed Following TSU Commencement." *Nashville Globe and Independent.* June 10, 1959.
13. David Williams. "The William E. Boeing Story." *Arcadia Publishing,* 2022. England. 73.
14. Jim Kershner. "Boeing and Washington's Aerospace Industry, 1934–2015." https://www.historylink.org/file/11111.
15. Jim Galasyn, interview with the author, January 23, 2021.

16. Sarah Davenport. "Battle at Boeing: African Americans and the Campaign for Jobs 1939–1942." https://depts.washington.edu/civilr/boeing_battle.htm.

17. State of California. California Birth Index, 1905–1995. Sacramento, CA: State of California Department of Health Services, Center for Health Statistics.

18. Cheryl Glass funeral program, July 22, 1997.

19. Washington State Archives; Olympia, Washington; Death Index Washington, 1940–1959, 1965–2017.

20. Anderson Almquist. "'Storm' of Cookies Will Aid Pool Fund." *Seattle Daily Times*. April 7, 1968. 101.

21. "Civil-Rights Groups Back New Trustee." *Seattle Daily Times*. July 25, 1969. 6.

22. "Trustee's Home Is Burglarized." *Seattle Times*. July 31, 1969. 38.

CHAPTER TWO

1. "Only the Flag Was Black and White." *AVENUES* (Indianapolis, IN).

2. Patricia Raybon. "The Fast Lane." *Rocky Mountain News* (Denver, CO). February 21, 1985. 13S.

3. Larry Lark. "She Cracks the Stereotype of the Race Car Driver." *Everett Herald*. September 27, 1980. 5D.

4. Stephen Hiltner. "Nascar's Future Depends on These 5-Year-Olds." *New York Times*. July 21, 2018.

5. https://www.painefield.com/130/Paine-Fields-History.

6. Louie Robinson. "Racing Against Odds." *Ebony*. January 1980. 112.

7. Louie Robinson. "Racing Against Odds." *Ebony*. January 1980. 114.

8. Tobey Butler, interview with the author, May 8, 2020.

9. WQMRA Driver's Annual Banquet program 1971.

10. Shirley Glass, interview with the author, July 30, 2020.

11. "Racing at Top Speed." Houghton Mifflin. Boston. 1985. 207.

12. Quarter Reporter. September/October 1973. 17.

13. Billy Kennelly, interview with the author, July 3, 2020.

14. Lisa Kelsie, interview with the author, August 22, 2020.

15. Marion Gartler and Marcella Benditt. *Off to the Races*. Prentice-Hall Inc. Englewood Cliffs, NJ. 1980.

16. Larry Lark. "She Cracks the Stereotype of the Race Car Driver." *Everett Herald*. September 27, 1980. 5D.

17. "The Achievers." TBS. February 1, 1988.

18. Jim Grantham, interview with the author, July 12, 2020.

19. "Sex, Race No Barriers for Driver." *Associated Press*. 1980.

20. Trisha Ready. "Driven to the Edge." *The Stranger* (Seattle, WA), December 11, 1997. 14.

21. "The Achievers." TBS. February 1, 1988.

22. "Model Beats Out 45 Men for Speedway Title." *Weekly World News*. December 7, 1980. 7.

23. James Grantham, interview with the author, August 22, 2020.

24. Louie Robinson. "Racing Against Odds." *Ebony*. January 1980. 112.

25. Jim Grantham, interview with the author, June 8, 2020.

26. Louie Robinson. "Racing Against Odds." *Ebony*. January 1980. 116.

Chapter Three

1. Clarissa Frank. "For Cheryl Glass, It's Life in the Fast Lane." *Design Coach Forum*. January 1992. 2.

2. James Gilroy. "Women in Motorsports: Their Past, Present, and Future." thedrive. com. March 8, 2018. https://www.thedrive.com/accelerator/17072/women-in-motor-sport-their-past-present-and-future.

3. Robert Cromie. "A.A.A. Refuses Bill Holland's License Plea." *Chicago Tribune*. November 20, 1952.

4. Wayne Grett. "Australian Drivers Hone Racing Skills at Knoxville." *Des Moines Register*. June 21, 1991. 5S.

5. "Race Fake Announced for Publicity Purposes." *Horseless Age*. October 5, 1910.

6. All quotes by Jerry Day from interview with the author, April 15, 2020, unless otherwise noted.

7. Payoff from Gold Cup 1979.

8. Allan E. Brown. *The History of America's Speedways Past & Present*, fourth edition. 2017. *America's Speedways* (Comstock Park, MI). 761.

9. Skagit Speedway program, 1981.

10. All quotes by Guy Mossington from interview with the author, October 15, 2021.

11. Lori Walker, interview with the author, July 26, 2019.

12. Garey Fauver, interview with the author, April 13, 2020.

13. Steve Royce, interview with the author, June 9, 2020.

14. Dick Rockne. "Cheryl Has Plans for AFTER She Wins the Indy 500." *Seattle Daily Times*. June 20, 1980. D3.

15. All quotes by Jim Grantham from interview with the author, June 8, 2020, unless otherwise noted.

16. "Loy Takes Feature Race at Speedway." *Bellingham Herald*. May 12, 1980. 2D.

17. Dick Rockne. "Cheryl has plans for AFTER she wins the Indy 500." *Seattle Daily Times*. June 20, 1980. D3.

18. Dave Griffith, interview with the author, August 14, 2020.

19. "Sports At a Glance." *Seattle Times*. July 30, 1980. E4.

20. Dick Rockne. "Dirt Cup Field Tops 80 Despite Boycott by Outlaws." *Seattle Times*. June 18, 1980. E6.

21. Connie Tedrow. "The 'Whiz Kid' from California Whizzing Again." *Bellingham Herald*. June 21, 1981. D1.

22. "Jimmy Sills Wins Super Dirt Cup." *Bellingham Herald*. June 23, 1980. 1B.

23. Jimmy Sills with Dave Argabright. "Life With Luke." *American Scene Press*, 2019. Noblesville, IN. 94 and 95.

24. Jimmy Sills, interview with the author, May 6, 2020.

25. Warren Rogers. "Pole Worth Big Money in Sprints." *The Billings Gazette*. June 28, 1980. B1.

26. "Washington Driver Wins Local Sprint Car Open." *The Independent-Record* (Helena, MT). July 1, 1980. 21.

27. All quotes by Steve Royce from interview with the author, June 9, 2020.

28. Garey Fauver, interview with the author, April 13, 2020.

29. Jim Hedblom, interview with the author, July 26, 2019.

30. "PI Sports Scoreboard." *Seattle Post Intelligencer.* July 7, 1970. C6.

31. Chet Cory. "Behind the Mike." *Racing Wheels.* July 30, 1980. 23.

32. "Tourond Gets First Win in Super Stock Feature." *Bellingham Herald.* July 14, 1980. 2D.

33. Chet Cory. "Behind the Mike." *Racing Wheels.* July 30, 1980. 23.

34. "Sprint Cars to Go." *Cottage Grove Sentinel.* June 23, 1980.

35. Ron Harris. "Cherry Glass: Racing and Winning." *Ebony Jr.* 1980. 38 and 39.

36. "Two Skagit Drivers Cop First Season Wins." *Bellingham Herald.* August 11, 1980. 3D.

37. "Two Skagit Drivers Cop First Season Wins." *Bellingham Herald.* August 11, 1980. 3D.

38. "Adams Steals Skagit Show." *Bellingham Herald.* August 18, 1980. 3D.

39. "Munn, Berrow, Huson Collect Skagit Wins." *Bellingham Herald.* August 25, 1980. 3D.

40. "Skagit Speedway Points." Skagit Speedway 1980 program.

CHAPTER FOUR

1. Patricia Raybon. "The Fast Lane." *Rocky Mountain News* (Denver, CO). February 21, 1985. 13S.

2. Jerry Day, interview with the author, March 19, 2019.

3. All other quotes by Jerry Day from interview with the author, April 15, 2020, unless otherwise noted.

4. "Glass Breaks Speedway Books on Final Night." *Skagit Valley Herald.* September 1, 1980.

5. "Rookie Steals Skagit Show." *Bellingham Herald.* September 1, 1980. 1B.

6. Shirley Glass, interview with the author, April 13, 2020.

7. "Glass Breaks Speedway Books on Final Night." *Skagit Valley Herald.* September 1, 1980.

8. Speech for Alpha Kappa Alpha National Convention, July 16, 1986.

9. Jerry Day, interview with the author, April 7, 2023.

10. Larry Lark. "She Cracks the Stereotype of the Race Car Driver." *Everett Herald.* September 27, 1980. 5D.

11. Letter from Lonnie, Susan, Morella, C. J., Joe. Undated.

12. http://nwsprintcarhistory.com/champions/track-champions/washington/skagit-speedway/skagit-speedway-410-champs/.

13. Trophy from 1980.

14. Shirley Glass, interview with the author, April 17, 2020.

15. Ranny Green. "Will Dirt Racing Lead Her to Indy?" Pacific, *The Seattle Times.* July 19, 1981. 12.

16. Letter from Linda Mansfield, *National Speed Sport New*s, October 10, 1980.

17. Larry Lark. "She Cracks the Stereotype of the Race Car Driver." *Everett Herald*. September 27, 1980. 5D.

CHAPTER FIVE

1. All quotes by Jimmy Sills from interview with the author, May 6, 2020, unless otherwise noted.

2. Jim Grantham, interview with the author, June 8, 2020.

3. "Celebrate Washington." Women of the 80s report. KTZZ TV 22.

4. "Black Girl Races Sprinter." *The Berkeley Gazette* (Berkeley, CA). October 9, 1980. 16.

5. "Sex, Race No Barriers for Driver." *Associated Press*. 1980.

6. Gordon Martin. "Woman vs. the Outlaws." *San Francisco Chronicle*. September 25, 1980. 75.

7. "Gold Cup Race Set for Chico." *Sacramento Bee*. September 25, 1980. C2.

8. Robert A. Carlson. "A True Sportsman." *National Speed Sport News*. October 29, 1980.

9. Ken Clapp, interview with the author, September 28, 2020.

10. "Cheryl Making Tracks in Racing." *San Jose Mercury News*. October 10, 1980.

11. Peter Harris. "A Woman in Auto Racing? Well, Why Not?" *Afro American* (Baltimore, MD). November 22, 1980. 9.

12. "Sellout Crowd Views Classic." *Register-Pajaronian* Watsonville (CA). October 12, 1980. 12.

13. All quotes by Jim Grantham from interview with the author, June 8, 2020, unless otherwise noted.

14. "Records at San Jose Speedway." *San Francisco Chronicle*. October 6, 1980. 54.

15. Gordon Martin. "Roberts May Quit 'Inferior' Yamahas for Four-Wheelers." *San Francisco Chronicle*. October 9, 1980. 68.

16. "Driver Widens Lead in Golden Classic with Third Triumph." *Santa Cruz Sentinel*. October 12, 1980. 59.

17. "Scoreboard." *San Jose Mercury News*. October 12, 1980.

18. All quotes by Lealand McSpadden from interview with the author, May 6, 2020.

19. "Boyd Captures First Thunder Park Feature." *Racing Wheels*. October 22, 1980. 1.

20. Verne Boatner. "Cheryl Glass: 9-Year Racing Vet at the Age of 18." *Arizona Republic*. October 21, 1980. C1.

21. Rick Martinez. "60 Cars Shoot for Western Title." *Arizona Republic* (Phoenix, AZ). October 22, 1980. D5.

22. Al Unser Jr., interview with the author, June 8, 2020.

23. Jerry Day, interview with the author, April 15, 2020.

24. Rick Martinez. "Billy Shuman Sets Mark in Western Qualifying." *Arizona Republic*. October 23, 1980. E5.

25. Shav Glick. "Glass Has Smashing Off-Road Debut: Crash into the Wall Takes Her Out of Saturday Gran Prix." *Los Angeles Times*. July 19, 1985.

26. Rick Martinez. "Swindell Runs Away from Field to Win Western." *Arizona Republic*. October 26, 1980. F4.

27. Jimmy Sills with Dave Argabright. "Life With Luke." *American Scene Press*. 2019. Noblesville, Indiana. 84, 85.

28. Lealand McSpadden, interview with the author, May 6, 2020.

29. "The Achievers," *TBS*, February 1, 1988.

30. Jerry Day, interview with the author, March 19, 2019.

31. James Grantham, interview with the author, August 22, 2020.

32. Jack Doo. "Glass Likes Life in the Fast Lane." *Modesto Bee*. October 24, 1980. 53.

33. Louie Robinson. "Racing Against Odds." *Ebony*. January 1980. 114.

34. Cheryl Glass racing reference.

35. https://www.museumofamericanspeed.com/billsmith.html.

36. Letter from Bill Smith, December 8, 1980.

37. Bill Smith, National Sprint Car Hall of Fame panel, June 30, 2013.

38. Letter from Bill Smith, January 3, 1981.

39. Johns, Clayton. "History Renewed." https://worldofoutlaws.com/sprintcars/outlaws-return-to-devils-bowl/.

40. Bill Smith, National Sprint Car Hall of Fame panel, June 30, 2013.

41. Tom Ford. "Glass Pursues Lofty Racing Goal." *The Tampa Tribune*. February 5, 1981. 5C.

42. Tom Ford. "Glass Pursues Lofty Racing Goal." *The Tampa Tribune*. February 5, 1981. 5C.

43. Dick Wallace Metcalfe. "Spotlight on Speed." *Racing Wheels*. February 25, 1981. 6.

44. Bobby "Scruffy" Allen, interview with the author, September 2, 2019.

45. Tom Ford. "Kauffman Wins at East Bay." *Tampa Tribune*. February 6, 1981. 6C.

46. Dick Wallace Metcalfe. "Spotlight on Speed," *Racing Wheels*. February 25, 1981. 6.

Chapter Six

1. All quotes by Jim Grantham from interview with the author, June 8, 2020, unless otherwise noted.

2. Letter from Seattle Seahawks, April 20, 1980.

3. Eugene Young Jr., interview with the author, August 17, 2020.

4. Bryn Berose. "Project Transforms Fairgrounds Racetrack." *The Daily World* (Aberdeen, WA). May 15, 1981. D3.

5. Jerry Fanger, interview with the author, May 25, 2020.

6. Jim Grantham, interview with the author, June 8, 2020.

7. Diana Bertram. "Munn Masters NSC Opener at Elma." *Racing Wheels*. June 3, 1981. 7.

8. Jim Grantham, interview with the author, August 1, 2020.

9. Bill Kennelly, interview with the author, July 3, 2020.

10. "Robertson Scores First Speedway Win of Season." *Skagit Valley Herald*. June 8, 1981. 9.

11. "SHRA, SSRA, Skagit Speedway Alger, WA, June 13." *Racing Wheels*. June 24, 1981. 12.

12. Guy Mossington, interview with the author, October 15, 2021.

13. "In Dirt Cup Sprints." *National Speed Sport News*. June 24, 1981.

14. "Auto Racing." *Seattle Daily Times*. June 27, 1981. D4.

15. "Auto Racing." *Bellingham Herald.* June 29, 1981. 2B.
16. "Trio Takes Elma Auto Racing." *Aberdeen Daily World.* July 6, 1981. Page B2.
17. "Speedway Championships Draw 7,000." *Bellingham Herald.* July 6, 1981. 2D.
18. Jerry Day, interview with the author, March 19, 2019.
19. Ranny Green. "Will Dirt Racing Lead Her to Indy?" Pacific, *The Seattle Times.* July 19, 1981. 8–15.
20. Letter from Kathy Benson, production assistant for *Seattle Today* show, July 31, 1981.
21. Ranny Green. "Will Dirt Racing Lead Her to Indy?" Pacific, *The Seattle Times.* July 19, 1981. 8–15.
22. "Cheryl Glass: The Profile of an Achiever." 1982 Knoxville Nationals program. 40.
23. "32 Seafair Princesses Reach for Crown." *Seattle Times.* August 1, 1981. A8.
24. "SHRA Sprints & Mods, Skagit Speedway, Alger, Washington." *Racing Wheels.* August 12, 1981. 11.
25. Steve Royce, interview with the author, June 9, 2020.
26. "Auto Racing." *Bellingham Herald.* August 3, 1981. 23.
27. "The Achievers," *TBS*, February 1, 1988.
28. Chet Cory. "Skagit Season Nears Conclusion." *Racing Wheels.* August 25, 1981. 4.
29. "Skagit Speedway Titles Still Up for Grabs." *Bellingham Herald.* August 28, 1981. 2B.
30. Denny Smith, interview with the author, July 26, 2019.
31. John Trussler. "Green Opens Golden Classic Series." *Racing Wheel.* October 7, 1981. 1, 3.
32. "Quick Change." *Open Wheel.* March 1981.
33. Jim Simmons. "Inside Racing." *Racing Wheels.* November 25, 1981. 8.

Chapter Seven

1. "Only the Flag Was Black and White." AVENUES (Indianapolis, IN).
2. Jerry Day, interview with the author, April 15, 2020.
3. "The Lady." Program for 1982 Copper World Classic.
4. "Auto Racing." *Arizona Republic.* January 31, 1982. E12.
5. All quotes by Steve Royce from interview with the author, June 9, 2020.
6. Ronnie Allyn. "So. Calif. Speed Secrets." *National Speed Sport News.* February 22, 1982. 26.
7. David Sink. "The Pink Lady." *Sprint Car and Midget.* December 2021. 58.
8. Ronnie Allyn. "Frey Repeats." *Racing Wheels.* February 10, 1982. 1, 3.
9. Robin Miller. "Cheryl Glass to Try Sprint Cars." *Indianapolis Star.* April 8, 1982.
10. Rod Reid, interview with the author, March 9, 2021.
11. All quotes by Charlie Patterson from interview with the author, June 10, 2020.
12. Dick Mittman. "'Little Gasoline Alley' a Big Deal." *Indianapolis News.* May 4, 1983. 21.
13. Robin Miller. "Hulman 100 Race Captured by Hood." *Indianapolis Star.* May 9, 1982. 2B.
14. Dick Mittman. "First Lady of Dirt Cars." *Indianapolis News.* May 10, 1982. 21.
15. Marvin Glass. "Public Forum: Cheryl Not Fired." *National Speed Sport News.* June 30, 1982. 4.

16. Steve Beitler, interview with the author, April 15, 2020.
17. "Cheryl Glass: The Profile of an Achiever." 1982 Knoxville Nationals program. 40.
18. Wayne Grett. "First Black, Woman to Race at Knoxville." *Des Moines Register.* August 8, 1982. 6D.
19. Eugene Young Jr., interview with the author, August 17, 2020.
20. Jim Hedblom, interview with the author, July 26, 2019.
21. https://www.knoxvilleraceway.com/pages/historic-results.
22. Wayne Grett. "First Black, Woman to Race at Knoxville." *Des Moines Register.* August 8, 1982. 6D.
23. Bill of sale, January 20, 1983.
24. Billy Kennelly, interview with the author, July 3, 2020.

Chapter Eight
1. "Race Car Driver Trades Helmet for Classy Veil." *Independent Record* (Helena, MT). September 25, 1983. 7C.
2. Shirley Glass, interview with the author, May 8, 2020.
3. Lori Walker, interview with the author, July 26, 2019.
4. "Race Car Driver Trades Helmet for Classy Veil." *Independent Record* (Helena, MT). September 25, 1983. 7C.
5. Eugene Young Jr., interview with the author, August 17, 2020.
6. Dave Griffith, interview with the author, August 14, 2020.
7. Cheryl Glass, Richard Lindwall wedding certificate, February 10, 1983, 830224.
8. Shirley Glass, interview with the author, June 11, 2020.
9. All quotes by Eugene Young Jr. from interview with the author, August 17, 2020.
10. Shirley Glass, interview with the author, April 17, 2020.
11. Elizabeth Rhodes. "What a Wedding!" *Seattle Times.* February 17, 1983. D1.
12. "Letters." *Seattle Times.* February 28, 1983. A11.
13. "Letters." *Seattle Times.* March 11, 1983. A13.
14. "Model Beats Out 45 Men for Speedway Title." *Weekly World News.* December 7, 1980. 7.
15. Sam Moses. "Racing Suits Willy to a T." *Classic Galleries.* October 17, 1983.
16. Cheryl Glass speech, undated.
17. Letter from Bertil Roos School of Motor Racing, undated.
18. Chris Economaki. "From the Editor's Notebook." *National Speed Sport News.* November 30, 1983. 2.
19. Shav Glick. "Ribbs Will Get His Chance at Indy." *Los Angeles Times.* December 15, 1983. Sports 14.
20. Dick Rockne. "Breaking the Barrier at Indy 500." *Seattle Times.* October 19, 1983. E1, E5.

Chapter Nine
1. Dick Mittman. "First Lady of Dirt Cars." *Indianapolis News.* May 10, 1982. 21.
2. Shav Glick. "Glass Has Smashing Off-Road Debut." *Los Angeles Times.* July 19, 1985. Part III, 3.

3. "Cheryl Making Tracks in Racing." *San Jose Mercury News*. October 23, 1980.
4. Letter from Robert L. Steil, Adam Berger, Jim Harvey, March 27, 1984.
5. Eugene Young Jr., interview with the author, August 17, 2020.
6. Clarissa Frank. "For Cheryl Glass, It's Life in the Fast Lane." *Design Coach Forum.* January 1992. 1, 2, and 3.
7. Kurt Ernst. "Fifty Years Later, There's Still No Racing Like the Original Can Am Series." *Hemmings.* February 2, 2016.
8. Cheryl Glass, filled out form to Can-Am Series, undated.
9. Undated letter, Shirley Glass Collection.
10. All quotes by Hersey Mallory from interview with the author, September 6, 2020.
11. Roger Campbell. "Grand Prix Preparations Nearing Finish Line." *Dallas Morning News.* July 5, 1984. 4B.
12. All quotes by Bill Tempero from interview with the author, June 8, 2020.
13. Roger Campbell. "Roe Leads Can-Am Qualifying." *Dallas Morning News.* July 7, 1984. 8B.
14. Roger Campbell. "Obstacles Mark Roe's Road to Victory in Can-Am Challenge." *The Dallas Morning News.* July 8, 1984. 21.
15. "A Wild Grand Prix in Dallas." *New York Times.* July 9, 1984.
16. Letter to Thomas N. Todd, February 20, 1987.
17. https://dw.courts.wa.gov/index.cfm?fa=home.casesummary&crt_itl_nu=S17&casenumber=84-3-07679-1&searchtype=sName&token=0A07C4BE03DAD3DDAB0FDBABEEC30320&dt=0EC8DCBCCCDCD3A5B1F97C29DDAAABBD&courtClassCode=S&casekey=13092128&courtname=KING%20CO%20SUPERIOR%20CT.
18. Robin Miller. "Youth Is Served in Sprint Cars." *Indianapolis Star.* May 23, 1985. 39.
19. Jonathan Tasini. "The Beer and the Boycott." *New York Times.* January 31, 1988. 19.
20. Ad. *The Atlanta Voice.* October 26, 1984. 12.
21. http://www.cherylglass.com/media/.
22. Patricia Raybon. "The Fast Lane." *Rocky Mountain News* (Denver, CO). February 21, 1985. 13S.
23. Letter from Cheryl Glass to Bill Sauter, January 29, 1987.
24. Marilyn Kirkby. "On a Fast Track." *Seattle Times.* May 23, 1985.
25. Renee S. Mitchell. "A Talented Designer Steers for the Top of Life in the Fast Lane." *Seattle Post Intelligencer.* July 19, 1987. F4.
26. Letter to Mike Summer from Ron Richards, June 20, 1985.
27. https://www.automotivehalloffame.org/honoree/mickey-thompson/.
28. Letter to Mike Summer from Ron Richards, June 20, 1985.
29. Les Unger, interview with the author, May 8, 2020.
30. Shav Glick. "Glass Has Smashing Off-Road Debut." *Los Angeles Times.* July 19, 1985. Part III, 3.
31. All quotes by Steve Millen from interview with the author, May 7, 2020.
32. Shav Glick. "47,205 at Coliseum for Races." *Los Angeles Times.* July 20. Part III, 12.

CHAPTER TEN

1. Shav Glick. "Glass Has Smashing Off-Road Debut." *Los Angeles Times*. July 19, 1985. Part III, 3.
2. All quotes by Hersey Mallory from interview with the author, September 6, 2020.
3. Cheryl Glass Coors flyer.
4. Shav Glick. "Purses for Indy Cars Could Reach $15.5 Million." *Los Angeles Times*. February 5, 1986. Part III, 13.
5. Letter to Phoenix International Raceway, undated.
6. "Bill Pickett Rodeo Honors Black Cowhands." *The Voice*. May 3, 1986. 6.
7. "Cheryl Glass Signs with Coors." *Los Angeles Sentinel*. August 29, 1985. B4.
8. "Accountant Picked Again to Run Center." *Kansas City Star*. May 19, 1986. 4B.
9. Typed out speech, undated.
10. Jim Galasyn, interview with the author, January 23, 2021.
11. Letter to Thomas Todd, July 2, 1986.
12. Cheryl Glass itinerary.
13. Eugene Young Jr., interview with the author, August 17, 2020.
14. Trisha Ready. "Driven to the Edge." *The Stranger* (Seattle, WA). December 11, 1997. 13.
15. Michele Glance. "From Nurse to World Crusader." *Detroit Free Press*. July 11, 1986. B1.
16. Carol Lawson. "Honoring 7 Who 'Do and Do.'" *New York Times*. June 19, 1987. A, 22.
17. Leonard Miller, interview with the author, April 12, 2021.
18. Letter to Bill Sauter, January 29, 1987.
19. Jim Grantham, interview with the author, June 8, 2020.
20. King County Superior Court 94-2-22422-1.
21. *The Achievers*. TBS. February 1, 1988.
22. Billy Kennelly, interview with the author, July 3, 2020.
23. *The Achievers*. TBS. February 1, 1988.
24. Invitation from Ted Turner to screening of Black History 88, January 7, 1988.
25. Charles Michael Opprecht, interview with the author, January 28, 2021.
26. Cheryl Glass and Charles Opprecht wedding certificate, 880719.
27. Letter from Dr. Stan Schiff to Tim Bradshaw, May 10, 1990.
28. Lisa Kelsie, interview with the author, August 22, 2020.
29. https://dw.courts.wa.gov/index.cfm?fa=home.casesummary&crt_itl_nu=S17&casenumber=90-3-00360-8&searchtype=sName&token=0876B6C678DBA4DDAB0FDBABEEC50320&dt=0CB9AEC4B7DDA4A5B1F97C29DDACABBD&courtClassCode=S&casekey=13036558&courtname=KING%20CO%20SUPERIOR%20CT.

CHAPTER ELEVEN

1. *The Achievers*. TBS. February 1, 1988.
2. Gordon Kirby. "The Way It Is." *Racemaker Press*. 2012.
3. Charles Michael Opprecht, interview with the author, January 28, 2021.

4. All quotes by Hersey Mallory from interview with the author, September 6, 2020.

5. Letter from Kirk Wines, July 31, 1990.

6. Dave Griffith, interview with the author, August 14, 2020.

7. Businesses expenses for 1990.

8. Lisa Kelsie, interview with the author, August 22, 2020.

9. Tillie Fong. "Women Racers Slowed by Macho Attitude." *Rocky Mountain News* (Denver, CO). August 26, 1990. 18S.

10. "Scoreboard." *The Daily Item* (Sunbury, PA). October 7, 1990. C12.

11. All quotes by P. J. Jones from interview with the author, July 3, 2020.

12. "Scoreboard." *USA Today* (Arlington, VA). October 8, 1990. 13C.

13. Cindy Hulford. "Cheryl Glass Looks for Grand Prix Win." *Huntington Beach News*. April 12, 1991. 2.

14. "Scoreboard." *USA Today* (Arlington, VA). October 22, 1990. 13C.

15. Marshall Pruett. "The Life and Death of Cheryl Glass." *Road & Track*. July 14, 2017.

16. Hersey Mallory, interview with the author, September 6, 2020.

17. Steve Irvine. "Glass Hasn't Been Broken by Obstacles She Has Faced." *Long Beach Press-Telegram*. April 14, 1991. B3.

18. "Cheryl Glass." *Racing for Kids*. July 1991.

19. Steve Irvine. "Glass Hasn't Been Broken by Obstacles She Has Faced." *Long Beach Press-Telegram*. April 14, 1991. B3.

20. Steve Irvine. "Glass Hasn't Been Broken by Obstacles She Has Faced." *Long Beach Press-Telegram*. April 14, 1991. B3.

21. "Scoreboard." *The Star Press* (Muncie, IN). April 14, 1991. C4.

22. Roger Bailey, interview with the author, October 6, 2020.

23. Eugene Young Jr., interview with the author, August 17, 2020.

24. "Scoreboard." *Detroit Free Press*. April 15, 1991. 7D.

25. Eugene Young Jr., interview with the author, January 18, 2021.

26. Randy Lanier with A. J. Baime. "Survival of the Fastest." *Hachette Books*. 2022. New York. 227–35.

27. Jim Galasyn, interview with the author, January 23, 2021.

28. Steve Brandon. "McMinnville's Smith Gets Pole for Indy Lights Race." *The Oregonian* (Portland, OR). April 21, 1991. D5.

29. "Scoreboard." *Arizona Daily Star* (Tucson, AZ). April 21, 1991. D6.

30. "Stats Extra." *The Edmonton Journal* (Edmonton, Alberta, Canada). April 22, 1991. D5.

31. Stuart Bramhall, interview with the author, January 25, 2021.

CHAPTER TWELVE

1. King County Department of Assessment records, parcel number 397170-1750.

2. Shirley Glass, interview with the author, July 30, 2020.

3. Charles Michael Opprecht, interview with the author, January 28, 2021.

4. All quotes by Eugene Young Jr. are from an interview with the author, August 17, 2020, unless otherwise noted.

5. Kate Shatzkin and Ignacio Lobos. "Racist Writing on the Wall." *Seattle Times.* August 10, 1991.

6. Kate Shatzkin. "Hate Crime Comes to Home of Black Race-Car Driver." *Seattle Times.* August 8, 1991.

7. King County Sheriff's Office, case number 91-242553.

8. Kate Shatzkin. "Hate Crime Comes to Home of Black Race-Car Driver." *Seattle Times.* August 8, 1991.

9. Benjamin Pimentel. "Rise of Fascist Groups Predicted in Northwest." *Seattle Times.* August 11, 1991.

10. King County Sheriff's Office report 92-037759.

11. Dustin Long. "Rookie Ribbs Has Heart But Engine Gives Out." *Journal and Courier* (Lafayette, IN). May 27, 1991.

12. David Benner. "Little Al's 'Neat' Victory Ignites Unser Celebration." *Indianapolis Star.* May 25, 1992.

13. Dan Duncan. "St. James Did What She Set Out to Do." *Indianapolis Star.* May 25, 1992.

14. Hersey Mallory, interview with the author, September 6, 2020.

15. Letter from Marvin Glass to Glen (no last name given), August 4, 1992. Shirley Glass Collection.

16. Shirley Glass, interview with the author, June 11, 2020.

17. Clarissa Frank. "For Cheryl Glass, It's Life in the Fast Lane." *Design Coach Forum,* January 1992. 1, 2, 3.

18. Shirley Glass, interview with the author, July 30, 2020.

19. King County court case number 92-008093.

20. King County Sheriff's Office report number 92-295454.

21. Trisha Ready. "Driven to the Edge." *The Stranger* (Seattle, WA). December 11, 1997. 15.

Chapter Thirteen

1. Trisha Ready. "Driven to the Edge." *The Stranger* (Seattle, WA). December 11, 1997. 15.

2. Eugene Young Jr., interview with the author, January 18, 2021.

3. All other quotes by Eugene Young Jr. from interview with the author, August 17, 2020, unless otherwise noted.

4. Letter from Jesse Wineberry and Martin Applewick, March 8, 1993.

5. Letter to Jesse Wineberry from James Montgomery, March 17, 1993.

6. All quotes by Stuart Bramhall from interview with the author, January 25, 2021.

7. Stuart Bramhall, interview with the author, January 25, 2021.

8. Notes by Eugene Young Jr., May 22, 1993.

9. King County Superior Court east 93-2-24928-4.

10. Eugene Young Jr., interview with the author, January 18, 2021.

11. King County Superior Court east 93-2-24928-4.

12. King County Superior Court east 93-2-24928-4.

13. Western Washington District Court 2:96-cv-01059-TSZ.

14. Trisha Ready. "Driven to the Edge." *The Stranger* (Seattle, WA). December 11, 1997. 15.

15. Federal Bureau of Investigations SE 44A068379-4.

16. Shoreline division 93-231150.

17. King County Superior Court east 93-2-24928-44.

18. King County District court west 93-014767.

19. All quotes by Lisa Kelsie from interview with the author, August 22, 2020.

20. Janet Maslin. "Film Review: Disclosure." *New York Times*. December 9, 1994. C1.

21. Eugene Young Jr., interview with the author, August 17, 2020.

22. Shirley Glass, interview with the author, July 30, 2020.

Chapter Fourteen

1. King County Superior Court 93-2-30022-1.

2. King County Superior Court 93-2-30022-1.

3. All quotes by Eugene Young Jr. from interview with the author, August 17, 2020, unless noted.

4. Trisha Ready. "Driven to the Edge." *The Stranger* (Seattle, WA). December 11, 1997. 16.

5. Federal Bureau of Investigations SE 44A068379-4.

6. Eugene Young Jr. notes, August 9, 1993.

7. Eugene Young Jr. notes, October 21, 1993.

8. Letter from Cheryl Glass to Jesse Wineberry, December 22, 1993.

9. Federal Bureau of Investigations SE 44A068379-4.

10. Constantine Angelos. "Ex-Auto Racer Accuses Police of Harassment." *Seattle Times*. April 6, 1994. B3.

11. King County Superior Court 93-1-074981-2.

12. Eugene Young Jr., interview with the author, January 18, 2021.

13. "Neighbors Back Their Neighbor." *The Skanner* (Seattle, WA). March 23, 1994. 1.

14. Constantine Angelos. "Ex-Auto Racer Accuses Police of Harassment." *Seattle Times*. April 6, 1994. B3.

15. Stuart Bramhall, interview with the author, January 25, 2021.

16. Trisha Ready. "Driven to the Edge." *The Stranger* (Seattle, WA). December 11, 1997. 17.

17. All other quotes by Shirley Glass from interview with the author, July 30, 2020.

18. All quotes by Lisa Kelsie from interview with the author, August 22, 2020.

19. Trisha Ready. "Driven to the Edge." *The Stranger* (Seattle, WA). December 11, 1997. 17.

Chapter Fifteen

1. All quotes by Stuart Bramhall from interview with the author, January 25, 2021.

2. Wayne Wurzer, Christy Scattarella, Helen E. Jung. "Store Clerk Denies Wrongdoing in Death. *Seattle Times*. December 22, 1993.

3. Trisha Ready. "Driven to the Edge." *The Stranger* (Seattle, WA). December 11, 1997. 16.

4. King County Superior Court 02-2-34771-1.

5. Western Washington District Court 2:96-cv-01059-TSZ.

6. Letter from Cheryl Glass, August 7, 1996.

7. All quotes by Jim Galasyn from interview with the author, January 23, 2021.

8. James Ross Gardner. "The Girl on the Bridge." *Seattle Met.* June 29, 2011.

9. King County Medical Examiner's Office autopsy 97-00832/Cheryl Glass.

10. Jim Grantham, interview with the author, June 8, 2020.

11. King County Medical Examiner's Office autopsy 97-00832/Cheryl Glass.

12. Shirley Glass, interview with the author, July 12, 2020.

13. Shirley Glass, interview with the author, August 1, 2020.

14. All quotes by Eugene Young Jr. from interview with the author, August 17, 2020.

15. Lisa Kelsie, interview with the author, August 22, 2020.

16. Cheryl Glass funeral program, July 22, 1997.

Bibliography

Books

Ashe, Arthur R. *A Hard Road to Glory: A History of the African-American Athlete Since 1946*. Warner Books: New York. 1988.

Brown, Allan E. *The History of America's Speedways Past & Present*, fourth edition. America's Speedways: Comstock Park, MI, 2017.

Gartler, Marion, and Marcella Benditt. *Off to the Races*. Prentice-Hall, Inc.: Englewood Cliffs, NJ, 1980.

Lanier, Randy, and A. J. Baime. *Survival of the Fastest*. Hachette Books: NY, 2022.

Mattish, Dennis. *History of San Jose Racing Part 2*. Wadsworth Publishing Company: Marceline, MO, 2016.

Mumford, Esther Hall. *Calabash: A Guide to the History, Culture & Art of African Americans in Seattle and King County, Washington*. Ananese Press: Seattle, 1993.

Sills, Jimmy, and Dave Agrabright. *Life with Luke*. American Scene Press: Noblesville, IN, 2019.

Williams, David. *The William E. Boeing Story*. Arcadia Publishing: England, 2022.

Magazines

AVENUES (Indianapolis, IN), April 1982.

Design Coach Forum, January 1992.

Ebony, January 1980.

Ebony Junior, September 1980.

Open Wheel, March 1981 to October 1982.

Quarter Reporter, September/October 1973 to September/October 1979.

Racing for Kids, July 1991.

Road & Track, July 14, 2017 to August 3, 2020.

Seattle Magazine, March 2013.

Seventeen, July 1979.

Sprint Car And Midget, December 2021.

Weekly World News, December 7, 1980.

NEWSPAPERS

Afro American (Baltimore, MD), November 22, 1980.
Arizona Republic (Phoenix, AZ), October 21, 1980 to January 31, 1982.
Associated Press, September 15, 1980.
Atlanta Journal-Constitution, November 25, 1990.
Atlanta Voice, October 26, 1984.
Bellingham Herald, May 4, 1980 to August 31, 1981.
Berkeley Gazette, October 9, 1980 to October 23, 1980.
Billings Gazette (Billings, MT), June 28, 1980.
The Canadian Press, July 18, 1992.
The Capital Times (Madison, WI), October 22, 1990.
Chicago Metro News, December 6, 1986.
Chicago Tribune, November 20, 1952.
Corvallis Gazette Times (Corvallis, OR), July 24, 1997.
Cottage Grove Sentinel (Cottage Grove, OR), July 30, 1980.
The Daily Item (Sunbury, PA), October 7, 1990.
Daily World (Aberdeen, WA), May 15, 1981 to July 20, 1981.
Dallas Morning News, July 5, 1984 to July 8, 1984.
Dayton Daily News (Dayton, OH), January 20. 1991.
Des Moines Register, August 8, 1982 to August 12, 1982.
Everett Herald, September 27, 1980 to February 7, 2005.
Hawthorne News Wire, July 17, 1985.
Huntington Beach News, April 12, 1991.
Independent-Record (Helena, MT), July 1, 1980 to September 25, 1983.
Indiana Gazette (Indiana, PA), February 13, 1981.
Indianapolis News, April 8, 1982 to May 4, 1983.
Indianapolis Star, December 10, 1980 to May 23, 1985.
Kansas City Star, May 19, 1986.
Long Beach Press-Telegram, April 14, 1991.
Los Angeles Sentinel, July 11, 1985 to September 19, 1985.
Los Angeles Times, November 1, 1980 to February 5, 1986.
Marietta Journal (Marietta, GA), June 21, 1987.
Modesto Bee, October 24, 1980.
National Speed Sport News, May 14, 1980 to November 30, 1983.
New York Times, July 9, 1984 to July 18, 2018.
News Journal (Mansfield, OH), October 26, 1945.
News Tribune (Tacoma, WA), June 16, 1980 to August 17, 2001.
The Orange County Register, February 1, 1988.
The Oregonian (Portland, OR), April 21, 1991.
Philadelphia Tribune, November 17, 1989.
Racing Wheels, July 30, 1980 to February 10, 1982.
Rocky Mountain News (Denver, CO), February 21, 1985 to August 26, 1990.
Sacramento Bee, September 25, 1980 to September 29, 1980.
San Francisco Chronicle, September 25, 1980 to October 9, 1980.

San Jose Mercury News, October 10, 1980.
Santa Cruz Sentinel, October 12, 1980 to October 9, 1981.
The Seattle Medium, October 5, 1988.
Seattle Post-Intelligencer, April 7, 1968 to July 19, 1987.
Seattle Times, April 7, 1968 to February 5, 2003.
Skagit Valley Herald, September 1, 1980 to July 13, 1981.
The Skanner (Seattle, WA), March 23, 1994.
Spokesman Review (Spokane, WA), July 31, 1969 to August 11, 1991.
The Stranger (Seattle, WA), December 11, 1997.
Tampa Tribune, February 5, 1981 to February 11, 1981.
The Tennessean, July 12, 1942.
Times-Picayune (New Orleans), December 10, 1989.
Tri-State Defender (Memphis, TN), January 10, 1990.
Tucson Citizen (Tucson, AZ), January 30, 1982.
United Press International, October 18, 1980.
USA Today, July 19, 1985 to October 8, 1990.
The Voice, May 3, 1986.
The Washington Post, March 28, 1988.
Watsonville Register-Pajaronian, October 11, 1980 to October 12, 1981.

PROGRAMS
California Golden Classic Series, 1980.
Cheryl Glass funeral, July 22, 1997.
Copper World Classic, 1982.
Gold Cup, 1979, 1980, 1981.
Knoxville Nationals, 1982.
Pacific Coast Nationals Sprint Car Championship, October 30, 1980.
Skagit Speedway, May 5, 1980.
Skagit Speedway, 1981.
Wendell "Greased Lightning" Scott 65th Birthday Celebration, August 29, 1986.

LETTERS
Letter from Don Anderson, April 20, 1980.
Letter from Tom Blattner and Bruce Flanders, October 9, 1980.
Letter from Linda Mansfield, October 10, 1980.
Letter from Judy Hales, October 25, 1980.
Letter from Bill Smith, December 8, 1980.
Letter from Bill Smith, January 3, 1981.
Letter from Kathy Benson, July 31, 1981.
Letter from Bertil Roos, 1983.
Letter from Squire Shop U-2, March 27, 1984.
Letter from Houghton Mifflin, June 3, 1985.
Letter to Mike Summer from Ron Richards, June 20, 1985.

Letter to Thomas Todd, July 2, 1986.
Letter to Bill Sauter of Coors, January 29, 1987.
Letter to Thomas N. Todd, attorney, February 20, 1987.
Letter from Willie Lewis Brown Jr., June 25, 1987.
Letter from Jim Burnley, 1987.
Letter from Robert M. McCallum, November 19, 1987.
Letter from Dr. Stan Schiff, May 10, 1990.
Letter from Kirk Wines, July 31, 1990.
Letter from Marvin Glass, August 4, 1992.
Letter from Jesse Wineberry and Martin Applewick to James Montgomery, March 8, 1993.
Letter to Jesse Wineberry from James Montgomery, March 17, 1993.
Letter to Cheryl Glass from James Montgomery, March 30, 1993.
Letter to Audrey Greyes, June 21, 1993.
Letter to Jesse Wineberry, December 22, 1993.
Letter to Cheryl Glass from Marilyn Gardner, July 20, 1994.
Letter to DeCharlene Williams from Cheryl Glass, November 11, 1994.
Letter to Montel Williams Show from Cheryl Glass, August 7, 1996.
Letter to Nori Hamilton, undated.

TELEVISION SHOWS
The Achievers, TBS, February 1, 1988.
Celebrate Washington, "Women of the 80s Report." KTZZ TV 22.

WEBSITES
https://depts.washington.edu/civilr/boeing_battle.htm.
https://www.historylink.org/file/11111.
https://www.blackpast.org/african-american-history/presidents-committee-fair-employment-practice-fepc/#sthash.dtFj9EL3.dpuf.
https://www.autoevolution.com/news/a-short-history-of-go-kart-racing-125891.html.
https://www.thedrive.com/accelerator/17072/women-in-motorsport-their-past-present-and-future.
http://nwsprintcarhistory.com/champions/track-champions/washington/skagit-speed-way/skagit-speedway-410-champs/.
https://worldofoutlaws.com/sprintcars/outlaws-return-to-devils-bowl/.
http://nwsprintcarhistory.com/historical-results/california/gold-cup-race-champions/1981-gold-cup/.
https://dw.courts.wa.gov/index.cfm?fa=home.casesummary&crt_itl_nu=S17&casenumber=84-3-07679-1&searchtype=sName&token=0A07C4BE03DAD3DDAB0FDBABEEC30320&dt=0EC8DCBCCCDCD3A5B1F97C29DDAAABBD&courtClassCode=S&casekey=13092128&courtname=KING%20CO%20SUPERIOR%20CT.

https://dw.courts.wa.gov/index.cfm?fa=home.casesummary&crt_itl
   _nu=S17&casenumber=90-3-00360-8&searchtype=sName&token=0876B6C6
   78DBA4DDAB0FDBABEEC50320&dt=0CB9AEC4B7DDA4A5B1F97C29
   DDACABBD&courtClassCode=S&casekey=13036558&courtname=KING%20
   CO%20SUPERIOR%20CT.
https://dw.courts.wa.gov/index.cfm?fa=home.casesummary&crt_itl
   _nu=S17&casenumber=90-3-00360-8&searchtype=sName&token=0876B6C6
   78DBA4DDAB0FDBABEEC50320&dt=0CB9AEC4B7DDA4A5B1F97C29
   DDACABBD&courtClassCode=S&casekey=13036558&courtname=KING%20
   CO%20SUPERIOR%20CT.
http://pilotosmuertos.blogspot.com/2007/03/cheryl-glass-1961-1997-usa.html.

INTERVIEWS

Bobby Allen, September 2, 2019.
Roger Bailey, October 6, 2020.
Steve Beitler, April 15, 2020.
Stuart Bramhall, January 25, 2021.
Tobey Butler, May 8, 2020.
Ken Clapp, September 28, 2020.
Jerry Day, March 19, 2019; April 15, 2020; April 7, 2023.
Jerry Fanger, May 25, 2020.
Garey Fauver, April 13, 2020.
Jim Galasyn, January 23, 2021.
Shirley Glass, July 16, 2019; April 13, 2020; April 17, 2020; May 8, 2020; May 25, 2020;
   June 11, 2020; July 12, 2020; July 21, 2020; July 30, 2020; July 31, 2020; August 1,
   2020; October 11, 2020; October 18, 2020; November 7, 2020; January 18, 2021;
   June 4, 2021.
James Grantham, August 22, 2020.
Jim Grantham, June 8, 2020; July 12, 2020; August 1, 2020; September 5, 2020.
Dave Griffith, August 14, 2020.
Jim Hedblom, July 26, 2019.
P. J. Jones, July 3, 2020.
Lisa Kelsie, August 22, 2020.
Billy Kennelly, July 3, 2020.
Hersey Mallory, September 6, 2020; October 4, 2020; January 18, 2021.
Lealand McSpadden, May 6, 2020.
Steve Millen, May 7, 2020.
Leonard Miller, May 13, 2020; April 12, 2021.
Charles Mossington, October 15, 2021.
Guy Mossington, October 15, 2021.
Charles Michael Opprecht, January 28, 2021.
John Panzarella, February 12, 2021.
Charlie Patterson, June 10, 2020.
Steve Royce, June 8, 2020; June 9, 2020.

Jimmy Sills, May 6, 2020.
Denny Smith, July 26, 2019.
Bill Tempero, June 8, 2020.
Les Unger, May 8, 2020.
Al Unser Jr., June 8, 2020.
Lori Walker, July 26, 2019.
Eugene (Skip) Young Jr., August 17, 2020; January 18, 2021; January 19, 2021.

SPEECH
Speech for AKA National Convention, July 16, 1986.

PUBLIC RECORDS
1940; Census Place: Dyersburg, Dyer, TN; Roll: m-t0627-03889; Page: 11A; Enumeration District: 23-8.
Cook County, Illinois Birth Index, 1916–1935.
King County Medical Examiner's Office 97-00832.
Social Security Administration; Washington, DC, USA; Social Security Death Index, Master File.
State of California. California Birth Index, 1905–1995. Sacramento, CA, USA: State of California Department of Health Services, Center for Health Statistics.
Tennessee State Marriages, 1780–2002. Nashville, TN, USA: Tennessee State Library and Archives. Microfilm.
United States, School Yearbooks, 1880–2012; School Name: Nathan Hale High School; Year: 1977.
United States, Social Security Death Index, 1935–2014.
United States, Social Security Applications and Claims Index, 1936–2007.
United States, World War I Draft Registration Cards, 1917–1918.
U.S. Public Records Index, 1950–1993, Volume 1.
Washington, Divorce Index, 1969–2014.
Washington State Archives; Olympia, Washington; Washington Death Index, 1940–1959, 1965–2017.
Washington State Department of Health Certificate of Death. Local file No. 6846, State file number 146 7 20248.

COURT RECORDS
King County Superior Court 88-2-13932-6.
King County Superior Court 90-3-00360-8 SEA.
King County District Court East 92-008093.
King County Superior Court East 93-2-24928-4.
King County Superior Court 93-1-074981-2.
King County District Court West 93-013207.
King County Superior Court 93-2-28628-7.
King County Superior Court 93-2-30022-1.

King County District Court West King County Superior Court 94-2-22422-1 93-014767.
King County District Court West 95-12649.
King County District Court West 96-002282.
King County Superior Court 96-2-28518-8.
Western Washington District Court 2:96-cv-01059-TSZ.
King County Superior Court 97-2-13602-4.
King County Superior Court 97-9-10797-6.

POLICE RECORDS
King County Sheriff's Office 91-242553.
King County Sheriff's Office 92-0003732.
King County Sheriff's Office 92-037759.
King County Sheriff's Office 92-288200.
King County Sheriff's Office 92-295454.
King County Sheriff's Office 93-160379.
King County Sheriff's Office 93-166805.
King County Sheriff's Office 93-173349.
King County Sheriff's Office 93-286043.
King County Sheriff's Office 93-287214.
Shoreline division 93-231150.
King County Sheriff's Office 93-318743.
King County Sheriff's Office 93-401548.
King County Sheriff's Office 94-000713.
King County Sheriff's Office 94-411934.
Federal Bureau of Investigation SE 44A068379-4.
Department of Justice 144-82-0574.
Seattle Police Department 97-301757.

INDEX

ABOUT THE AUTHOR

Bill Poehler is an award-winning investigative journalist who has spent his career as a reporter at the Salem *Statesman Journal*, covering issues ranging from the COVID-19 unemployment crisis to dead rats floating down streams to abandoned buildings. Honing his craft as a sports reporter, Poehler now covers Marion County and Polk County for the newspaper, among a wide swath of other topics. He is the author of *The Brown Bullet: Rajo Jack's Drive to Integrate Auto Racing*, which was published by Chicago Review Press in 2020. He is an unrepentant snob about baking, is addicted to superhero movies, and fixes other people's cars without their permission.

Bill Poehler.
TED MILLER JR.